My Life with Kangaroos

My Life with Kangaroos

A Deaf Woman's Remarkable Story

Doris Herrmann

with Michael Gaida and Theres Jöhl

Translated by Paul Foster

Gallaudet University Press
Washington, D.C.

Gallaudet University Press
Washington, DC 20002

http://gupress.gallaudet.edu

The illustrations and photographs have been kindly supplied
from the private collections of Doris Herrmann and Ursi Weiss.

Library of Congress Cataloging-in-Publication Data

Herrmann, Doris, 1933-
My life with kangaroos: a deaf woman's remarkable story /
Doris Herrmann; with Michael Gaida and Theres Jöhl; translated by Paul Foster.
p. cm.
Translated and revised edition of: Känguruherz. Berlin : Pro Business GmbH, 2009.
ISBN 978-1-56368-559-0 (paperback: alkaline paper)—ISBN 978-1-56368-560-6 (e-book)
1. Kangaroos—Behavior. 2. Kangaroos—Australia. 3. Herrmann, Doris, 1933-
4. Human-animal relationships. 5. Deaf authors—Switzerland—Biography.
6. Deaf women—Switzerland—Biography. I. Gaida, Michael. II. Jöhl, Theres, 1957-
III. Herrmann, Doris, 1933- Känguruherz. IV. Title.
QL737.M35H47 2013
599.2'22—dc23
2012047495

Cover art: "Kangaroo," an Aboriginal dot painting by
Indigenous Australian artist Stanley Geebung, ochre on card, circa 1995.

To the memory of my parents,
Trudel and Siegbert, and also to
Rosa Hunziker, my "Auntie,"
and to my brother, Peter

Contents

Preface

IN SOME fairy tales, animals talk, human beings are bewitched, and other strange things occur twixt heaven and earth. Moreover, the people in them frequently play roles in which the limitations that constrain them in life, either material or physical, play a decisive part. These characters have access to invisible powers that watch over them and determine their fate. Many of these actors are people we might call naïve, yet they possess what we would call a natural simplicity, a certain uninhibited candor.

I cannot say for a moment that I am an expert on fairy tales, for indeed I have not read many and, apart from this, regard myself as a scientist who prizes sobriety. Having said that, however, when I look back at certain events in my life, it seems as though magical forces have been at work from time to time. Simply to pass them off as coincidence is rather difficult, especially in view of the fact that a number of these events were revealed to me first in the form of a dream.

Since I have been aware of my close association with kangaroos and their Australian homeland, an association that one may well regard as determined by fate, I have always felt that, finally, nothing has been in vain even if, on occasion, life seems to have been full of obstacles and fraught with sadness. Added to this, I can say that the older I become, the more clearly I have come to realize that many of the steps I have undertaken—not only those pursued in personal crises but also those embarked upon at sunny times in my life, have

been guided by an invisible force. To be unerringly guided—this
indeed is something I have experienced several times.

Although it is true that I have been deaf since birth and that
my vision has deteriorated almost to total blindness in the meantime, these restrictions have in fact been the means whereby I have
learned to concentrate on what for me was essential. At the same
time, these disabilities have been instrumental in helping me gain
a perception of the world that—and here I'll choose the word to
apply to myself—one could call "naïve." Although I, like many
others, have often been burdened by prejudice, I have nevertheless
managed to maintain a sensitivity to and an understanding of the
little things in life, which, for a "normal" person without disabilities
merely go unheeded.

Although it may seem strange to say, I have my disability to thank
in particular for that finer sense of perception when it comes to dis-
cerning the mysterious, imperceptible bond that exists between
human and animal and natural forces in general. Put somewhat paradoxically, it seems, among other things, that out of the inability to
hear and, lately, the loss of sight into the bargain, I have developed
a veritable sixth sense. Despite the fact that, due to my deafness,
I have never been able to properly appreciate language in all of its
nuances, I have, nevertheless, been able to comprehend one of its
wonders. From the time I was first able to strenuously learn how to
form words and syllables with my voice, I also began to grasp the fact
that meaningful sound not only links one's mind to the real world of
things but also pertains to the realms of thought and feeling. How
much more of a torture it is, then, to encounter nameless things that
are full of life, which I have experienced several times and describe
in this book.

It was the kangaroo—or shall I say the spirit of the kangaroo—
which so enthralled me in my childhood and later shaped my life
into a kind of mental symbiosis. One can say that the kangaroo has
in many ways dominated my life. On the other hand, it has provided
me with an even keel in difficult situations. As a person with a disability, I am constantly confronted with the challenge of having to

get myself under control each day and so face up to life's demands openly and positively. Precisely because of this, I have been able to appreciate every bit of assistance I have received from this animal. These were always good deeds, so to speak, gifts that my soul comprehended directly and without hindrance.

Why and how all this happened, I do not know. And in so saying, I find myself back at the fairy tale. There, too, the characters have difficulty in telling us exactly what happened to them. It is just this that I refer to as the fairy-tale aspect of my life. The powers at work during my association with kangaroos in the end remain an enigma, and sometimes I have the impression of having been born in a different zodiac right under their sign. Anyway, it is a good feeling to know that this great secret will remain inviolable.

1

Kangaroos as Yet Undiscovered

A THIN skein of cloud has spread over the delicately blue sky illuminating the red-tiled roofs of our Swiss town on the Rhine River. I am nearly three years old. Getting out of bed, dressed in a shirt and pants, I stand at the half-open balcony door, where a waft of cool air brushes past me. I sense the coming of a beautiful, warm sunny day. Then I run off to the bathroom, where I bend and stretch and twist, reveling in the joy of being alive. In so doing, I feel my body and look at myself and run my hand through my curly hair. Suddenly Mummy is there in front of me. She smiles at me lovingly and strokes my head. Astonished and a little taken aback at her total nakedness, I become aware of my own flat chest with its two tiny pink points—I've discovered myself!

These are the first, consciously recorded pictures in my memory. Apart from these there are others that are witness to many long walks through the hilly countryside with my mother or with the governess until my little legs were so tired that I had to be placed in the baby carriage.

My first intense impressions of color, form, and aroma were such that one night they made me dream how and from where I had "suddenly" appeared in this existence. Weightlessly and devoid of a body, I hovered in the air above wonderfully green woods and fields in the warmth of the sun under a blue heaven and was nothing more than pure, receptive feeling.

AS OFTEN as I could as a child, I watched the interplay of change and variety in the sky. What impressed me greatly was the infinite kaleidoscope of color variation. These impressions were so strong that I dreamed from time to time that the clouds changed their colors to pinkish-red, orange or yellow-brown.

On one occasion when I was out on a walk with Auntie,[1] we were surprised by a storm. Bewildered, I looked at Auntie's face, pointing first at the clouds and then at her black dress because at that time I could make neither sounds nor words. On later excursions, after I was able to form short sentences, I absorbed the mountains, the sky, and the clouds and was made happy by the alpine flowers. Up in the hills I would say, "Sky moves. Clouds move. Sun moves." If the mountains were shrouded in mist, I would say, "The mountain has gone." On one of these walks I witnessed my first sunset. Just to watch the fiery red sun sink behind the horizon was a profound experience for me. "The sun has fallen into a hole!" I cried in great excitement.

Auntie Rosa Hunziker, Peter (on her shoulder), and me.
Auntie loved to take Peter and me for walks outside.

1. Auntie was my teacher and nanny.

All That Shoots Forth, Ripens and Blooms

I SUPPOSE it must have been during one of those childhood walks that I first immersed myself so deeply into the microcosm of nature that I quite forgot myself. It was hot at the time, and the poppies bloomed a deep, bewitching red along the paths and edges of cultivated land, but even in the fields, standing there among the yellow corn, their brilliant signal could be spotted at many places. In order to initiate me a little into the secrets of nature, my mother opened one of the large, green buds to show me the still tightly folded petals inside—a sight that transported me with delight.

From then on I discovered the as yet unrevealed inner life of these buds. I looked at them all, large and small, and as I did so, the same brilliant redness met me. The repetition was a kind of meditative ritual, if one can use such a term to apply to a child, but the fact was that it worked in a way to gradually change my consciousness. Something within me opened my eyes to the world in miniature to see more exactly and receive what I saw in a spirit of devotion. In this way, I learned the stages of growth and development of the poppy up to its fullest moment. And indeed, my concern for plants grew and developed. I stopped opening buds that were not yet ready to break and instead began concentrating on their development. I noticed, for example, how the very slightly haired buds grew on the branching stalks; I also watched the still snow-white little petals get bigger. My imagination was stimulated when I considered that these petals would be induced by secret forces to burst forth and that they were also "painted" in the darkness of the closed bud by the same secret strength.

I realized that it was a slow, uniform process of "painting," one that would pass through a stage of white to reddish-white, from there to a delicate, light red, and then to its brilliant scarlet consummation. I had come to learn as well that the bud loosened first along its side clefts before slowly unfolding its large, four-leaved blossom. The poppy's red was always the sign of summer for me.

The poppy was not my only teacher, however. On my journeys of discovery in the garden, I soon noticed how quickly the tulip stalks

grew and, along with them, the firmly closed flowers that would
ultimately unfold to display their differently colored "goblets" to
the spring skies. I loved these dearly. Every morning I delighted in
watching how the sun's rays brought these flowers to their prime,
almost, one might say, to radiate. These impressions did not leave
me in peace, and just because they failed to do that, I could not
leave the tulips in peace. I would break the stalk carefully at the
bottom and then march around waving my multicolored "flag" in
triumph until, that is, my mother caught me and firmly slapped
the back of my hand. After that, she placed the flower carefully in
a vase.

My sadness at this did not last long because I then began to
understand that everything that grew out of the earth was not a
toy. Berries were another matter, though. After all, they thrived
everywhere among the hedges and bushes and simply asked to be
devoured. There were wild strawberries in great numbers practically everywhere. I learned as a kindergarten child that masses of
little blossoms bearing small, hairy, yellow berries would appear in
springtime. I would watch expectantly how, from the wilted blossoms, miniature white fruits and then red strawberries eventually
appeared. To confirm my observations, I would test what had happened at every stage by eating them. Nevertheless, the world of
flowers, and especially that of blossoms, was always nearest to my
heart.

EVERY summer and winter we spent our holidays at a chalet in the
Berner Oberland region of central Switzerland. For me, this meant
enjoying the superb green of the alpine fields with their glorious
array of flowers and errant butterflies in the summer and in winter
the glittering splendor of snow and icicles hanging from porches and
eaves. These impressions gave me great pleasure.

Once in winter, just before dusk, my parents took me for a walk
in the snow, and it was then that I experienced ecstasy for the first
time. The wonderful spectacle of the evening sunlight tinting the
mountains a soft pink and the reddish violet sky above thrilled me to

the marrow. These fiery colors in the heavens have remained part of me since that moment, and sometimes it has even seemed as if this natural display of light and color actually gave me strength.[2]

Noises More Felt than Heard

I REMEMBER quite clearly that, despite my lack of hearing, I was nevertheless very sensitive to noise in my early years. For a long time my parents did not realize why I whimpered at a radio that was too loud. When I was about three, my parents took me to the autumn festival in Basel, where, they thought, I would be able to enjoy the same busy fun as the other children. However, the wild confusion, the vibration caused by the merry-go-rounds, the explosions at the shooting arcade, the booming music, and the general upheaval only served to fill me with fear and anxiety. My mother seemed not to sense what I felt, and when I cried or whimpered, she merely shook my hand in impatience. But the noise was not the worst.

My fears, which of course could all be traced back to my lack of hearing, were to last for a time yet. Indeed, for a while they even increased. If, for example, I believed I was absolutely alone in the woods, I would scream like mad for my "vanished" parents or for Auntie, who would come running and reprimand me. Being alone in a room, for instance, even if only briefly, was unbearable because I could not hear the movements of the people in the adjacent rooms. When I could no longer feel the vibrations they created on the floor or the stairs, I panicked. At that moment I sensed a deathly stillness, which I interpreted as nobody being in the house but me.

However, terror could also overtake me when I was in the street, at home, or even on a streetcar. These panic attacks would apparently come about quite independently of an identifiable cause.

2. Later I was to feel similar emotional stirrings on watching the sun rise and set in an incredible nuance of color while in Australia, and on each occasion I recalled my early experience of such magnificence in Switzerland.

They even occurred in the presence of Auntie or my parents. At such times I would jump and then convulsively clutch at their clothes or their arms and stare fixedly at their faces but remain silent. My appearance during these episodes must have seemed strange, perhaps even funny, and I was always urged to explain my behavior, but I never revealed my "secrets."

Today, when people ask me in astonishment whether I can hear, I reply that my ears do not hear but that my body as a whole serves as a means of "hearing." Thanks to this finely tuned reception to sound felt on the surface of the skin, I can detect various forms of vibration such as thunder and the gentle pulsing or stronger reverberations made by engines, footsteps on wood floors, and knocking on doors and walls. The same is true of the noise my neighbors make with their strident music, and I am also able to pick up loud conversations and the barking of dogs. Noises whose frequencies lie in the middle and lower ranges, which produce noticeable vibrations in the air, on the ground, or in a table or other objects with which I happen to be in direct contact, don't affect my ears but have an impact on my whole body. They run from my head to my feet or vice versa, and I thus become aware of them. On the other hand, violent, crashing noises actually penetrate my inner ear. The drumming and the Guggenmusik that accompany the Basler Fasnacht,[3] for example, the rumbling inside a railway tunnel, or the scream of turbine airplane engines are intolerable. On the other hand, the high-frequency sounds that issue from a violin or those of a similar nature are quite out of range for me.

Nameless Things That Move

WHEN I was four years old, vocal communication was as yet impossible. I suppose the only "words" that I could produce were gestures to indicate yes and no. My mother or the maid would

---

3. A three-day festival that takes place each year in Basel in celebration of the medieval rite of driving out the evil spirits of winter.

point to objects, and if I didn't want them, I would shake my head no; if I wanted an object, I would nod and take hold of it. If I felt miserable, it was easy to make this clear to anyone, but differentiations such as fear or discontent were not so easy to demonstrate. If I encountered objects made of wood or metal, glass or rubber, which, because of their mechanical potential, seemed to me to move of their own accord, it was impossible for me to ask how they worked. So it was that no one explained the meaning of a small, green, constantly pulsating "light spirit" on the radio chassis, whose uncanny "living" presence never failed to send shudders down my spine.

Once, during the winter at a place called Arosa (in the Bündnerland region of Switzerland), I screamed nonstop during lunch on the balcony and would not be comforted. Finally, my mother scolded me and sent me to bed. It was not until ten years later that I learned what had upset me: a small bubble of air in the glass pane of the door. I had been sitting next to the open door, which was flat against the wall, and had noticed a very small but extremely bright reflection of this air bubble. It constantly changed, now larger, then smaller, now thicker and then thinner, according to my movements as I moved the door back and forth. I was terrified by this "fiery little devil" living in the glass.

One evening about four years later, while I was at the farm that belonged to Auntie's relatives, I began drawing to amuse myself. Each of my pictures had a related story that concerned children who were afraid of the radio in their parlor. More precisely, they were afraid of the small green light, the so-called magic light that used to flicker and frighten the children so much that they would retreat to the far corners of the room. Eventually, they plucked up their courage, seized the offending radio, put it in a box, tied up the box with string, and took it to the post office so to say "good riddance" to this tiny demon forever!

When I had finished my "œuvres," I found that I could appreciate Auntie's laughter because both the children in the drawings and I myself were no longer afraid.

The Search for the Two-Legged Animal

EVEN as a small child, I was very fond of playing and can still vividly remember romping with the neighbors' children in our large courtyard. I didn't realize at the time that one of the reasons for our occasional violent squabbles was my inability to hear, which often resulted in completely dislocated communication between my play-mates and me. They would often wrench the bucket and shovel out of my hands, and this angered me. I felt that they were constantly pushing me aside. Then I would sit there apathetically, not saying a word, but often in tears. Because I didn't know how to deal with the stronger kids, I did not protest. Moreover, their ugly expressions frightened me. If either my mother or the governess took me away from the scene, I would run straight back to the children since I favored their company despite their many rejections. It was not until I was about nine years of age that I fully realized that I was deaf.

From a very early age I was often surrounded by the cats and dogs of our neighborhood, and I used to seek out the company of other animals near our vacation chalet and was soon familiar with them all. The same was true of those animals I encountered in the zoo not far from where we lived.

Soon I had come to trust my association with these animals to the point that, to me, they became the most important creatures in a world of living beings. A secret wish grew in me one day to find a species of mammal that could stand and run on two legs and be the playmate I so desired. Certainly this was because I found animals to be friendly companions, quite contrary to the human kind.

Even as a child I was very interested in animals, and my desire to know more about them began to develop at this time. Each day and with rapt attention, I used to watch the birds peck at the seeds Mummy had spread on a board on the balcony. One day, however, I wanted to try an experiment, so I made a snowball, placed it on the board, and waited. Soon a titmouse flew from somewhere, settled on the snowball, and began pecking for food. Then, all of a sudden, it surprised me by spitting out bean-sized particles of snow before it resumed pecking. And so it went on: peck-peck, spit-spit, peck again, all very quickly. My mother and I couldn't stop laughing.

Insects fascinated me, too, especially the very small, creeping, crawling kinds like ants, and for hours I would lie on my stomach on the carpet and watch these little creatures go about their business. I often became so absorbed in my observation that I would cry when one of the insects disappeared into the carpet, never to be seen again.

Many years later, when I was about twenty, this living microcosm still captivated me. I watched ants as they played their parts, so to speak, on the "stage" provided by the shelf over my bed. It was like a miniature theater as they crept here and there among the books and small statues in the light of my bedside lamp. They didn't disturb me in the least as they went about their affairs. On the contrary, it gave me great pleasure to scatter a little sugar for their delight and then note their reactions.

I HAVE only an indistinct memory of my first encounter with kangaroos. Nonetheless, it remains firmly entrenched in my memory. I was about three years old, I suppose, when I suddenly stood rooted to the ground at my first sight of these animals at the zoo. Breathlessly, I gazed at these upstanding beasts on the other side of the fence. They were a good deal taller than me, and their "hands" hung loosely over their bellies—and they stood on two legs. I was delighted! My child's eye had not yet taken in their thick tails, their pouches, and the curious bend in their legs.

A long time ago and to my surprise, I discovered a photograph of my mother taken at the Basel Zoo. The snapshot showed her sitting with relatives on a bench in front of a huge tree. Pregnant with me at the time, she was crocheting a baby jacket. I was strangely enthralled and touched by this scene, and it occupied my thoughts in a peculiar way. A few years before my mother died, she admitted that in her youth she had known nothing at all about kangaroos until the day she first visited the Basel Zoo. Perhaps she saw a kangaroo there for the first time. I pressed her for details, but she insisted

Group of kangaroos, my lifetime friends.

that, try as she might, she could not remember anything more about the visit. Was that perhaps the magic moment in which the "spirit of the kangaroo" had entered my mother and therefore me as well? The question is weighted with all kinds of speculation, and I will probably never receive a valid answer.

A few more years were to pass before I would be in a position to understand these animals and feel for them. For the time being, there was an abundance of other nicer and more important things to discover and experience. I would have to learn about them and try them out for myself, as this was essential for my development.

IN MY playroom were a number of dolls and stuffed animals, among them a dog, a bear, and a giraffe, but no kangaroo. Had nobody, then, noticed my "discovery" at the Basel Zoo? Or was it that these sensational feelings of mine were invisible? Had I not shown any emotion in all of this?

Today I am pretty sure that, had I possessed one of these unusual two-legged creatures at the time, my love for them would not only have stayed with me but would even have grown. From that time on, a toy kangaroo would have become an inseparable companion, one that I would have taken with me everywhere.

2

School Years

AFTER my family moved to the Basel suburb of Riehen, I was sent to a kindergarten for deaf children. While there, I was much more interested in the wonderful colors displayed on the blackboard than in the lessons or playtime. When I discovered that chalk could be rubbed off, I put this knowledge into action by erasing a picture on the board. The teacher, displeased by this, sent me out of the class and closed the door behind me. Shocked by her punishment, I ran through the halls, opening every classroom door, but no one would let me in. Eventually I found myself in a long hallway where all the doors were locked. Not knowing what else to do, I sat down and cried.

This, to be sure, was an ominous beginning, but since my mother did not find the personnel at the kindergarten particularly congenial, she removed me and hired a private teacher. Despite this, I went in fact from the frying pan into the fire. This teacher, whose face I have forgotten, would frequently lock me in the bathroom when my parents were not at home, and here I was terrified that I would never be able to open the door. All my shrieks of distress were in vain. Happily, though, my parents soon realized what was going on and dismissed this individual.

Then, on May 1, 1938, a woman named Rosa Hunziker arrived at our house. Having come from a large farming family in the canton of Aargau, she became my nanny and teacher. After just a few days, even before I had really begun to speak, I lovingly named her Auntie.

Auntie taught me the names of my parents, relatives, and friends, as well as those of animals and important objects, and how to say them. She drew and painted clear, bold pictures of things of the most varied kind and attached the corresponding word to each. In this way, I could remember them more easily. This so inspired me that I began to invent new words. One morning I pointed at the sun, drew a picture of it, and then tried to find a suitable word for it. Under it I wrote *or.*[4] At a loss for the real word, I pressed my pencil into Auntie's hand, and she wrote "sun" for me.

IN THE spring of 1940, people were afraid that German troops would violate the Swiss/German border near Basel. The threat was so serious that we moved to Grindelwald for safety. I was six years old and hardly aware of the war going on beyond the frontier. Only the huge suitcases and the large wicker hamper were indications that the family would be away for several months. At first it was quite strange to be living in the chalet with Auntie and Peter, my younger brother, who was also deaf. I missed not only my parents, who had not yet arrived, but also my beloved playthings, which had been forgotten in the haste of packing. Happily, our parents later joined us in the mountains, and Mummy gave me a heavy shoebox. I could hardly contain my joy; inside was a locomotive that one could wind up and set down on the floor to run. I was very fond of it, viewing it as a little animal on wheels, made of tin and with a small engine inside instead of organs. When we went for walks, I took this tin creature along and held it lovingly under my arm. I even took it to bed with me.

Every day after lunch I would "study" Otto Schmeil's *Animal Life* and thought about the illustrations. One evening I said, "The bird has no arms" (I didn't yet know the word "wings"). "The bird has no ears," I added. The illustrations of skeletons, teeth, and the

---

4. Decades later I learned to my astonishment that *or* in French is "gold" or "golden" in English and appears in Italian as *oro*. I was not so wrong after all.

anatomies of human beings and animals interested me greatly. I knew, for example, that the abdominal cavity contained intestines but wanted to know from Auntie where chewed food actually went. She explained to me simply that the stomach turned things like fruits and vegetables into juices, which then passed into the blood-stream, while the rest went on through the intestinal tract and were excreted.

Of Bewitched People and Inspired Matters

THAT things and human beings could be transformed into some-thing else was something I took for granted. My daddy was drafted into service as an auxiliary soldier again. I had no idea why he had to stay away for so long, and each day that passed I missed him more. His personal presence as head of the family did much for my well-being.

One afternoon Mummy wanted to take me for a walk, but I wanted to run down to the small train station to watch the trains and the way they revolved on a turntable. As a result, I was a bit surly, but Mother knew how to put me in a better mood, and soon we were off

My beloved Father at the age of sixty-six. He was a good listener with a great sense of humor. We used to have many a laugh together.

on a long walk through the meadows, sprinkled with flowers. On the way home, she suddenly stopped and listened intently. She then ran to a hole in a nearby stone wall, looked into it, and lifted me to show me what was inside. In the half-light I became aware of an odd-looking thing tottering on two spindly legs, round, quite naked, and with a quaint little head and a large mouth. My mother mouthed the word "baby" and made a waddling movement. I was paralyzed with horror. My whole body itched. On lipreading what my mother had said, I understood the word "Daddy" and was now convinced that my father had been magically transformed into this repulsive dwarf! I knew nothing of baby birds. However, I soon recovered from this incredible news and accepted what seemed to be an irrevocable fact.

Soon afterward, my father and I were able to enjoy watching the growth of the baby bird at the stone wall. On warm days, Auntie would hold her lessons in either the meadows or the woods. During breaks and at every other opportunity, I would be drawn to my favorite spot, a wonderful, untouched glade in the wild forest, with stones and moss, alpine herbs, cranberries, and wild strawberries. There was always activity here. All sorts of beetles, colorful butterflies, snails, and worms inhabited the place. At first I was hesitant to get close to these creatures, but curiosity soon triumphed. I never tired of sitting or lying there, letting ants and other insects crawl over my arms and hands while I watched them intently. Once I took a basin from the kitchen with me, filled it with dirt, stones, moss, and plants, and put all kinds of these creatures into it, took it home, and added a lot of water to the pan without suspecting that the creatures in it, among them worms and caterpillars, would not survive the deluge.

Thanks to this happy time in the mountain village, Auntie's good company, the presence of the family, and my discoveries, which sharpened my awareness of these new surroundings, I developed rapidly. Before falling asleep, I needed someone to talk to about the day's events and impressions. This somebody would have to be very patient since I would go on and on, for the most part incomprehensibly talking about iron, overhead monorails, the animal world, anatomy, and a thousand other matters. By the end of our stay I was familiar with the terms for most common objects and with the vocabulary for a variety of activities.

Where Does a Little Child Grow?

DURING my stay in the country I discovered much that was new and beautiful, like how milk flowed from a cow's udder, something I had not grasped as a small child. Later I was allowed to be present while a mother breast-fed her baby and could hardly comprehend that it was milk that flowed from her breast.

Like all children of my age, I was curious to know where babies came from and constantly asked Auntie this question. To this she was ever ready with the answer: "From God" or "They are miracles wrought by our loving God" or "It's one of God's wonders and a great secret." This of course did not satisfy me for a moment, so I tried to figure out the answer myself. Perhaps babies grew in the clouds? Or in a secret place known only to God, where it is cared for before descending to the world to surprise its parents with its appearance?

One day, when our little poodle, Topi, presented us with its newborn offspring, I was perplexed by how these had come through the window! There were other questions, too, as to whether it was really God or some other heavenly being that had placed the eggs into birds' nests in the woods and fields, not to mention our own canary's nest. Once, after Auntie had carefully explained how blue titmice build their nests and then care for the babies until they fledge, I burst out joyfully, "It's true, isn't it, Auntie? You hatched us, Peter and me, until we could fly!" Constantly being with her, for school and in the free time (she was my teacher and nanny), had convinced me that she must be my real mother, and it was not until I was about ten that I knew who my actual mother was.

That's How Big the World Is!

AUNTIE prepared an especially interesting lesson to communicate the idea of measuring distances to me. She produced a meterlong stick and marched along a path with it from one small patch of woods to another. I helped her with measuring and counting, and it wasn't easy to remember the numbers, but finally we were very satisfied with our success. I was astonished by the fact that we had been able to measure this considerable distance by ourselves. On another occasion we took a ten-meter-long rope and walked along a straight road with it. I held one end firmly, while Auntie went ahead with the rope until it was taut. She then pressed her end into the ground, while I proceeded down the road, passed her, and did the same thing. We did this alternately and counted as we went: ten, twenty, thirty . . . one hundred, one hundred and ten, twenty, and so on for a kilometer, which, in those days, seemed really far!

As a child I believed the world was flat and infinitely broad, topped by a blue sky like a mantle sprinkled with a moon and stars. When Auntie read the fairy tale "Mother Hulda," I decided that, many kilometers under the earth, there was a kind of "basement," which had a wonderful green landscape and a blue sky like ours. The sun would travel over the earth during the day and then go down a huge shaft in the evening, then come out of another shaft the next day on the other side of the world.

Although I frequently looked at our large atlas with particular pleasure, especially for its many colors and to locate our very small country, I knew nothing about the earth being round since we didn't have a globe in the house. I was all the more perturbed at night after learning from Auntie during my first Bible study about the eerie, pitch-black depths that had no sun or moon or stars, where the creation of the earth had begun, as this in no way corresponded to my conception of an endlessly flat world. I was shocked.

The story of paradise, on the other hand, pleased me—until the Fall of Man. Hearing about this dashed my spirits since, in my imagination, Adam and Eve, on being cast out of God's paradise, would have had to trudge through a harsh desert over sand, stones, and boulders. Concerned, I asked Auntie how these two had departed. "On foot," she replied crisply.

One evening I put on a show called the "Creation of the World." The audience was my family, including my grandparents, and the household staff. The sliding doors served as the stage curtain and the salon as the stage, from whose darkness creation emerged. I, as God the Creator, turned on all the lights, placed indoor plants on the floor, and put both my stuffed and porcelain animals between them. Finally, I placed a beautiful apple on the rubber tree. Then I vanished behind a wing chair. At my bidding, my mother took the apple, bit into it, and expressed great shame until I, in my wrath, appeared and cast her out of paradise.

Boundless Curiosity

ON RAINY Sundays at our home in Riehen I often sat on the sofa and looked at my picture books. These mainly had to do with popular adventures, which had dominated my child's world. I probably have to thank these for their information on kangaroos, whose thick tails, pouches, and short arms now made a stronger impression on me. I was eight years old when we visited the kangaroo compound at the Basel Zoo. Again, by extending her skirt, Auntie drew my attention to the mother kangaroos. I looked at every one of them carefully, without, however, really noticing their progeny, who were peeping out from the mothers' pouches. I was more interested in their characteristic movements, which are peculiar to them. First, they place their forepaws on the ground in front of them and lift their back legs, which then follow the movement of the forepaws. Then the tail is placed between the back legs and pushes the animal forward. Then the forepaws are placed on the ground again, and the sequence continues.

This odd form of locomotion, a kind of half-hopping, was nevertheless smoothly executed and considerably impressed me. This visit was very exciting, but I decided not to say a word about it, even doggedly keeping quiet over our tea and cake in the zoo restaurant. I uttered not a syllable. Despite a number of attempts to divert my attention, I managed to keep mum about my experience until the following evening. After my bath, I decided to try out this peculiar yet elegant form of ambulation for myself. However, kangaroos have a powerful tail that helps propel them forward, whereas I could manage only a clumsy rabbit hop!

Once during winter in the mountains, a magnificent, infinitely blue sky stretched over the landscape. The powdery snow stood several meters high, glittering in the powerful rays of the sun, its crystals dancing like so many millions of delicate flares. I was about eight at the time, tramping up from the village with my parents by various routes on the way home. It would not be long before dusk caught up with us, and the long, steep path seemed endless. I was exhausted, which didn't help my mood, so I kept my eyes glued to the path. The road had been well rutted into regular patterns by sleighs passing this way. I plodded on valiantly in my nailed snowshoes: two steps up, two steps down; two steps up, two steps down, and so on. The glaring white of the snow all around and the monotony of my movements put me into a near trance, and in this absent state of mind I suddenly saw a kangaroo in front of me. It was traveling in the same direction, and in graceful slow motion, this alien fellow traveler moved forward, first placing his forepaws on the mounds of snow, and then lifting his hind legs while the muscular tail did the rest in heaving his rump forward. Thus, hop for hop. This graphic image gave me new energy, and I reached the summit in good spirits. Of course, I knew even then that kangaroos don't live in snowy regions,[5] although I could not have told you where they really lived!

My strong feelings for this animal had now found a firm place in my life. However, I wasn't really aware of this yet because many other things were more important to me. There was school, for example, with its daily exercises in articulation and other subjects. Nevertheless, images of kangaroos would appear in my mind's eye from time to time but then quickly vanished. Of course, it was likely that this gelling of my interest could be explained by my very personal, private yearnings and was something shared by all children. One of these was my avid desire to go to a "normal" school with

5. I was all the more astonished some fifty years later to find several dwarflike, dark-brown kangaroos in a small, snow-covered zoo at a high elevation in Switzerland. These were Tasmanian wallabies, which could manage thirty centimeters of snow in a single bound and left sweet little tracks behind them. For me, the sight was like a dream. I understood at once that these were probably representatives of the colder regions of Australia, namely in the south, and perhaps of Tasmania itself, which occasionally receives some snow.

"normal" children. Even though I was lovingly cared for by Auntie and the rest of my family, I was often bitter when I was ordered—sometimes with the encouragement of the cane—to be more obedient and less stubborn.

ONCE, when I was about nine years old, I went to a large department store in Basel with my brother, Auntie, and mother to see the Christmas display. There was a circus with life-sized figures, animated by clockwork behind the scenes. The clown's face was so grotesque that I burst into tears. A little annoyed, Mother gripped my hand. As I obediently looked on, and to my utter surprise, I suddenly perceived hopping kangaroos on the other side of the balustrade. The vision calmed me down instantly. I never said a word about this, however. It was as though I had to safeguard these images and their effect on me and so protect them from the horrid world outside.

Some time after this, I experienced something unusual, which was later to influence my life as a kangaroo researcher. One Sunday I went with my father to the Basel Zoo, where we visited the kangaroos in their pen. As we stood watching them, one of the animals suddenly pulled himself up and threw his body so far behind him that I shuddered for a moment. Despite this, I remained where I was. This strange episode followed me later in my dreams, which startled me and frequently interrupted my sleep, pursuing my child's spirit with the question of whether good and evil existed among kangaroos.

Budding Imagination

OTHER matters soon displaced these thoughts. Auntie and I often visited Basel's Ethnological Museum, and she often read stories or fairy tales from other regions of the world as a supplement. This was my favorite lesson because it supplied the themes that my expanding imagination needed. Once at home, I drew or painted the objects I had seen in the museum in either grotesque or imaginary representations. Auntie was less pleased than she might have been with these endeavors and urged me to indulge in "more sensible activities," but this didn't diminish my pleasure. The reason for her distaste very probably lay in my exaggerated fantasy, which led me to believe that the masks, costumes, and clothing made from wood, straw, palm leaves, clay, or animal skins were real faces of flesh and blood. So sensitive was I that, in my vivid fantasies, the sight of a black man walking along with a broad head and huge, goggle-eyes hanging from stalks shocked me, and I was able to calm down only by looking at his legs, which were those of a normal human being!

During the course of World War II, the delivery of coal to heat our home was cut off. As a result, three wood stoves were installed in the house. Even these fired my imagination! On one occasion, I drew vertical and horizontal flue pipes all over the blackboard and rooms full of fire on top of them. To complete the scene, I added people stumbling about inside the black pipes until they toppled into the fire. Laughing, I showed these pictures to my mother, who flatly refused to look at them. I couldn't understand her vehement reaction. After all, I had not the slightest idea of the reality of the Holocaust. My Mummy felt it best not to tell me anything about these matters so as not to alarm me, but my family lived each day in fear of a possible German invasion of Swiss territory. The child that I was, though, sensed a mystery in the air.

At this period in my life, my one great passion was acting, either alone or with others. Material for performances came from fairy tales, marionette shows at big theaters, movies, or picture books. However, for the most part the plots were ones I invented. These were performed for an audience, which was partly amused but also partly horrified as my brother was buttoned up into a comforter cover on a stage made of chairs and boards. I called this scene "How robbers Dragged a Kidnapped Child into a Barn to Spend the Night in the Hay." The fact that Peter took all this in his stride throughout the scene and also showed no resistance kept me from being punished by the viewers! Costumes were devised from cloth remnants found in a large box on the top story of the house. After delightedly looting this "treasure trove," I sewed various pieces of cloth together or used sofa covers. For makeup I found that colored crayons or Mother's lipsticks worked well. On another occasion, I beguiled the home audience with a "witches' show," which included wild dances and several changes of costume.[6]

These "witch shows" were also essentially a means of overcoming my many fears. They were an expression of the insecurity that I suffered from for many years. They enabled me to remain alone in a room and not to panic when the adults went shopping in the village. In addition, it was a strange feeling for me to know that there was no one in our large family house apart from me. At such times, I felt myself surrounded by "spirits."

With the Scouts

ONE afternoon I went with Auntie to visit the history museum in Basel for the first time. As we inspected the great Knights' Hall, Auntie said, "Look, there are the soldiers in the heavy armor that protects them from stabs and sword blows. Over there on the wall, you can see the halberds, maces, daggers, and rapiers, crossbows, and shields. Not far away are the cannons and the cannonballs to destroy the houses—and look, there are some pictures of battles!" The many instruments to kill and maim were just too much for me, and it took me days to get over the visit.

On a beautiful spring day a few weeks later, Auntie and I went on a long walk. We went from house to house, collecting money for the Red Cross. I watched her very closely and at last asked her what all this was for. She began telling me in simple language and at length about World War II but without mentioning the background to it.

"Today war is everywhere," she said, "and only in Switzerland is there no war. The wicked German soldiers have marched into many countries and destroyed homes with their cannons and killed lots of

6. Even as an adult, I was delighted by fancy dress. In 1983 at an artists' masked ball in Basel, I performed as a witch dressed in an old silk, green-striped skirt purchased at a flea market. My head was adorned with an absurd, self-made crown plaited from wire and pearls. My face was painted dark red, my cheeks sported vertical white lines, and the tip of my nose proudly displayed a pitch-black spot. This somewhat odd presentation, it must be admitted, can be understood only by one initiated into "kangaroo lore" since, in essence, and if somewhat stylized, it was meant to characterize the outer appearance of the large red kangaroo. However, fearing ridicule, I was chary of letting people know about the resemblance. This was of prime importance to me.

people. There are many people and many children who don't have a home anymore. They're poor. They wear torn clothes and worn-out shoes. That's very, very sad, and we have to collect money for them so that they can live in a house again and have clothes and shoes and something to eat."

"Do German soldiers have suits of armor?" I asked quickly.

"No, soldiers don't use armor anymore. It's much too much to carry," Auntie answered with a slight smile.

War was part of my world from this day forward, so I had the feeling that I had been born into a warring world. I did not know yet when it had begun and assumed that it would never end. I was deeply affected by the newspaper pictures that came my way and by Auntie's explanations. At the table, many questions that arose ended more and more frequently with the refrain "war this, war that." Military parades, march music, and the uniforms worn by Swiss soldiers fascinated me, so I often dreamed of marching forth myself in a fine uniform. When we went on a trip somewhere, I always wore a headscarf around my shoulders and waist as I had seen the soldiers wear their rolled-up pelerines.

AT TEN, I learned that children, too, could wear uniforms. The ones I encountered were khaki shirts worn by boys and blue blouses worn by girls. Both sported cowboy hats and gaily colored ties. I talked about them every day, and my greatest wish was to be one of them. In the spring of 1944, I joined the Girl Guides (the Pfadis[7]). This particular group, called "Despite Everything," was a special unit for girls with disabilities. Even during the week, I looked forward to our meeting on Saturday afternoon, which took place either in a pub room in Basel or in a forest. The greeting we exchanged as guides, a hand touching our hat, had considerable significance for me. I learned how to read tracks, make a fire, prepare soup, and play a number of games.

Although I was a member of the group, the sight of so many young people with disabilities—bodies in wheelchairs, legs in splints, and

---

7. One referred to the scout movement members in Switzerland as Pfadis.

arms with crutches—during our summer camp made me very sad. At first, I felt that I had to show deep sympathy rather than cheerfulness to those around me. Accordingly, one merry evening while we were playing our games, I disappeared from the hall without being seen, changed in the dormitory, and returned as an "angel" with a halo constructed from a Girl Guide tie. Then I planted myself in front of the company, folded my hands, and, in words that were difficult to understand, prayed that everyone present would be cured. I imagined that they would all be healed by the intensity of my prayer and be able to abandon their crutches, splints, and wheelchairs on the spot. The reaction stunned me: Almost everyone cheered. It was only later that I realized that most of them would have to bear their disability for a lifetime.

I felt at home from my very first moment at the Girl Guide Camp, and this was probably because of the kindness of our leaders and perhaps the relaxed discipline. It was a very different atmosphere from that at home. These were good times. The group had a number of adventures in the mountains, where we camped in tents, and once we even went to Holland to see the ocean. For the next ten years I worked my way to the top by passing all kinds of tests, for each of which I received a badge that was later sewn to my blue blouse. Finally, I became a group leader. For another five years I was a regular member of the nondisabled team, the Rangers, one of the higher orders of the organization. Here I was fully accepted and was allowed to lead the field exercises on occasion.

THE dangers of war increased during the winter of 1944–1945. Practically every night we saw the flashes of gunfire, lighting up the horizon. During the day we saw the rising clouds of black smoke following the bombardments. These were the result of heavy fighting, as the Allies drove the German troops out of Alsace and later marched into Germany themselves. The disturbing sound of bomber squadrons in the air and the subsequent explosions went on all night and kept us wide awake. When I cried, Auntie would come into my bedroom and comfort me. "The good ones are driving the wicked Germans into the fire," she used to say.

The area along the Swiss frontier was subject to very strict black-out rules because of the threat of air attack. There were no blinds in our hallway or in the bathroom, so we had to make do by covering the lamps or using blue light bulbs. These created such a strange atmosphere that for some time I was afraid to get up at night to use the bathroom.

Then, one day in May 1945, we were sitting at breakfast when Mummy announced that either today or tomorrow the war would be over. The next afternoon, Auntie, Peter, and I took the streetcar to a place near the border to watch the last stages of the tragedy. But when we got there, there was nothing to see. It was a beautiful day. The orchards were in bloom, and the fields we walked along were superbly green. From the streetcar on the way back, we could see what was going on in the city. There were long columns of refugees, people eager to distribute special issues of a newspaper, others with large placards, and still others animatedly discussing the most recent issues and much more. I think I can recall people joyfully celebrating victory in the streetcar, but I do remember Auntie suddenly saying to me, "Now the war is over!"

Once back home, I asked Auntie and Mummy whether there would be bananas and oranges from now on, as I was fed up with eating only apples and pears year in and year out! But they disappointed me by saying that it would be a long time before these found their way onto the market since the railroads had been destroyed and new tracks had to be laid.

Courage and Independence Are Steadily Growing

THOSE nearest and dearest to me tried to shield me from my attacks of fear, and I, too, wanted to become braver. They encouraged me to go out on my own, to take the streetcar and find my way home. But anxiety always thwarted my efforts. Then, one day when I was about fourteen, Auntie devised a plan to rid me of my anxiety once and for all. She lovingly persuaded me to take the streetcar into the city by myself for the first time. There we would meet at a restaurant and have lunch together as a reward. So that she would not be called upon at the last moment to offer her helpful services, Auntie left the house some hours before I did.

I set off bravely and knew before I had gone very far that this time things were going to be different. I breathed more freely and, apart from a slight excitement, did not feel the usual fears. In the streetcar I found that I could even smile. It seemed then that my insecurity and my awkwardness had simply been blown away. On my way through the city I found that I could orient myself well, and without difficulty I located the restaurant, where Auntie was waiting for me. I was so happy and proud of myself!

Because of this experience I began going shopping in the village by myself and even took trips into town. I was no longer so eager for someone to accompany me. I also felt more independent and was even able to venture into the countryside. One fine Sunday morning I wandered through Riehen's woods alone. I walked happily through the Wenkenpark, past the pond, and from there to a path that I knew led into the woods. There I paused for a moment and took my bearings. I looked for a fork and the footpath, which now lay under broken twigs and decaying leaves. I had often dreamed that there were fearsome ghosts here that were intent on possessing my soul. In other dreams this narrow, "holy" path led to the dancing court of the kangaroos. This particular Sunday I had no fears as I set off on the path. My parents had never accompanied me on this route, probably thinking that it led nowhere, but I knew better—thanks to a map I had read.

And so I walked on until I reached a hillock at the end of the forest path. I climbed up it. I immensely enjoyed the feeling of being by myself. Since the trees were not very close together, the sun was able to shine through and illuminate the bushes and other plants in their finest green. There were blackberry bushes with their white blossoms, woodruff, wood anemones, and, to my great delight, yellow cowslips and the reddish violet lungwort all growing together. I didn't pick anything because I loved it all, this splendid vegetation, thriving on the damp, pungent-smelling earth. It was better to admire it here than to possess a pale reflection of it stuck in a vase in my room. At every turn I was obliged to kick my way through thorny blackberry creepers, which threatened to cling to my clothes. Once at the top of the knoll, I sat down for a while not to rest but to look around. The warm rays of the sun caressed my bare arms. A tiny beetle was also sunning himself there.

Almost overcome by the surrounding beauty of nature, I stood up and cautiously went down the hill. Feeling joy in every fiber of my being, I walked home through the woods and meadows and passed a small village on the way. Then I increased my pace. Soon I would be home, where a delicious lunch from mother's kitchen was awaiting me.

My World of Dreams

AS FAR as I can remember, I was three years old when I first discovered the picture cabinet in which, by both day and night, living scenes passed before my eyes as though conjured up from nothing. I still have my dreams even today, and that alone would be nothing much to comment on, but, contrary to many of my fellow human beings, for me these dreams are important. Consequently, I have always given them my special attention even if they have sometimes been oppressive or have tormented me by their repetition.

I can still remember my mother asking me once at dinner why I laughed so often in my sleep. For a long time I remained unresponsive. But my mother didn't let up, so one day I blurted out, "Last night I dreamed about . . ." At that moment the bird was out of its cage, and from then on I loved to talk about my dreams in all their detail with a roguish smile on my lips. These stories of mine became a source of enduring interest for the adults listening to them. When I became familiar with the biblical stories of Joseph and the significance of his dreams, I tried to understand my own and found that I was able to do so quite well.

3

Under the Spell of the Kangaroo

ONE day after the war had officially ended, Auntie told me for the first time about the origins of World War II. To help explain, she took me into her bedroom and showed me a large map of the world that indicated the theaters of the war. She also pointed out the seven continents, including a huge, purple-red island. "That's Australia!" she said. I peered at this richly contoured shape. It was not only totally foreign to me but also seemed to be at the edge of the world, and I could not have even told you whether any living creatures existed there! Regardless of this, the shape of the island stuck in my mind like a seed planted in my memory. Of course, at the time I had no idea that Australia would one day hold a central place in my life.

One superbly sunny day in May, Auntie sat opposite me at the table, opened the school reading book, and smiled down at me. "I've got a long zoo story for you today," she announced. I was four years old at the time. She began reading, and I followed the story word for word from her lips.[8] This was a hard job, but I enjoyed this exciting animal story. At first, there were stories about apes, elephants, various predators, and other inhabitants of the zoo. And then Auntie read about the kangaroos.

---

8. This is how we always communicated. We did not use sign language.

At this word, Auntie looked at me kindly and made kangaroo hops with her hands. In doing so, she demonstrated to me how high these animals can jump even with a full pouch. I laughed with her!

Some days later we visited the Natural History Museum. Auntie instructed me to draw various animals, an assignment I didn't much care for. After completing sketches of several animals, we packed up our things, but as I was heading for the exit, Auntie gently tugged at my sleeve and signaled that I should go back. She placed my stool in front of a glass window and, with a cheeky smile, suggested that I draw this one last animal. It was a kangaroo. Still a little unwilling, I nevertheless sat down and drew what was there. Not overly pleased with my rendering, Auntie took the pencil and corrected some of the outlines. Then she had me copy the description on the display. I scribbled down the text. A moment later I was astonished to read that kangaroos eat only plants.

"Do they eat tulips, cowslips, and sunflowers, do you think?" I asked.

"You know they eat only grass!" Auntie replied, her forehead furrowed.

A few days after this we went to the zoo again. Auntie hurried along in front of me, carrying a list of animals that she wanted to show me. We rushed past several pens in the process, including those containing kangaroos. However, I just could not help glancing at them, and it was at this very moment that something passed through me like a flash of lightning. It may sound rather strange, but so it was. Without wanting to, I jumped into the air! The inner spark had become a flame, and a close relationship with kangaroos had been struck. This was how it was to be in the future.

On another occasion, Auntie and I went for a walk in the brilliant sunshine. All of a sudden, I stopped for a moment and then began hopping over puddles so that my braids just flew! "Kangaroo! Kangaroo!" Auntie called the moment I turned toward her again. Looking back on that moment, I can say that my enormous affection for the species was first promoted by Auntie, who understood me and cheerfully accompanied me everywhere.

From then on, our school lessons went along in a more cheerful way, and on every suitable occasion I talked about kangaroos.
It wasn't long before the blackboard, my exercise books, the edges
of newspaper reports, and even the pavement outside were full of
kangaroo portraits. With assiduous practice, I soon became a master
of kangaroo portraiture. I drew them standing, hopping, and playing, with full or empty pouches. When we went on walks, I would
hop over the fields and through the woods until Auntie would call
out that tonight she would have to inform a keeper at the zoo that
one of the kangaroos had broken out and was jumping around in the
meadow.

I wanted to know everything about this animal. One day I interrupted our handicraft lesson to put the burning question to Auntie
as to how a kangaroo baby could be so well looked after in the pouch
and what it did in there all day. (This was a subject I investigated
later during my scientific research.) Auntie looked flabbergasted for
a moment. Then she said that I should first finish the crocheting I
was doing and then she would show me something. I was intrigued.
She brought out a copy of Schmeil's *Animal Life*, which had been
with me since childhood, and thumbed through the pages until she
found what she was looking for.

The young kangaroo is barely two centimeters long when it is
born. Just after its birth, the mother conveys it with her lower lips
(Auntie didn't elaborate here) to the inner folds of the pouch. Once
there, it suckles until it's about seven months old, when it looks out
from the pouch for the first time.

I was bowled over by this information and looked at Auntie, quite
unable to comment on this very odd procedure. Auntie then showed
me a picture of a newly born kangaroo, which still looked for all the
world like a fetus. For weeks I thought about the kangaroo mother's
care of her baby, which seemed to me no less than a miracle.

I asked Auntie where the kangaroo comes from, and without a
moment's hesitation she said, "From Africa." However, on our next
visit to the Natural History Museum, I discovered from the "habitat" sign a huge island marked in bright red called "Australia."

One Sunday morning Daddy and I were happily playing when he suddenly raised his eyebrows and looked at me quizzically as though he suspected that I was up to something. After a very short pause, I said, "When I get to Australia, I'll grab a kangaroo, stroke it, and give it some grass." He creased his eyebrows at this. "You won't be able to touch them. They're very shy, and they'll run away just like that!"

"I'll run after them, and perhaps I can catch them," I replied, quite convinced of my powers.

One of my mother's acquaintances who was staying with us for a time said that in 1900 her father had been in Australia, where he had traded in sheep's wool. At the time, he had sighted a whole herd of kangaroos that had vanished very quickly. Up to that point I had read in various books and magazines that the kangaroo was a friendly, trusting animal. And now that! This news was a huge disappointment for me. Nevertheless, I did not want to accept it as the last word on kangaroos. Australia remained my dreamland even if my encounter with kangaroos seemed so distant as to be impossible. On top of this was the astronomical cost of such a journey, especially just after the war. Clearly, for the time being at least, it had to remain a dream. Despite the seemingly unattainable, I saved like mad!

WHEN summer came, my family went to the mountains again. Auntie and I rambled past the waterfall, Abbachfall, and then went farther uphill. As we gazed on the wonderful alpine meadows, I asked myself and then Auntie whether a kangaroo would be able to hop down these slopes. She laughed heartily and said it would probably mean its end. It was far too steep and much too far. I was later to learn in Australia that such judgments can be very deceptive.

At home, there were several fairly steep steps from the front door to the path and garden gate. Because of my balance problems, which are due to Usher's syndrome (see note 40), these steps presented something of a challenge to me, and I always tackled them with care until one day when Auntie called out, "Look how quickly the other children jump down the steps, Doris! You're much too slow! Hoppity-hop! Jump like them!" I noticed that all of the others had reached the bottom long before I did. Then I was seized by ambition; I wanted to be like them, so I'd go down the stairs like they did! Thus inspired, I was soon able to get down the steps as fast as the others. Greatly encouraged and full of pride at my achievement, I began to jump down several steps at a time or, like a kangaroo, hopped recklessly into the village and over a small brook without landing in the water. I even jumped from high walls and over small haystacks at harvest time. Jumping was no longer a problem.

On my birthday, Auntie gave me a small kangaroo carved out of wood. I was very happy with her gift, which I carefully studied from all sides. It wasn't long before I had mentally noted its form and had started "carving" my own kangaroos from hard cheese and kneading them from bread. They then appeared as "decorations" on the table at every evening meal. My family and any dinner guests were partly delighted and partly irritated by this innovation. On one occasion I abruptly announced that two kangaroos were outside in the hall and then hopped up and down, stamping my feet. "Don't be so noisy!" Mother said, a little annoyed. I laughingly retorted, "But it's true; they're outside and are hopping about!"

If I happened to come across pictures or stories of kangaroos in illustrated magazines, I would try very hard to hide my excitement, but, despite this, others in the house would notice my enthusiasm and make fun of me. This used to offend me because it touched a soft spot.

WHEN I was seven years old, Auntie taught me how to pray. I would fold my hands each evening and say, "Dear God, let thy hand guide me through the night. Amen." At some point, Auntie allowed me to pray in my own way, and on these occasions I would say the following: "Dear God, bring the sun and a blue sky. Amen." Then there was another prayer in which I included my brother. "Dear God, grant that Peter can soon speak. Amen." I felt solely responsible for the content of my prayers, and I concerned myself intensively with the idea of a loving God.

As a result of my association with Auntie and the servants in the house, I was familiar with Christian traditions. Auntie thoroughly instructed me in the meaning of Christian holy days and holidays and their biblical background. I took a lot of this to heart and, like my fellow Christians, looked forward to the approaching Christian festivals not only because these were public holidays and meant no school but also because they were occasions that I could celebrate, too.

Contact with Judaism

BY THE time I was eleven, World War II was over, and the danger for us as Jews had passed. Mother now took the opportunity to tell me about the Jewish faith, a religion that I soon found captivating. In order to familiarize myself with Judaism and its culture, I became friends with Paula, a girl of the same age, who came from a very devout Jewish family. We met regularly at playtime. Thanks to this contact, I one day made an astonishing discovery, although at first it irritated me.

It was summer, and Paula and I wanted to go swimming. I asked my mother for a little pocket money so that we could buy some ice cream. But this she denied me, saying that Paula would not be allowed to eat it and that this applied to all other foods that were not "pure" (I didn't know the word "kosher"). Among others, pork was an example. Why not? Why no pork or ice cream? I didn't grasp what mother was trying to tell me and wondered why Paula was not allowed to eat ice cream. Was it because of the sugar? If that were the case, there was certainly no sugar in pork! I just couldn't find a common denominator.

I soon learned about the Jewish dietary laws and saw for myself what was served at the Orthodox table. How appalled I was to learn how often pork was served at home! This meant, then, that we were not particularly pious people. I believed this kind of thing had to stop. I decided from then on to do as Paula and her Jewish friends did and announced there and then my intention to be a pious Jew. I vowed never to touch pork again—and not only pork but also other meat that was possibly questionable. In so doing, I did indeed pick out the pieces of bacon rind or other meats and put them on the edge of my plate, thereby keeping my oath. However, on one occasion, out of forgetfulness I ate something I shouldn't have eaten. When I realized this, I burst into tears.

My mother frequently urged me to adopt the eating habits of my Christian friends and Girl Guides. However, I stuck to my guns until I realized that my "eating sins" went quite unpunished by "God above." After this, I adopted a philosophy that I have maintained to this very day and which has allowed me to avoid unpleasantness. If, for example, on being invited somewhere, I am obliged to decline nonkosher foods, I almost always experience discomfort at being discourteous to my hosts. If, on the other hand, I am polite and eat foods that are forbidden, I'm no longer plagued by discomfiture. This is because I have imposed this practice upon myself and entirely of my own accord and follow it to the letter when I'm alone. As it is my own, independent decision, I feel that in the company of others I am free to choose.

However, one evening, a fateful aspect of life in all its desperate reality broke in on the family and threw a shadow over our lives. After our meal, and with a very serious air, Mother read a long letter to us. Many of the words in it had been struck out in black by the censoring agency. I noticed how worried she was and asked what the letter was about. She told me that at last a letter had arrived from her relatives in Holland, who, with the exception of my great uncle, had survived the horrors of Bergen-Belsen. Totally impoverished, they had now returned to their home country. Mummy said that she would have to speak to Daddy to find out how they could be helped. I couldn't understand what it was all about; after all, the war was over.

Mother explained to me that the Nazis had dragged off millions of people to concentration camps and there put them to death. The majority of these victims were Jews. It was only through her painstaking explanation that I learned that we were Jews. I was eleven years old. Up to that time, I had grown up in what one might call a Christian "cocoon," one woven, so to speak, from Auntie's presence, Auntie's family, our maid and neighbors, and, of course, the Pfadis.

In all of this, the pictures and decorations associated with Christian festivals and feast days also played a large role. There was little to bear witness of a Jewish atmosphere in our house, although I had seen Jewish rites and ceremonies performed by my relatives in their homes. However, I knew little or nothing of their significance.

Without knowing the meaning of it all, I do remember the morning prayer once recited at my grandfather's house, which had left a strong impression on my young mind. I was about five at the time and on a visit to my grandfather on my mother's side. On this occasion, I watched how he emerged from the bedroom early in the morning with his prayer robe, the tallith over his shoulders, the tefillin (prayer bands) with its box secured to his head, and the other band wound around his left arm. In one hand he held a book stemming from the time of our great grandparents and then bowed several times. Inspired by this procedure, I recall trying to imitate it, using pieces of string and shoelaces to wind around my head and arm.

Years later, my grandfather failed one day to come down to breakfast and lunch, which seemed unusual. However, he returned to the table at dinner, and this made me happy. I asked him where he had been, and he replied with something I didn't understand. I looked questioningly at Auntie, who, instead of using the word "synagogue," a word I found difficult to decipher, said simply, "in church." It must have been the Day of Atonement (Yom Kippur), a Jewish festival whose significance became clear to me only years later. I also remember how he once put the prayer book under my nose, and I noted with astonishment how familiar he was with these, for me, completely alien Hebrew letters.

From then on, Mummy and I often talked about our own Jewish tradition. Finally she decided to revive these in our own home. She had often been urged to be baptized a Christian, especially during the war, while others had even more strongly suggested emigration. The fact was that she felt a little lost in her almost exclusively Christian environment.

Hanni, a Dutch relative of ours, spent six months with us after her release from a concentration camp. I recall this girl with her smooth, blonde hair and remember how thin she was and how ill she still was, but thanks to the warmth she received from the family and to the care she was given, she quickly recuperated.

We were both eleven at the time, but since Hanni was a relatively inexperienced young person and still a child in many ways, her ordeal remained inaccessible to me. Her suffering could not be imagined and stayed hidden behind her merry laugh and her cheerfulness. My mother often scolded me, at the same time pointing out that Hanni was always ready to help in the house, whereas I was frequently grumpy and unwilling to lift a finger. Hanni and I soon managed to communicate very well with one another because I was proficient at lipreading, and I of course tried to awaken an interest in kangaroos in her, but she could not muster much enthusiasm for them. Nevertheless, she showed her friendship for me by composing jolly little ditties about my "mania," which I enjoyed. Once I fell ill with influenza and had to stay in bed. It was at this time that I was offered some smoked sprats to eat. I refused them. Hanni giggled at this and immediately scrawled on the board: "Kangaroos would certainly have eaten them all up!" On the other hand, I got to know the Star of David through her. She drew a number of these with me and, to my greatest joy, wrote the word "kangaroo" neatly in the middle of them.

Through Hanni I soon became acquainted with a religious way of life unknown in our family. We lived as "assimilated" Jews, not as Orthodox. Auntie explained that Hanni did no housework or knitting on Saturday since that day for her was the Sabbath. From then on, I wanted to observe the Sabbath like her and work on Sunday. This proved to be ticklish, however, but more later.

WHEN Hanni eventually left us to join her family in Holland, Mummy sent me to a Jewish woman teacher for religious instruction. Before long I could read and write Hebrew quite well, but I couldn't speak it. Delighted with this new dimension in life, I began covering everything with Hebrew letters, not least, of course, my schoolbooks and the blackboard. Naturally, I wrote the name of my favorite animal everywhere and wanted dearly to magically integrate the creature somehow into my newly discovered religion.

Shortly before we visited the synagogue for a service there, my mother told me that we were going to a "Jewish church." However, the word "synagogue" soon imprinted itself in my mind. Once inside, I felt somehow at home as I saw the Torah, the Torah scrolls, and the men praying in their talliths. Reading the axioms and quotations on the walls and dome inspired me, and the colored windows with their Eastern designs made my heart beat faster. I was delighted to belong to this oriental community. But I was astonished not to see an organ—something that is not generally part of synagogue furnishings. Nevertheless, I was able to feel the choir singing next to the Torah. The dignity of the rabbi, preaching from his pulpit, earned my respect, and I was deeply impressed by it all. During my visits to the synagogue at services and on religious festival days, my mother would quietly make the rabbi's words clear to me. These moments were stamped on my soul. Here I felt quite different from the way I felt elsewhere on ordinary days. There was a stillness in which I was quite alone, and there were the prayer books in German. Of course, I could not hear the voice of the man leading the prayers or the quiet murmuring of the congregation, but all of it was nevertheless beautiful and moving. It was balm for my soul, and it was also at these moments that I discovered empathy for all the creatures of God's creation.

Or perhaps not for everyone? Once, when I was in the city with Auntie, I said quite spontaneously that I could no longer love the Christians. Since the time I had become fixed on the Jewish religion and was convinced that this was the one true faith, I believed that the followers of other religions were by that much inferior. At least, that's the show I put on, having no corresponding knowledge.

Auntie stood still and regarded me with an accusing expression. She was dumbfounded by my remark. Then I was thoroughly scolded and told that I was a bad Girl Guide. Both Jews and Christians are good people. There are heathenish, bad people everywhere, and it is better to keep out of their way. Ashamed of my remark and a little confused, I looked at the people going past. The next evening

I asked my mum whether she loved Christians, and she promptly replied that she did. I was much relieved.

PUTTING me in my place and her subsequent confirmation were both important for me, and I have much to be grateful for with regard to this and to my upbringing in matters of belief as a whole. Because of this tolerant, reserved attitude within the family, doors everywhere were open to me in the future. Mutual respect and acknowledgment are for me the most important principles in things religious. As for me personally, I try to maintain a religious independence, one free of dogmatic regulations and any form of orthodoxy, which I find oppressive. On the contrary, I enjoy every form of cultural exchange with people of other religions and indeed even with atheists. In the case of the latter, it has often occurred to me that the rejection of a particular confession or church must not automatically imply a lack of faith. Often it is these ostensible "heathens" who are much finer tuned in their thinking and who show much more general interest in religious matters than do the representatives of some hard and fast religious system.

But to return to the synagogue or, for that matter, to kangaroos. One Sunday in the summer, my daddy came resolutely toward me and declared rather pompously that our visit to the zoo would have to go by the board. The reason was that Rabbi Weil and his wife would be paying us a visit within the hour. I was to help Mummy set the table in the garden and put out the drinks and snacks. Further, I was to be good and not talk about kangaroos since, and this he emphasized, these people were very pious. In any case, he went on, I had been warned on several occasions not to bore household staff and my comrades with my kangaroo stories. I was not pleased.

During the conversation that followed between my parents and the rabbi and his wife, the rules of proper behavior held me in steel bonds. However, eventually I developed a liking for this rabbi, not least for his beautiful sermons in the synagogue, which Mummy translated for me. Years later, my mother encouraged me to follow Rabbi Weil's suggestion to help decorate the synagogue yard at the traditional Feast of Tabernacles. After hesitating, I decided to jump in and help after my visit to the zoo. At the same time, I didn't dare to excuse myself for the possible "kangaroo smell," which possibly hung about me. Could the rabbi smell this at all? Had the aromas of grape, nuts, and autumn leaves succeeded in masking it? In any event, in the presence of my parents he invited me into the tent for the midday meal in order to thank me for my efforts. I was given a place of honor near him, which filled me with pride and happiness.

ONE night I dreamed I was on my way to the synagogue, when I suddenly felt a voice from above saying that it was strictly forbidden to pray for kangaroos. Perturbed, the very next morning I told my mother about the dream. She comforted me with the words that I was allowed to pray for all of God's creatures.

I was ardent in my prayers and used to read the thick prayer book avidly. Every time I came across the word "animal" my heart would beat strongly, similar to the way it had felt in my dream. Especially when I came to the moving words "the hills shall leap like goats," I was immediately overcome with the delicate smell of the kangaroo, which made me tingle strangely from head to toe.

Somehow, the knowledge of my preoccupation with kangaroos must have been passed from Rabbi Weil, who had died, to Rabbi Adler, his successor. This man invited Mummy and me for a visit one evening before Passover. The table was richly decorated, and imagine my surprised delight at finding an expensive present lying at my place. I was speechless. It was a black enamel broach in the shape of a kangaroo, inlaid with opal. This was the rabbi's small gift to me! I was filled with gratitude. For me, it was a symbol of the atonement between my beloved religion and my beloved animals. Finally, my concern for the kangaroo became too much for my parents, and they insisted that I say farewell to them once and for all. Their concern did not change much; things remained the same even when Daddy took pains from time to time to make it clear to me that God had created other animals in the world apart from the kangaroo!

4

Thwarted Courtship

AT SIXTEEN, my intensive reading of work that was written in simple, comprehensible German awakened in me a burning desire to write. Indeed, one could almost speak of a "rage to write." I was so overwhelmed with this desire that I didn't really grasp the fact that my ability to express myself was rather inadequate. I could draw upon only a relatively small treasury of words and expressions, so I went off to buy a fat notebook and began with enormous gusto to write my "principal opus," namely, "My Life with the Kangaroo, 1950–51." The first chapter began with these words: "I was a happy-go-lucky, deaf, young country girl of eleven."

I almost filled this notebook, and yet all the people that read it—my parents, Auntie, the Pfadis, and other friends—hardly knew what to say about it, apart from making jokes. A few years later, when I came to realize what rubbish I had put on paper, I got rid of the notebook, and it almost passed into oblivion. But it turned up again later and quite by accident as I was busy clearing out my library. I felt so embarrassed at finding it once more that I hardly dared turn its pages. I simply couldn't understand how my experiences and impressions at home, at school, and at the Girl Guides, as well as my experiences with the Jewish religion, my dreams, and my observations at the zoo could all be impossibly mixed up with all kinds of weird kangaroo sayings. The "diagnosis" was clear: Here was someone who was suffering severely from kangaroo fever!

The Struggle against Pressure

ONE day on a walk with my family, my father, who happened to be in especially good spirits that day, asked me just how long this "kangaroo love" was going to last. A little suspicious of his tone, I answered him in the same terms.

He then went on to make me fully acquainted with the Chinese belief that such an unalterable relationship would likely outshine death itself and go on into eternity. I felt that he was right. To this day, pictures of kangaroos pursue me day and night. Should I chance to be wandering in the countryside as an artist, I often find myself so engrossed in my own private fantasy world that I am overcome with the desire to let my imagination run away with me after the manner of a Marc Chagall painting, for example; kangaroos and donkeys in heaven, lions in a snow-covered garden, and many other freely envis- aged forms float before my inner eye. If I note the aroma of, say, the woods around me or of the meadows beyond, especially if these are combined with leaves of fox red from last autumn, then the smell of the kangaroo rises up in me and into my nose, producing a feel- ing akin to a current of electricity shooting through my body. I have found that an aromatic mixture of fresh leaves and humus evokes these strange sensations.

I ALWAYS found myself in a state of desperation when either my parents or my friends tried to destroy my private feelings for the kan- garoo or divert my attention to other topics. How could I go through life without these animals? To discard these feelings would be to remove an important element in me, and I would lose my inner bal- ance. And so it was that I fell into ever more frequent psychological turbulence according to whether my fellow human beings showed understanding for my affection for these animals or opposed it.

I needed to strengthen my sense of self-esteem in order to free myself from this all-too-powerful outside influence. Accordingly, and despite all external hindrances, I spoke quite frankly about my needs and about the things that moved me. I could do this best and in the most relaxed way during chats with my mother just before I went to sleep. However, sometimes even these conversations were unsatisfactory. On one of these evenings my mother tried to instill a greater sense of responsibility in me by citing my friends, some of whom were also deaf. She said that they had a much more developed sense of duty in caring about their parents' problems and worries. For her, she said with a smile, the kangaroo is just a toy. "I'm not less responsible than they are!" I screamed. "Don't make such a fuss!" my mother said, much taken aback by my reaction. I stared at her for a long moment, tears welling up in my eyes. Then a thought shot through my head, and I probed: "Am I much more retarded than my friends?" I asked. "No," she replied. "You've certainly made progress, but on the other hand, you're still a child." For me, these were hard words, and I didn't feel that I was being taken seriously.

On another occasion, my mother and I talked about famous contemporaries, and I asked her whether I could become famous with kangaroos. She turned her eyes heavenward at this and said that such a thing was impossible as these animals were just boring. It was possible that I could make a name for myself by helping other people who had disabilities, so that people would talk about me—but with kangaroos, no, that was impossible! Even so, I stood my ground. Weeks later, I spoke to my mother again about my wish to become an author. I told her that, along with doing my job, I was prepared to devote every free minute to writing. My theme would be—yes, kangaroos. Astonished, but with a loving smile, my mother told me that I was exactly like Anne Frank, who was also preoccupied with the idea of world fame, and this encouraged me.

Of course, Auntie was one of those persons I entrusted with my thoughts, but there were also a few friends. I realized, though, that I needed many more people with whom I could seriously share my enthusiasm for kangaroos over a long period. One of these was Brigitte, who listened to my accounts with a sympathetic ear. I met her while studying sculpture and drawing at vocational school, and even today I can still rave about kangaroos and Australia with her. She worked at the Basel Zoo in the bird department for a year but then trained as a music teacher, later as a violinist, giving concerts here and there. On seeing cartoons in the newspaper showing kangaroos playing this instrument, I called her "Wallaby" (a small species of kangaroo) from then on, meaning that I was thinking of her as a "great girl."

A "Liberator" Comes on Stage

DURING a car ride, Mother told me something interesting. My uncle in Tel Aviv had by coincidence met a certain young man named Simon, who, like me, was deaf. He worked for the military as a specialist in the manufacture of machine guns. My uncle had asked him to write to me. On returning home, I noticed that a letter from Simon was already on the hall table waiting for me. Without much enthusiasm, I slit it open and read the following: "I don't know what you're like, but write from your heart if you're really interested. I'm 26 years old, have a sense of humor and a zest for life."

I was just sixteen, and the feelings that overcame me at this moment were highly conflicting. The most dominant was the realization that I would have to prepare myself for a life far away from kangaroos.

I began corresponding regularly with Simon and sent him so-called care packages since at that time provisions were in short supply in Israel. I also fulfilled his wishes where bicycle parts were concerned. All this was done from a sense of duty; there were no feelings of affection on my side. I felt strongly that we had no common interests. He had sent a photo, which aroused no great interest in me, either. On the other hand, the photos I sent him seemed to appeal to him, for he called me a pretty young woman. Moreover, Mother pressed me to take an interest in Simon and to inform him about everyday matters rather than kangaroos since he could make something of the former and nothing of the latter. Virtually none of my letters went to the post without Mother having read it first. Everything was controlled. Not only were they checked for correct expression but also for the views I expressed, which, according to her, Simon would only find ridiculous. I found this "censorship" an irritating restriction and, moreover, felt myself being drawn into a personal relationship against my will.

Four years later—I was then not quite twenty—my struggle for independence of thought and action had reached a critical point. Sometimes I would have such "wars" with my mother that I'd even become frightened of myself! On one occasion I did feel some warmth for Simon, and I asked her how a marriage could come into being. She replied that he would have to ask me whether I wanted to be his wife. I was filled with apprehension at the thought of what Mother would do to organize the founding of a family. All I really wanted was for this business to remain exclusively my own. Under no circumstances did I want others to involve themselves in my affairs and so push me into an unhappy marriage. Although I felt a strong instinct at times to enter into wedlock, it was nevertheless a basic condition as far as I was concerned to be with someone who had mutual interests and who respected his partner. On the other hand, from Simon's letters I was able to acquire a pretty accurate idea of life in Israel as the "Promised Land," and this was most congenial to me. What he wrote in his letter on the war of 1948 was very touching.

In the meantime, at the vocational school, where I was studying handweaving, graphic design, and modeling, I got to know a young Hungarian who could hear and was also studying graphic design. We used to meet during school breaks, and I was always pleased when he would greet me first. I had to hold myself back in order not to reveal my feelings for him too openly. Our communication took place on a verbal level and was about our life at school and peppered with quite a lot of fun. He talked of his interests and about the political destiny of his country under communist oppression. I was fascinated and learned much that was new to me. His sympathy for my interest in kangaroos was not so important as the harmony I felt between us, an accord that did my soul good.

I used to tell my parents about these pleasant encounters but earned not much more than a faint smile. My parents were of the opinion that a deaf person should not marry someone who could hear. In addition, marriage between Jews and Christians was not without its problems. After final examinations at school, I lost sight of my Hungarian friend, and Mummy never tired of telling me how good Simon would be as a husband.

Four years after this, my relations with Simon took on a more serious nature. I was almost free of parental control by then and wrote to him of my plan to live in Israel. First, though, I wanted to go to Britain to work at a social institution so as to improve my English. I wrote that I was eager to meet him, to which he replied that I should first come to Israel, as he was curious, too, to get to know me. To this, I said that I would have to go to eastern Switzerland first to learn domestic science, so that I could arrive in Israel suitably qualified to work in a kibbutz. I also mentioned kangaroos in more detail in this letter, hoping that Simon would show a little interest in this direction.

While at this college, in which I was the only deaf person, for six months of the spring and summer, I received a letter from Simon one morning that Mother had sent on to me. I opened it in haste. It read as follows: "You are sick. It's an addiction to the kangaroo called [here he used a made-up, pseudomedical term, which I can no longer remember]. Try to get off this hobbyhorse so that you can come and live with me as a cured person. I wish you all the best in the attempt."

Everything around me began to spin; I felt dizzy. I tucked the letter hastily under my pillow. I had the greatest difficulty in hiding my utter dejection. Simon's words had wounded me more deeply than any others before. Having said this, I was also relieved that I was not at home, where family members would probably attempt to change my mind in Simon's favor.

The next day I wrote to Auntie, my only confidante in intimate matters, and told her about the whole affair. She answered that I shouldn't worry unduly about making plans to marry just yet. After all, a single person can live independently and be just as happy. (She herself had never been married.) This consoled me a little, but I still worried that my parents might take me to task about Simon.

As for me and my kangaroos, everybody from students to the staff and from there to the school administration soon knew of my passion! They were all pleased. Once a week, a student was given an opportunity to talk to the others about one of their interests. When I was in a position to communicate verbally with practically everyone, I was also eligible to speak. Delighted to do so, I talked of my experiences with kangaroos at the Basel Zoo, and everyone applauded my efforts. I could hardly believe my luck! The talk counted among my dearest memories, as it was the first time that I had had an opportunity to air my feelings in public.

During a short school vacation I went home alone by bus and train. My parents warmly greeted me at the bus station, and my fears of admonition instantly disappeared. However, at four o'clock tea, I discovered a letter from Simon waiting for me on the table. I turned to stone. Wordlessly, I looked at my mother, who smiled back and asked how things were between Simon and me. I needed all the strength I could muster at that moment to tell her that I hadn't corresponded with him for months. I opened the letter with conscious deliberation and then read his sharp words: "Dear Doris, I believe that you are now healthier and quite cured of your sick feelings. . . . Have you made plans by now to come to Israel so that we can meet up?. . . Do write to me soon!"

CALMLY but with a wry smile, I gave Mother the letter to read. In order to divert her attention, I asked her to look at me to see whether the blisters I'd had earlier from chicken pox had all healed. She examined my face and, smiling, told me that my complexion was all right and that the remaining spots were the result of the overconsumption of cheese and nuts. I then plunged into accounts of my experiences without letting her get a word in edgewise. Breathlessly, I recounted my adventures at the domestic science school, reported on making bread, roasting oats—and of course my first public lecture on kangaroos. My parents listened with rapt attention. Without hesitating I also informed them that I had decided after all not to go and settle in Israel. As a result of my quick narration, I had managed to gather enough courage in the telling that I found it relatively easy to add this last announcement.

Fortunate Outcome

TO MY utter astonishment, my decision did not have the negative effect on the household that I had anticipated. I had expected accusations, but instead my parents shared my views. I felt, too, that this was because they were pleased to have me at home for a little longer. My father in particular was so pleased that he exploded into all kinds of jokes and funny anecdotes.

While our evening meal was being prepared, I explained the whole business between Simon and me in detail. We all laughed about his odd views. At the same time, a huge burden fell from my shoulders. I felt free. My mother advised me to write to him in peace, and I did just that. He never answered the letter. Happily, I returned to school for the last month of study.

I was just about to tackle a huge pile of dirty dishes when I sensed a kind of rattling. Shocked, I looked around to see a horde of students rushing toward me. They encircled me and told me that the new teacher in household studies had just arrived. She happened to be a Swiss woman who had spent years in Australia. I was so thrilled that I almost let the pots fall on the floor! I couldn't wait to meet this new teacher. For the first time in my life I would be able to talk to a person who had been to Australia. Thanks to this teacher, whom I bombarded with questions, I came a little closer to my beloved continent. I even began to forge plans for a future visit. What's more, I didn't take umbrage when she admonished me for careless work from time to time. Much more important to me was the fact that I would be leaving the place at the end of the month, when the course would be over. As a farewell present, this teacher gave me a few Australian coins with kangaroo images on them. My mother had one of them gold-plated and surprised me with it on my twenty-first birthday.

IN THE autumn of 1954, I got my first job as a handweaver. There was a small handweaving business near the famous Spalentor (Spalen Tower), in the city's Old Town, situated in a charming, three-story house from the eighteenth century. I had been on good terms with Lotti, the manager, for some years, and could communicate with her perfectly. I wove, warped, tightened threads, and spooled happily all day long. I was also glad to serve customers, friends, and acquaintances when they dropped by and also decorated the shop display window. Coffee breaks were especially exciting for me when I was able to chat with Lotti and the other employees about "my" kangaroos.

While working at the loom, I was able to look down from the second story at the people below in the very small inner courtyard. Once the reel slid from my hand and fell into the yard, and I had to run down and retrieve it. Not long after, this event returned to me in a dream. I related it to my mother, not without a certain feeling of anxiety:

> *Just as I am busy serving a customer, Simon appears in the shop. He showers me with accusations, rips the kangaroo chain from my neck, and demands that I go off with him. Unable to help myself, I run upstairs and throw myself out of the top-story window into the courtyard below so as to escape an unhappy future by my death. Although I crash onto the stones below, I feel no pain and am apparently uninjured. I stand up, only to find that the door has vanished. Searching in vain for the exit, I come upon a small hole and quickly creep through it to find myself outside in a broad expanse of wonderfully green meadowland.*

My mother suggested that the significance of this dream was that I had found a means of escape from possible unhappiness into a free, fulfilled life. This I found very encouraging.

5

Dora

WHEN I was fifteen, the need to actually touch a kangaroo grew from day to day. However, there were insuperable obstacles to my doing so. The reasons lay in the infinitely deep feelings that these animals stirred in me. No other animal aroused such emotion. Whenever I visited the Basel Zoo to watch the kangaroos, shivering overwhelmed me, took complete control of my body, and was sometimes so strong that I could do nothing about it. It was not only a very odd phenomenon but also uncanny; it was as though something alien had overpowered me and was tormenting my soul. From time to time, I complained of this to my mother. Her reaction was to try to cheer me up by playfully suggesting that this symptom belonged to a true kangaroo lover. On other occasions, she tried to soothe me by quoting something or other along the lines of "The roses one loves have thorns, too!"

My inhibitions lasted until the day I encountered a class of schoolchildren at the zoo. The children crowded and crouched in front of the pen and stroked some of the less shy among the kangaroos. Seeing this produced an irresistible urge in me to do the same, and I pushed forward and stretched out my hand to touch one of them. An indescribable feeling of pleasure coursed through my being as I ran my shaking hand over the animal's coat, amazed at how soft it was. It was even softer than that of a cat! It was precisely this bodily contact that calmed my excitement. After a few months my shivering ended.

Kangaroos in the Basel Zoo.

One Sunday as we were in the zoo section for antelopes, where the kangaroos also lived, I asked my mother to speak to the keeper, Glücki, and tell him about my passionate interest in these animals. She readily agreed, and we had a lively conversation with him. Then my mother told me that Glücki wanted to surprise me and had something up his sleeve that would make me happy. We waited, all keyed up for what was in store for us. Then the keeper appeared with a two-and-a-half-year-old female kangaroo. For a moment or two it struggled but then settled down comfortably in Glücki's arms. It had a beautifully formed head and sweet brown eyes that watched me carefully. I looked at it for a while and then began to stroke it gently. I was amazed to learn that this little animal already had a baby in its pouch about the size of a mouse!

A little later, I began visiting the zoo regularly to see a group of nine giant gray kangaroos. Several times a week I would get up at half past five in the morning, hurriedly prepare my breakfast, set off by streetcar for Basel, and then walk on the zoo, which opened at seven in the morning. I spent almost half an hour there looking at the kangaroos before going to the vocational school, which was about twenty minutes away on foot. On these occasions I always had soap and a towel with me so that I could wash my hands before class. I was very eager not to emanate an animal smell in the classroom. Despite these precautions, my clothing had absorbed the various scents of the antelope house, in which not only the kangaroos but also the giraffes, okapis, gnus, and, of course, antelopes lived. In the winter, when the zoo opened an hour later, I would sacrifice my free time and my holidays to make these visits.

Glücki, who was responsible for all the animals in this section, soon became my friend. I grew fond of the mischievous spark in his kindly eyes and his warmhearted smile. We eagerly discussed the matter of looking after kangaroos either verbally or with the help of pen and paper when there were questions to be answered. What I learned about kangaroos at this time was carefully jotted down in a notebook I had with me and which I took great care of. Here is an example of one of these entries, together with the mistakes: "I went to the kangaroos and took carrots to the keeper. I had washed them at home, peeled them, and cut them fine, so that they would be all right for the kangaroos to taste. They must not have dirt in them because of worms in the intestine. An okapi died last year because of worms." I suffered under the delusion that one day all of the kangaroos at the Basel Zoo would die because of me, thereby leaving none that I could visit.

Every time I came by, Glücki would gratefully accept my small offering for the kangaroos, but not without a private grin. It was strictly forbidden to feed the animals, but when no other visitors were present, Glücki let me have bananas, pieces of apple, or even bits of onion to give to the animals. That they liked onions was a big surprise. From then on, I purloined an onion or two from the kitchen at home or bought them by the pound but noticed, too, that friendly relations with kangaroos could be built up without the onion bribe.

One Sunday I wanted to show my father the trust the animals had in me. I did this by putting my hand into the cage and calling them. They came! I turned to my father for acknowledgment of this feat but found him doubled over with laughter. This was a big disappointment. He said that no animal would come over to me just like that and remained skeptical for a long time, insisting that encounters between me and the kangaroos were only a matter of coincidence. It was something quite different from that between a dog and its master. Nonetheless, I insisted again and again that there was a friendly bond between the kangaroos and me. Finally, he, too, had to admit this.

One day, after returning home from the zoo, I happily told everyone at the table about my favorite female kangaroo, the one that I had stroked first, and also informed them that this animal still had no name. So I asked them all to help me choose a suitable name for this young female. "Doris!" my mother called out cheerfully. What? A kangaroo with my name! No, that didn't appeal to me at all. But why not a name that had some connection to us—so what about "Dora"? We all agreed.

With the passing of time, Dora and I built up a firm relationship with one another. Physical contact was more frequent. I stroked her and she snuffled my hands. Sometimes we just looked at each other. Of all the kangaroos, Dora became the most devoted in the course of time, whereas the others in the compound were more or less neutral toward me. One of Dora's characteristics was that both her ears were nicked, and Glücki explained that while she was still young, one of the older siblings had probably gnawed at her ears while she was sticking her snout into the pouch to drink.

I was soon able to distinguish between the animals quite easily. It was clear, too, that Dora could quickly single me out from others as I approached the cage. Daddy continued to insist that dogs responded much more easily to a call or an order than kangaroos. He stubbornly stuck to this opinion when I told everybody at the table about the familiarity I enjoyed with Dora. At home we had a large, black sheepdog, which my father had tried in vain to educate. The dog would beg during meals and was otherwise quite undisciplined. I was always trying to get the animal to behave by gesticulating wildly and shouting at the top of my voice. On one of these occasions, my father remarked, half in earnest and half in jest, that we should go to the zoo together and that I should do exactly the same thing with Dora as I did with his dog. At first I was a bit taken aback, but then I grinned with him in agreement. I knew that Dora and I had built up a trusting relationship.

Among the Kangaroos

MY NEXT great desire was to be allowed to move among the kangaroos in their pen. I received special permission from the director of the zoo, Professor Hediger, to go into the inner and outer areas of the kangaroo compound. Hardly had keeper Glücki opened the gate for me when Dora was at my side and supported herself with her forepaw on my shoulder.

The smells of textiles and leather were particularly interesting to her. She found them animating. She was always busy sniffing my clothes or trying to chew them. When we stood belly to belly, she would often play at tenderly scratching me. None of the other animals had the slightest interest in me apart from the time when all of them displayed great interest in my shoes. With undivided attention, they would nibble at what was evidently pleasant-smelling leather, so I had occasional difficulty in moving. Sometimes I gripped one of them under its armpits and lifted it off, but this didn't help, either.

The hoped-for eye-to-eye ploy simply didn't take place. I found this a bit disappointing since for me it implied that the relationship between humans and animals was less plausible than I had hoped. However, as I was to learn later, I myself contributed to this lack of mutuality in that I made the mistake of standing up straight and walking around in the same posture. Finally, I learned to walk around in a slightly bent position so as to more or less mimic the size of the kangaroo. I discovered that eye-to-eye contact could be achieved if I lowered my height to coincide with theirs. This required me to bend my knees or put one knee on the floor. Once in this position, I would refrain from stroking any of them. After a discreet interval, the animals were glad to be stroked and scratched at the neck and at the back of the head, areas that were inaccessible to them and which thus served the objectives of body care.

I was also able to modify my steps to their hopping, so they soon took little notice of my presence. I had become one of them, so to speak. Life in the group then resumed its normal, undisturbed course as though I were not there at all. They ate and attended to their bodies, while the males carried on their "battles" with one another. This was an ideal situation for the observations I wanted to make.

Everything went along nicely until I unwittingly made a serious mistake that put the group into an uproar. At this stage I was relatively inexperienced with regard to kangaroos and therefore did not recognize the early signs of the mating season. Thus it was that one day, in my slightly bent posture, I entered the compound and was making my way to Dora by moving carefully among the kangaroos lying on the floor. Without warning, the whole group suddenly got to their feet. A young, fully grown male came toward me and hit me hard in the face with both paws. My glasses went flying, but I quickly retrieved them and retreated before Glücki could come to my aid.

After a good year or more, my regular visits to the compound came to an abrupt end. A few weeks after this incident and after yearlong attempts to produce offspring, the young kangaroo males were exchanged for others. These new animals proved to be something of a problem for the zookeepers and were a bit of a danger.

Pouch Cleaning

ALTHOUGH on the farm and in movies I had seen how young cats or calves are licked clean by their mother, I still didn't know how kangaroos could do this. How was it possible to keep both the pouch and its tiny occupant clean until it was ready to climb out and fend for itself? The first encounter with Dora awakened strong emotions in me.

Beginning in February 1950, I had an opportunity to study Dora's experience of motherhood while her baby was hidden away in her pouch. It was still winter, but there was a warm wind, and the animals were allowed outside on pleasant days. A little way off and not far from the bars around the compound, Dora cleaned baby and pouch very carefully. The unusual sight of her body bent far forward made me shiver, but I realized that hygiene was important for the baby's survival. I was witness to the basic procedure of the mother-baby relationship. Could it be that as a result of a cosmic impulse I was awakened on this occasion to an understanding of maternal love? Looking back, I believe that, had I not had this experience with Dora, I would probably never have made the breakthrough in my research on kangaroos.

After this experience I immediately began making systematic observations. Other females were carrying young in their pouches as well, and during the course of a long period of such monitoring, Dora became a mother on several occasions. What I witnessed was documented by a series of photos that recorded the exact direction of movements and served as a valuable basis for my later scientific papers on pouch cleaning. I have Dora to thank especially for my early observations and research. She would allow me to touch the edge of her pouch in order to determine the baby's position.[9]

To conclude with one of my dearest memories: Dora is lying in the warmth of the sun with the little one peeping from her pouch, its snout toward its mother. She puts her head gently toward the small nose to sniff—a moment of tender contact.

Surprises

CAN one call a kangaroo by name? No, not usually; a kangaroo is not a dog, and in this my father was right. A kangaroo reacts to other

---

9. Later in the Australian countryside, I was able to feel the whole of the outer pouch while a half-wild kangaroo cleaned the inside. This was a remarkable experience. I was astonished that, as I did so, the baby neither kicked nor wriggled. It was less active than a human baby during diaper changing.

acoustic signals. Dora, for example, responded to "Hello, here I am!" or to "Ha ha!" and often to mere humming. This was sufficient to alert Dora and the other kangaroos to my presence, and their ears would point in my direction. Interestingly, the other animals did not react. For example, Trudi, another kangaroo that I observed at the zoo, refused to react to several calls even though she stood only a few meters away from the edge of her pen. Dora behaved quite differently. At that time, she was a strong, impressive female who held sway over her group, and, surprisingly, she was also the only one to respond immediately to my call even when I was more than, say, five meters away from where she was standing. Very often I didn't need to call her at all; as soon as she was aware of my presence, she would come over to me.

Once something entirely unexpected happened. It was a cold winter day as I entered the antelope house. So many people had drifted to the kangaroo area that I could see little. Despite this, Dora fixed her eyes on me. Excited by this attention, I asked a few people in the crowd if I might go a little closer. I was surprised and delighted as Dora came straight over to me. How could she have recognized my face among so many? Or did something besides my face enable her to identify me? It was clear that none of the other kangaroos was either willing or in a position to do the same.

Dora possessed other capabilities, too. Among other zoo visitors, she was able to recognize me from a distance of some ten or even twenty meters, and then she watched me as I walked along the visitors' path. I was very eager to know whether this behavior was simply "cupboard love" or whether there was more to it. For this reason, I seldom had any food with me to give her. I could later say with certainty that she came when she wanted to because on other occasions she didn't come even if I had tasty pieces of banana in my hand. There was no doubt about the fact that she needed personal contact with me.

It was never possible to get her to approach me when she was eating, resting, busy caring for her offspring, or cleaning herself. It was quite natural that she didn't want to be disturbed during her regular activities. Nevertheless, Dora was definitely aware of my presence since, once these natural concerns were seen to, she would come over to me. In addition, she would also make an extra effort to move closer to me when she was making for the straw dump or the food trough or heading away from them. If, for instance, there were obstacles in the way, like a couple of thick branches, she would go around them in order to greet me. Even if many other animals were between us, she would nevertheless push her way through them to be near me.

The pleasantest memory I have of her has been entered into my notes:

> On one occasion, Dora stood with her back to me about four meters away in her stall. She was busy cleaning herself and looked over her shoulder toward me every now and again. I reckoned that it would be quite a while before she came over, so I looked in the other direction, but a second or two later I felt a nudge in my back. I stepped back in fright only to notice that Dora was already there and had butted her nose into my back for attention!

It was wonderful, too, to watch Dora care for her last baby in 1963–1964. After almost every pouch cleaning, she came over to me without my calling her.

My "conversations" with Dora lasted ten to twenty minutes on average. The ceremonial climax of our reunion was always the rubbing of noses, whereby we exchanged our breath for a few seconds. This corresponds exactly to the specific behavior of kangaroos. Comprehensive, olfactory information is received and processed in this manner. It is also a means of coping with conflicts. For me, on the other hand, the act of coming together like this in a dignified, intimate way was the confirmation of a strong spiritual bond with these animals we call "kangaroos." In addition, Dora allowed me not only to stroke her body but also to feel the empty interior of her pouch, and in this way I became familiar with its form and temperature. Dora was pretty demanding when it came to strokes and general attention. If I stopped for a second or two, she would encourage me to carry on by nudging me.

For the next fifteen years I was obliged to stay away from the interior of the compound because of the potential danger of attack from the male kangaroos, who are naturally aggressive toward humans. They often attack the zookeeper with their front paws and can cause serious injuries. As a result, there was a burning desire within me to renew my relationship with Dora without the intervening railings.

After talking this over with the new zoo director, Professor Lang, it was agreed that I might try again, but this move ended in great disappointment. Once I was inside the pen, Dora behaved as if she didn't know me. She made not the slightest move to come toward me. It was as though I were a stranger. Surprisingly, when I then went back behind the railings, some of her intimacy returned. Paradoxically, I had the impression that Dora felt near me only when there was a barrier between us. Of course, it is possible that she had simply forgotten our former free association with each other.

The Beneficial Effect of Cooling

ONE memorable—and very strange—incident occurred because of kangaroos' need to cool off. It is a peculiar characteristic of these animals that, to cool their bodies, they resort to spreading spittle on their arms and shins and sometimes even their lower abdomens when in extreme heat, on becoming greatly excited, during the mating season, and during conflicts. It is easy to distinguish between activity for bodily hygiene and this cooling habit. For the former, the coat is "combed" with the teeth or, alternatively, nibbled at, whereas in the latter the limbs are treated with saliva in generous amounts by using the tongue.

It was on a very hot June afternoon that a number of animals, having completed their mating rituals, began applying saliva to their limbs. Those that had not joined in the mating procedure remained in the shade of the trees. About half an hour later, when the animals were back in their stalls, Dora came over to me and drank the water from a bucket at one end of the fence. After she had slaked her thirst, she came to me, and we greeted each other in the time-honored way. And then she began to lick my right hand until it was thoroughly wet with saliva![10]

At our evening meal, I proudly related this astounding proof of confidence when my father asked me with a smirk whether I would not have preferred to put my arms under the tap.

I still ask myself why Dora wanted to cool me off. Was it a friendly gesture? Or was it a kind of service rendered in return for my stroking her?

As far as the usual bodily hygiene techniques kangaroos employ are concerned, one notices that mothers and their half-grown young mutually nibble at each other's coats, but adults rarely do so.

DURING my time in observing kangaroos, I have never seen a kangaroo apply saliva to another, so that what Dora did on this occasion was unique, and I am sure that this act did not just concern licking the salty sweat off my hand.

Saying Farewell

IT WAS a summer day in 1971. The radiant sun transformed the zoo into a place of beautiful color, and everywhere was a mood of cheerfulness. However, I could not share this good cheer. I was miserable. I had just returned from my first visit to Australia and had gone to the zoo to see Dora. The kangaroos were outside with the antelopes. Dora limped slowly and with difficulty toward me, directly in front of the steel fencing, drew herself halfway up, and looked at me dejectedly. In deep sadness, I saw how age had robbed her of her vitality. She was in poor health. I stroked her and was appalled to feel the bones under her coat. We stood there together and looked at each other for a long time. At that moment, I knew that it would be our last meeting. While I stood there dumbly looking at her, an

---

10. When water is at hand, these animals often avail themselves of this opportunity.

inner struggle was taking place in me, resisting the looming fear that
I would not know how to live without her. Dora stood for a long
time without moving, as if she wanted to say, "I would like to give
some proof of our long-standing relationship, for this will be our last
good-bye."

The following day, I found my mother sitting at the table with a
red face and tears in her eyes. I did not dare to ask her why but knew
that something final had happened the previous day. She told me
that Dora had died. She was concerned about me since she knew
how much the loss would mean to me. However, I tried to be brave
and lighten the burden of her death by recalling that Dora, with her
twenty-three years and five months, had truly reached the age of a
Methuselah in kangaroo years and that this was certainly the time
to depart.

6

A Firm Decision

OUR yard bordered on some ivy-covered wasteland that harbored a few tall trees. From time to time, one could catch sight of a roe deer, and the birds, whether large or small, were often at war with one another over nesting places. Hedgehogs, too, emerged from their hideaways under the elderberry bush and appeared on our lawn. A brook flowed at the outer edge of this land left to nature, and its banks hosted a riot of wild plants, which I loved so much that I successfully forbade my parents to "improve" anything. For me, this patch of land was a paradise where I could watch the animals' activities every day, sometimes from my bedroom window, armed with my field glasses, and sometimes from our yard. In this way I laid down a good foundation for my later intensive activity in the field. Among these were my observations of marmot colonies (in the Engadin region of Switzerland) and of chamois near the Aletsch Glacier, in the Jungfrau region.

One warm summer day one I was sitting with Auntie on our wonderful garden seats, when she observed that I was interested not only in kangaroos but also in all sorts of other wildlife that lived in woods and gardens. She was right. My interest was in nature as a whole in all its variety and wasn't restricted to kangaroos. The latter would have meant specializing and could well have earned me a reputation of being a bit eccentric.

On one occasion Father came to me in the best of moods and reported that Uncle Fritz in Tessin had told him that there was a German student observing kangaroos at the Zürich Zoo and had written a report on them. A man after my own heart at last! That was the one thing that I had wished for. His name was Karl H. Winkelsträter, a man who hailed from Saarland and was a few years later to become the director of the zoo in Saarbrücken. A few months after hearing this, we began corresponding with each other and talking shop about kangaroos. He recounted his failed attempt to observe the birth of a kangaroo and mentioned the kangaroos' strange habit of licking their limbs until they were thoroughly wet.

As a result of this contact, I was initiated by an expert into a number of important facts, scientific questions, and problems, and this stimulated my thirst for knowledge. It also prompted my mother to scold me to spend more time in the office and less time sitting in front of the kangaroo compound. Regardless of this, I was determined to continue. In further clashes she tried to make it clear to me that, without a university degree, I wouldn't make much progress in my exertions. This made me furious, and in desperation I ran to my father for consolation. In his cheerful and humorous way, he tried to comfort me, but he, too, suggested that I shouldn't spend all my time watching kangaroos.

In those days, deaf persons were unable to study at a university, a regrettable but unalterable fact. But it was just this that impelled me to find alternative solutions, and I have not least to thank Dr. Winkelsträter for helping me discover a course of independent study.

In 1962 I took a part-time job as an assistant in the occupational therapy department at the Jewish senior citizens' home, La Charmille. I worked there two days a week with elderly people. Despite the difficulties some of them had in communicating because of their age, these people were eager to learn handcrafting and other skills such as painting and weaving, and for the most part they were successful. As my boss knew little about weaving, I was glad to be able to help her. But weaving was not all I did; I also painted and illustrated a children's book. The text was inspired by and based on an Aboriginal animal story called "Laughing Water."

In 1956, after giving up my work as a handweaver around the age of twenty-two, I was employed in the office of my father's business. I had already learned how to type and now began to learn how to run a firm. I worked only a few hours a day in this capacity and so had plenty of time for my zoological studies. Added to this, I received regular lessons from zoology students, whose fees were paid by my parents. However, these lessons were not satisfactory in the long run, and I aspired to a higher standard. Moreover, I couldn't entirely dismiss the impression I got from these young people that, as a person with a disability, I could not really be taken seriously.

Not long afterward, I received another piece of good news from Uncle Fritz in Tessin. A young student had visited him to have a look at his colony of woolly monkeys. He had asked this young woman to get in touch with me as soon as possible so that we could talk about the particularly interesting areas of zoology, thereby more fully introducing me to the subject. And so it was. She often dropped by, and we were able to communicate perfectly well with each other. She stimulated my interest by lending me one or two books on animal psychology. I consumed these and other books and specialist papers, together with those I borrowed from the university library, with great interest. All of this information was by no means limited to the kangaroo. What fascinated me above all was research on animal behavior, all the way up from studies of the single cell to fish and birds and the higher mammals. I read works by Nobel Prize–winner Konrad Lorenz, N. Tinbergen, H. Hediger, A. Portmann, I. Eibl-Eibesfeldt, and others. With the help of Dr. Lilly Schönholzer, I was able to extend this knowledge to include a wide variety of subjects related to zoology and behavioral science.

With Wild Cattle at the Mediterranean

MY PARENTS were proud of my growing knowledge and sought to find me a suitable place for fieldwork. Soon I received a letter from Professor Lucas Hoffmann, a zoologist in Basel, who ran a research station in the Camargue, not far from the coast. He invited me to go there as an assistant volunteer, and so it was that I traveled to France in July 1958, together with Auntie, who wanted to vacation at a place nearby.

At first, there was much that was strange to me, but it wasn't long before I adapted to the new conditions. Along with German-speaking researchers, there were also several students who spoke English. I was fascinated by the technique of putting bands on birds and helped in freeing them from the nets after examination. Later I went out into this superb seaside landscape to set them free again.

A Swiss zoologist, Dr. Schloeth, was working at this same research station. He was studying the behavior of bulls in establishing their herd hierarchy in the huge fenced-in compounds there. I soon became intensely interested in his observations, and we had a number of long conversations. He showed me several notepads full of illegible entries on "his" bulls, each of whom had a number. He could skillfully distinguish one from another. In addition, he showed me how to conduct fieldwork and took me out on horseback, which I, a nonrider, bore with courage and without complaint for several hours. From this elevated position I was able to observe the bulls and make notes. These animals were large and impressive, but I had no fear of them—not even when I found myself all alone on the grassland. The swarms of horseflies were much more menacing!

Every day I did my stint of work for three to six hours, watching these bulls for more than a fortnight, but the time in the Camargue was far too short. In my enthusiasm, I wrote a long report of my experiences and sent it to Dr. Schloeth. Not long after, he replied with his critique. I would have to read more and think more, and to these remarks he added an example of my lack of knowledge. What I had taken for mere playfulness (when the bulls mounted each other) was in fact specific, sexual activity, something that, to date, I had little knowledge of.

In addition, Dr. Schloeth advised me to get in touch with a person whom I could trust and from whom I could request frank information. To this day I am grateful to him for not only showing me the right way to study but also for encouraging me to look into the sexual conduct of humans and animals.

The Prospect of Australia Comes Nearer

ARMED with my expanded knowledge, some of which I had picked up from texts in English, I now eagerly looked forward to meeting people in Australia who worked with kangaroos and were also familiar with the country's flora and fauna. I requested the addresses of organizations in Australia from the Swiss Association of the Protection of Nature (now Pro Natura Suisse). Rather late in the day, I received a response that enclosed one or two periodicals. In one of these and to my considerable surprise, I came across the following lines: "Doris Herrmann from Switzerland, who is very interested in kangaroos, would like to make contact with people in Australia." I banged my fist on the table with joy, startling my parents. A second later I pushed the article across to them and indicated the lines in question. They were delighted and actually amazed that I had managed in this way to come a little closer to this faraway country. They wished me luck but at the same time warned me that I would have to be patient since it would likely take longer than usual to receive replies.

Then came the winter of 1959, and I had just streaked down the mountainside on my skis when, on retracing my course on foot to the top, I met my parents coming toward me with smiles on their faces. My dad was waving a letter that had arrived by airmail. Excitedly, I took the envelope and read the address on the back. Overjoyed, I found that the letter was from a certain Geoff Giles, a schoolteacher in New South Wales, whose name I had taken from one of the journals in which my own name appeared. I felt that this person was the right one for the yearned-for correspondence. I learned that not far from Geoff's house was a psychiatric clinic that had numerous large and small pavilions scattered over a thickly wooded area. The kangaroos from the nearby bush regarded this neighborhood as their natural grazing land. Accordingly, the patients fed them, and this served as a welcome diversion. However, this "symbiotic" relationship had a negative aspect: This situation made the animals easy prey for hunters.

We corresponded regularly, and as a consequence I learned about Geoff and his family, about the animals and plants there, and also about Geoff's adventures in Australia's outback. All this had its effect on my dreams, and I longed more and more to visit the country. I often told my mother that I wanted to set off soon for Australia by ship, but she put me off by saying that dreams were always nicer than reality, and of course I was disappointed but nevertheless made up my mind to go.

After a long correspondence with Geoff, during which we exchanged not only letters but also journals and the like, our conversations became less frequent, as, unfortunately, he was obliged to do less and less for health reasons. In the meantime, though, I also corresponded with two other Australians, a Mrs. Molly O'Neill, an active environmentalist who was mainly interested in spiders, and a Mrs. Beryl Graham from Sydney. My folder had begun to bulge with airmails. For me, they were a piece of Australia, which became more vivid with every missive.

Breakthrough

FOR a long time, the special relationship between a mother and her young had given me much to ponder, especially the mother's fastidiousness with regard to her pouch and its occupant. I combed through research on this subject only to discover a large gap in the studies done so far. Thus I began to do some intensive and systematic work at the Basel Zoo. After compiling a number of suitable notes on the subject, I summarized these in a provisional document and submitted it to Professor Hediger, the then director of the zoological garden in Zurich. It was my intention to revise this essay later and finally publish it. The months went by without a reply, and, consequently, my initial expectations were somewhat dampened.

As a newcomer to the science, had I deceived myself in the assumption of finding the right connection? Did this mean that I would have to return with a heavy heart and in all humility to my everyday life? Could it be that someone else had already formulated all the "discoveries" I had made? Disappointment overwhelmed me, and I began to consider my work as worthless. Totally discouraged, I abandoned all further activity in this direction and didn't know what to do with myself.

However, one evening when I came home from my job at the office, I could hardly believe my eyes. Under the many letters delivered that day was one from the zoo in Zurich. My fingers trembled as I slit it open and read the contents. Then, in uncontrollable excitement, I ran into the kitchen and showed the letter to my mother. Moments became eternities—everything seemed incredible even when my mother, overjoyed at what she read, called me a worthy researcher. Professor Hediger fully acknowledged my research and articles about pouch cleaning. Because of this research, several pouches were able to be cleaned at just the right time at the Zürich Zoo; as a result, several mothers and their offspring managed to survive a horrible poisoning caused by various remedies. Now, at last, the ice was broken even if I had had to wait quite a long time for my work to gain official recognition. From this moment on, I could rightly regard myself as admitted to the circle of kangaroo researchers.

A few days later my mother and I went to Zurich. The sunny May weather and the freshness of the green landscape beautifully complemented the roused feelings that now propelled me forward. I was to take a look at the kangaroos at the zoo and after that visit Professor Hediger. This man encouraged me go on with my research. Accordingly, I continued with my work, completed the manuscript, and, finally, thanks to Professor Lang, the director of the zoo in Basel at that time, was able to publish it in a specialist periodical.[11]

11. Here is a note I wrote at the time:
It is necessary first to note that the kangaroo mother undertakes cleaning of the pouch at the moment the baby defecates. The next important matter to notice is (see, for instance,

Even on my first regular visits to the zoo, I had noticed that a kangaroo's feeding was often accompanied by an extraordinary, rhythmical contraction of the body before chewing. When I hypothesized what it might be, I contacted Professor Lang at once and explained to him, with the help of pencil and paper, that this behavior was nothing other than a fake "chewing the cud." This was such astonishing news to him that at first he didn't believe my theory. He then strongly suggested that I write a paper about this observation. Both the article on pouch hygiene and the one on eating were published in Switzerland, Germany, Australia, and other countries. This peculiar form of chewing was also described in *Grzimek's Animal Life Encyclopedia*. Of course, I was very proud of these field studies. In this way, my mother's words were confirmed. She had said on that occasion that "Research is to discover something new!" and I took these words to heart.

I REPORTED all this to Molly O'Neill, who had recommended me to Professor Geoffrey Sharman, one of the best-known researchers on the life of kangaroos at the Commonwealth Scientific Industrial Research Organization (CSIRO), the Division of Wildlife Research in Canberra. I sent him my research papers, and after a short correspondence, he announced that he was coming to Basel. It was hard to believe that this man, world famous in his field, making his first visit to Europe, would take the trouble to interrupt his journey by coming to Basel.

The day finally arrived, and I found myself waiting for Professor Sharman in the lobby of his hotel in Basel. After a while, I found myself in the company of a man who was dressed very simply and had a weather-beaten, friendly face and who lightly tripped down the steps to the foyer. He had a small attaché case with him. We greeted each other and then entered into a lively discussion in English

G. B. Sharman, "Reproduction in Marsupials," *Nature* 173 [1954]: 302–303) that massaging of the intestine then takes place. Since the cleansing of the pouch from the inside can never be accurately followed, observation has to be limited to the exterior to gain some idea of the process of maintaining the baby's hygiene.

using pen and paper. Professor Sharman was not at all put off by my inability to communicate in the usual way, and with patience and understanding he shared the results of his kangaroo research with me. He then took out a large roll of film from his case, and on reading the label, my heart beat faster. It was the first film of the birth of a kangaroo. He had made it himself. (This film was presented to kangaroo specialists all over the world and also shown on TV.) My anticipated pleasure stimulated my intuition and suggested a way to conjure up a projector. We then went to the zoo, where I wanted to show Professor Sharman the kangaroos, and while there, we looked up Professor Lang. He in turn set about procuring a projector and organizing things so that, in addition to my parents, one or two professors from the institutes for chemistry and zoology could also be invited.

I was breathless with anticipation. The film began by showing the procreative act involving two red, giant kangaroos and later the birth of the offspring. In size and form, one couldn't help thinking of a worm issuing from the birth canal. It then freed itself from the umbilical cord and, using its forepaws, wound its way like a lizard up the mother's belly and into the pouch. All this took place without the mother's taking the slightest part! The film clearly showed that the forepaws had already developed sufficiently strong claws for this task, while the hind legs and the tail were as yet underdeveloped. I later learned that Professor Sharman had slightly anesthetized the mother a little before, which made photography easier.

This unique documentation at one stroke refuted previous assumptions that the transport of the baby to the pouch was facilitated by the mother's lips and forepaws. The film made it quite clear that the newborn animal needed neither the help of its mother nor a previously prepared path of saliva along which it could slide from the birth canal to the opening of the pouch, for example. Only its fully developed sense of smell guided it into the pouch and to its mother's teats. That evening, when my father came to say goodnight, he asked how I was, and I could only reply that my head was so full that I could hardly say anything. "But now you're famous!" he said proudly. "Professor Sharman will certainly mention your work on pouch cleaning when he visits the USA."

That night I had no thought of sleep; the film fully occupied the passing hours. However, my father saw to it that all this didn't go to my head, and in this applied his own particular talent, a mixture of hearty cheerfulness with a drop or two of good-natured mocking that the title of "Dr. Kangaroo" would eventually be bestowed on me! For all that, somehow things were under way.

Five Kangaroo Heads for Doris

PROFESSOR Sharman and I continued to correspond with each other on our respective research. I asked him about secretion glands and the way in which kangaroos mark their territory. I was of the opinion that the glands must be situated under the eyes. Professor Sharman contacted Dr. Roman Mykytowycz about this since he had done some work on these glands in rabbits and various marsupials. The latter came up with the stunning idea that I should find out for myself where they were and offered me five kangaroo heads to experiment on. I was a bit taken aback by this proposal but accepted. The pricks of conscience were to some extent lessened by the realization that the stock of kangaroos would have to be reduced in order to prevent damage to farmland. My parents and friends also encouraged me on this point, but for all that, I felt pretty uncomfortable. On Yom Kippur, the Day of Atonement, my mother happened to ask me in the synagogue when the heads would arrive. I was flabbergasted. From then on, I refused to talk to anyone about the business.

Import regulations required a number of obstacles to be overcome. Then, after two months by ship from Australia, arrival in Bremen, and a trip down the Rhine to Basel, a wooden chest appeared at Basel's Zoological Institute "For the attention of Doris Herrmann."[12] I carefully lifted the heads from the chest, one after

12. Since scientific material of this kind was not allowed to be sent to private addresses, Professor Adolf Portmann (1897–1982), director of the institute and a distinguished publicist, had kindly provided me with this address.

the other. They were contained in glass jars of formalin, all of them without a neck and with half-open eyes. The sight of them gripped my innards. It seemed as if they were all looking at me accusingly.

Each jar had a label with information about the head it contained. I pulled myself together, tried to be brave, and entered this information in previously prepared tabular form: area of origin; sex; weight, and so on. Zoologists and students were more than willing to help prepare the tissue for examination under the microscope. However, even though all of our careful investigations failed to reveal any organs of secretion, my disappointment was limited, for the research was constructive in establishing good relations with Dr. Mykytowycz, whom I privately referred to as "Myky" from then on.

Still No Green Light for the Big Adventure

MONTHS later, Myky unexpectedly announced his intention to come to Basel en route to other places in Europe. I felt greatly honored. During lunch with him and his wife after their arrival, I hinted to my parents and relatives that I would like to visit Australia one day and, while there, do research on kangaroos in the outback at the CSIRO station. At this, Dr. Myky looked rather serious. Then his face lit up, and he declared that there was no place in the world as beautiful as Switzerland. Jokingly, he said that it was much less risky and also considerably less expensive to remain here with my microscope and do research on the life of the flea. However, a moment later, he began talking enthusiastically about a lonely vacation resort on the east coast of Australia, where one could carry out investigations on half-tame, free-range kangaroos. It was called Pebbly Beach. "Wouldn't that be an opportunity for me?" I cried.

"You shouldn't cram too many things into your head," mother countered. I looked carefully at the faces of those present in the hope of finding a glimmer of encouragement in their expressions, but, quite to the contrary—and mother translated everything perfectly correctly—Myky tried to discourage me with all kinds of warnings about fieldwork on kangaroos. On entering the compound, for example, there was always the danger of being attacked by aggressive males, and so accidents had to be taken into consideration. In the outback, these animals were rarely seen, and just to observe them in local zoos was hardly worth such a long journey.

Myky's descriptions and his efforts to dispel my dreams of Australia were cause for depression for many weeks afterward. Would I never be able to visit this continent then? But despite this despondency, the name "Pebbly Beach" would not go away.

Even though I continued to study zealously and carried on my observations at the zoo, I also worked in my father's business. I didn't neglect my work at the loom, either. As early as 1957 I had managed to get hold of an old Swedish loom, which I put together myself. At first I wove linen and later learned to plait and knot. I worked on carpets according to patterns that I had designed myself in chalk or watercolors. Evening sunset scenes were my favorites because of their fiery tints. In 1964, and to my surprise, I won third prize in the Basel art competition for the design of a large collage of many-colored tissue papers featuring a sunset over the sea, which I had once experienced while in Israel in 1962. A design for a wall carpet for a hospital in Basel also stemmed from my inspiration. I liked more than anything, though, to assemble mosaics of broken stones in the garden. One of these represented the creation of the world, another symbolized the process of cell division, and yet another that of splitting the atom. The yellow Bernstein that I had found in Tessin I formed into sunflowers. Another of these showed a kangaroo standing in front of a sunset.

I noticed even as a young person just how much is destroyed in nature by human hand. One couldn't overlook it. So I asked myself what I could do against it. What kind of contribution could I add to its preservation? I had just become a member of the Swiss organization of the National Society of the Protection of Nature. But was I then to take part in conferences and meetings or in demonstrations perhaps? No. My handicap was in the way. I was just not suited to that kind of thing.

But there were other possibilities open to me that were much more suitable, and one of these was my artistic talent. So I began there and then by portraying nature. In so doing, I earned myself a good deal of appreciation which, of course, did me a lot of good. At first, I painted sunsets. The flowers followed, all of them cheerful pictures full of color, and later I painted a special motif for a small carpet—the building of a stone wall. In this way, I wanted to protest against the ruination of the landscape. Then came ten woven pictures having the theme: The Creation of the Earth up to Its Catastrophic End—in other words, the apocalypse.

When I visited Australia for the fourth time and took a look at a particular lake, I was appalled to realize that money played a far more important part in the life of some than untouched nature, rich in flora and fauna. I decided at that point to couch my protest in artistic terms. I constructed a sculpture from metal plates, plaited jute, and thick hemp

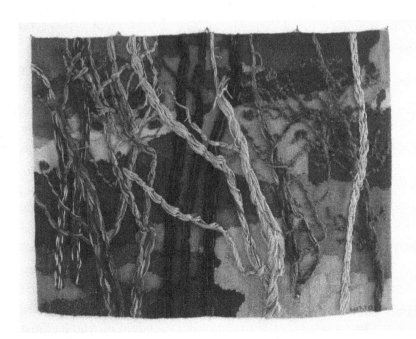

Wall hanging (woven, knotted and braided) titled "Sunset in the Australian Bush." I created it after my trip to Australia in 1970.

under which I placed the title: *Money Eats Landscape*. It was publicly exhibited, and my hope was that people would come to their senses.

The next stage of my creative work was the presentation of pictures displaying beautiful, untouched countryside. They were primarily evening impressions of the Australian bushland in all its colorful variety. These were not always painting of things and places, but abstract representations. On the other hand, I have never tried to represent kangaroos in the abstract. I loved them too much to subject them to such experiments.

ONE DAY I arrived home to find father standing at the door. He was very pale. About a year before he had been diagnosed as having leukemia, and this made life difficult for him. I saw the tears in his eyes, and yet he smiled, and the smile was a cheerful one. I knew that this derived from the joyful anticipation of my projects, which he hoped to live long enough to see. "Today I've got important news for you. Guess what it is," he announced. Then he told me about a long telephone conversation he'd had with Professor Lang, whom I had to thank for arranging the upcoming publication of the book *Laughing Water*.

An Unexpected Encounter

WHILE watching kangaroos at Basel Zoo one day I had a pleasant experience that helped to lessen my long-standing depression. I was sitting on my stool a little to one side of the visitors' path with my camera on a tripod, when I noticed the keeper, followed by a young blonde. He showed her the list that I had made of the kangaroo stock and pointed out individual animals, ones, of course, which he knew as well as I did. At first I thought she was a professional photographer, then the two looked over toward me. Curious, I could no longer concentrate properly. After a while, the two of them came over to me, and we greeted each other. It turned out that the young woman's name was Vreni Meyer, a zoology student of who had just begun her dissertation on kangaroo behavior. I learned later that Professor Portmann at Basel's Zoological Institute had drawn her attention to my work, and this I found very flattering. At our regular meetings we found that we could communicate with each other very well. These exchanges were to be very valuable to us both.

Often we observed the kangaroos together and then compared notes. These were wonderful hours spent together, and it wasn't long before we became fast friends. Vreni gave me lessons in physiology, evolutionary theory, and other areas of biology and helped me prepare comparative studies on kangaroos in the wild and in captivity.

I had hoped to complete this work on my own in Australia, but without careful preparation this would hardly be possible. Nevertheless, I was confident that I would be able to make this long journey with my mother in the coming years. Father had wished this for me, but his health steadily deteriorated. Pain was written in his face. Finally, he took to his bed. The moments I spent alone with him at the edge of the bed were among the most heartfelt of my life. Much that had happened to him in the past and had been forgotten he now vividly recalled, and I lived these with him. He would tell me of his youthful escapades in Schwabach, near Nuremberg, where he had lived with his parents and three brothers in a large old house dating back to 1561. We also talked about our trips to Israel. I fell into sad reminiscence. We were on a bus ride along the Dead Sea, and the sun was setting. I sat cuddled up to him and felt that God was near. Then, as if in a vision, he experienced unimpeded access to the Wailing Wall in Jerusalem. (Later, the Six-Day War was to justify his insight.) There was a deep spiritual affinity between us.

But soon our communion with one another was cut short by morphine, prescribed to keep him from inordinate pain, and this made him remote. Even so, there was a kind of elementary communication between us right up to the end. Now and again Daddy would humorously correct my indistinct pronunciation and at this would raise his long, bushy eyebrows, and I would quickly disappear to weep alone. One evening I helped the district nurse prop him up in a sitting position and stroked the thick eyebrows above the emaciated face and told him how nice they were. He smiled at me in his friendly way. During the night of the following day, when he was almost seventy, he died peacefully at home. That was in June 1967. His death was a great loss. I could find him again only in my dreams.

My mother and I managed father's business, which had to do with the exchange and repair of office machines. I was proud of having learned so much from him, and, together with my mother, I was well prepared to take the helm. While mother looked after the telephone and corrected my business correspondence, I was responsible for calculating prices and making out bills. At that time, fax, email, and other electronic devices had not yet been developed, so I was always dependent on my mother's help; nonetheless, everything went better than we would have believed. After all, mother used to insist, we ought to be glad about running the family business; otherwise, financing a trip to Australia would have been impossible.

I am working with my computer and reading device—my technical companions, which I now cannot imagine living without.

7

In the Land of My Dreams at Last

I AM at one with the movement of the waves, now rising, now falling; it's as though I were myself a wave. Up we go, and then down, a little to the left and then to the right until the ocean becomes a great smooth mass extending to infinity. Then the winds come again, and the waves begin to roll, and me? I am but a small human child, bravely maneuvering a boat no larger than a nutshell with a mast and sail of matchstick and postage stamp and the finest cobweb for rigging. There I sit, all alone in my odd little boat, hardly bigger than a housefly, my bags and my food stowed away in the wrinkles of the nutshell. Even the biggest waves cannot capsize my little vessel, and not a drop of water falls inside. I take up my telescope, which is no bigger than an apple stem, and scan the far horizon, but the land of red earth is still not in sight, not yet. It is midnight, and I awake from the dream.

Final Preparations

OUR first plan was to travel to Australia by ship. This would take more than a month but would be much cheaper than going by air. The Suez Canal was blocked in the sixties, which meant that ships had to take the much longer route via the Cape of Good Hope.

Late summer. It was Sunday again and the weather was calm. My mother and I were in the yard. While she sat perusing the newspapers, I was studying scientific articles when I suddenly thought of my brother, Peter, and my heart missed a beat. How would he survive for so many months without us? At the moment he was in a psychiatric clinic in the mountains. He suffered from depression. The news of Father's death had reached him by unknown means. Perhaps he had felt it somehow, but he would have to remain at a distance. He could not be informed personally as he lacked the ability to communicate. And because he was unable to speak, he could not express his feelings and thoughts; thus he had experienced immense emotional pressure that had brought about this depression.[13]

I got up and went over to my mother, now quite determined to change our plans and go instead by plane to Australia. This way,

Peter, in his thirties is happy even though he is deaf, can't speak, and has very bad eyesight. He likes to work as a laundry aide and irons extremely well.

13. I have dedicated a whole chapter to my brother; see chapter 19.

we could return quicker, should Peter need us. We shouldn't for a moment allow financial considerations to get in the way here, I pleaded. After, all, I went on, business had been good enough to enable us to travel by air. Mother thought for a while and then agreed.

We spent almost six months organizing everything. Our employees were to take over the responsibilities of reliably running the business in the meantime. A travel agency managed the details of our journey very competently, and then, finally, mother shook hands all around, which signaled both her integrity and the fulfillment of her promise. Now all we had to do was to board the plane.

We took off at the end of March 1969 and flew to Perth via Athens, Beirut, Karachi, New Delhi, and Bombay. I was thirty-five. Nonstop flights were not possible at that time. Our first stopover was Bangkok, where we wanted to stay for a couple of weeks and also do some sightseeing in Cambodia. We had learned so much from newspaper articles, movies, and television that we wanted to see the land of a thousand temples for ourselves. This was a time of ever-present political problems, and we had our own thoughts and worries about peace in the world.

What a breathtaking foreign culture surrounded us! On many nights I failed to sleep, not so much because of jetlag but more because my mind was full of the impressions of temples, golden statues, the many unfamiliar images, the provocative attractiveness of the Buddha figures, and the charmingly beautiful Thai girls gracing the temple forecourts, wearing light, sharp crowns of gold, dancing to the magic of another world.

We traveled by boat over the many canals that crisscrossed the city to floating markets, and we rattled through the teeming streets in a rickshaw. We also took a bus trip into Cambodia to visit Angkor Wat and other sites. This magical world was all very well, but then impatience gnawed at me, and I longed to set foot on Australian soil. At last we returned to Bangkok, where we boarded a Quantas jet and began the last leg of our journey.

On Australian Soil

IT WAS midnight when we landed in Perth. Two officials came aboard to spray disinfectant over our heads as the usual protective measure taken against the possible presence of unwanted insects and the like. After this "bitter overture," I greeted the mild Australian air outside the aircraft. I filled my lungs and my heart beat strongly. Now, at last, I had my "second home" under my feet, and a long-cherished dream had come true.

At customs, our bags were checked for an unreasonably long time and thoroughly searched. The customs official asked us darkly about the object of our visit.

"We come only to visit the kangaroos," my mother said in clumsy English. The official's face brightened. "You can stay!" he said cheerfully, and we were allowed to pass through the barrier. After a very short and much-disturbed sleep, I awoke to see my mother opening the curtains in the hotel room.

"Now we're in Australia!" she said. I could see a radiantly sunny sky, tinted in an unusual turquoise. It was to be a typical Australian color, which I would eventually get used to. Still a little sleepy but happy, I smiled at my mother. Our stay in the land of my dreams had begun.

WE SPENT the morning walking through the town, and a few hours later a Swiss acquaintance dropped by and invited us to stay with him for a week. He drove us to a remote place in the country a few miles from Perth. Here I had an opportunity to see the Australian bush firsthand. Up to now, this had been only a figment of my imagination. In powerful sunlight, the colors of the landscape varied excitingly with the interaction of the earth, the grassy areas, trees, bushes, and farmland. The trees—their trunks, branches, and twigs as part of the abundant vegetation—now and again were crazily spiked and twisted.

I peered out of the window. My mother nudged me with her elbow and said that there was no sense in my looking for kangaroos.

Our host had seen a few just before dawn. I was a bit disappointed to learn that kangaroos were seldom seen during the day. Later, at dinner, we all—as if on cue—turned our heads toward the window to better hear a noise coming from that direction. My mother informed me that she heard some strange noises, and someone went outside to see what was going on. On his return, he signaled to us to follow him—quickly. We stormed outside only to be told that to keep quiet. "Shhhh!" someone hissed. Full of expectation, I looked into the dimness but could see only a couple of small birds sitting on a branch making comical movements. They were two kookaburras. This encounter with Australian fauna was unquestionable proof that I had arrived in the country of my longings.

The next day the two birds managed to rip every branch off the shrub that my mother had given our host as a present and which she had placed in water! We all laughed. Mother ran into the kitchen and brought back a few pieces of the cake she had baked but which had failed to rise and placed them at the edge of the spring. The birds reappeared, danced along the edge of the water and splashed in it like happy children, and plucked at the nearly denuded shrub but ignored the cake completely. Then, quite abruptly, they got out of the water, seized the cake, and flew off to the nearest telephone pole. Once there they started laughing in their peculiar way. So infectious was their laughter that Mummy could hardly contain herself. Had these two found out that her cake was an utter failure?

Wild Kangaroos

A FEW days later our friends took us one evening to a golf course, where we hoped to see kangaroos. Once there, we walked over the empty, extensive course until I discovered kangaroo tracks. I stood glued to the spot. There were cherry-sized droppings all along the side of the freshly mown grass. But where were the big hoppers?

It was getting dark, but we continued our investigations. Then I felt my mother thump me in the small of my back, and through my field glasses I spied one . . . two . . . three kangaroos emerging from the bush. Soon a whole group of them emerged from the wild! Before the heavens turned a marvelous red like the red-hot coals of an ebbing fire and before the animals were transformed to black silhouettes against the sunset, the most exciting adventure of my life had begun. "Look over there! There's a male with its mate—and over there a female with a full pouch! The others are young animals. With their dark coats, they remind me of those in the Basel Zoo!" I called out, full of pride. But it was really a "zoo" I now found myself in!

Jokingly, my mother asked me whether it wasn't time to go home now that we'd seen what we came for, but I was so engrossed in my first encounter with living kangaroos in situ that I missed the humor in her suggestion. "What a nutty idea! Never!" But as I replied, I understood her irony.

We flew from Western Australia to Sydney in the east, and we were determined to make a few excursions into the outback on the lookout for kangaroos far from the madding crowd and its high-rise concrete blocks. However, my earlier correspondents informed me that it was rather difficult to find places where one could encounter kangaroos with certainty. I was downcast to learn this but realized that I had entertained too high hopes and expectations.

For a time we stayed with Mrs. Beryl Graham, the woman with whom I had corresponded. She and her family lived in a house with a yard in a suburb of Sydney. She was a most hospitable person and an ardent environmentalist. We visited a number of museums and private zoos and under her expert guidance learned a lot about Australia and picked up a lot of useful tips. The heavenly scented white gorse in water bowls that used to decorate our bedside tables remain in our minds as symbolic of Australia, a small touch that I later missed very much.

In the Research Station

ONE fine day we took the old suburban railway out of Sydney and left the sea of houses for Cowan, where Professor Sharman was expecting us. He was there to greet us cordially, and we drove in his car to the research station, situated in the Australian bush. He showed us the laboratory and introduced us to the koala forest, which had a six-foot-high fence around it made of wood, wire, and metal, an insuperable obstacle for these small bears. Here one could wander around at will and feel free to discover things for oneself and also stroke the tame kangaroos that were housed there. We admired the variously colored mushrooms, but we wisely didn't pick any, as they were quite foreign to us.

We went on with Professor Sharman to visit another compound that housed other kinds of marsupials. He cast an expert eye over them and at one point ran his hand over their coats to determine whether they were in tip-top condition. The animals submitted to his examination without complaint. In the case of the red giant kangaroos, he gave us a good idea of the real body mass of the male, something I had had only a vague idea of up to that moment. Sharman opened the cage and went straight up to the animal. Immediately, the kangaroo rose on its hind legs: It was as much as a head taller than the professor. Professor Sharman ran out of the cage at once and locked the gate behind him. The irritated kangaroo, for its part, drew itself up even further and threw its head back until we could see only its broad chest. Then it stretched its muscular arms skyward as if calling on the gods for support! Something demonic about this pose sent a shudder down my spine.

Inside the compound we also came across the so-called wallaroos, a species of mountain kangaroo. We sat down right away in order not to irritate the animals. The wallaroo is smaller than the large, red-coated kangaroo and has a bushy coat suitable for the harsher climate in the rocky hills of its habitat. When in very hot weather, they retreat to caves and are able to survive for days without water.

With a few professional movements, Professor Sharman and his assistants caught one or two animals and placed them in a gunny sack, carefully turning the edges of the sack to reveal the abdomen of the animal. In this way, the interior of the pouch could be more easily controlled. In one case, the pouch was quite empty, but in another we found a flesh-colored baby about five centimeters long, which was still hanging on to the mother's teats. In another, we discovered a growth, probably a cyst, at the pouch opening, and the professor said that this would have to be operated on without delay.

He slung the sack and its patient over his shoulder and marched off. We followed. My mother touched my chin and pointed in the direction of a group of koalas sitting comfortably on a branch staring down at us with apparent amusement. I looked around then and was startled to find an emu pursuing us. The assistants, however, managed to calm the creature down and told us that we need not fear this bird, big as it was.

Once we arrived at the laboratory, the wallaroo was gently set down on the floor. Professor Sharman pulled the tail carefully to its full length and, using his thumb, tapped the veins at the base of the tail, where he then injected an anesthetic. The effect of this was fairly rapid. I quickly focused my camera on the proceedings and recorded the removal of the growth and the subsequent stitching up of the wound. Somewhat later the animal was taken back to the compound, where it swiftly recovered from the effects of the narcotic.

Although I was able to carry out my observations independently at Cowan, it was not a suitable place for my studies, and I felt disappointment gradually welling up within me. Could it be that Myky was right when he told us some time ago in Switzerland that he had a few reservations about a trip to Australia? Where could I find a better place for my observations? The truth was that I was pretty dejected by the prospect that this might be true and wept at night out of desperation. The trip out here could, after all, prove to be a wild goose chase.

Do They Speak Pidgin ... or Something?

I HAVE to admit that I had some difficulties with English. Later I was in a restaurant and wanted to order a glass of orange juice, but the waitress couldn't understand me even after several attempts to make the order clear. Finally, I had to resort to pen and paper. It was depressing to realize that no one understood me here. Prior to this, I had conversed with a number of English speakers without the problems I was encountering here. Mum said that even she, too, was having trouble in Australia. The difficulty lay in the different accent. This peculiar offshoot of Standard English presented me with an almost insuperable task. My mother, on the other hand, was able to accustom herself to the accent after a few weeks. As a consequence, I found it a real burden to have forever to appeal to her for a translation. Happily, this situation was soon to take a turn for the better.

One evening, my pen friend, Geoff Giles, surprised us with a visit. He proved to be a cheerful character with a small beard. He came by not so much to see Beryl as to invite us to accompany him to a place called Morisset, about 250 kilometers north of Sydney in the middle of the bush. We were all for it, of course!

The sun went down slowly over the wide-open bush landscape, but soon we couldn't even see the bare outlines of the trees and shrubs. It was pitch dark. Here Geoff decided to stop somewhere in the middle of it all. We stumbled rather than walked a little way until we saw lights in the distance. They issued from the windows of Geoff's wooden house, which, because of the uneven terrain and the humidity, stood on stilts. It was large enough to accommodate his big family. I got to know the various members as we sat together over a late meal eaten by lamplight. There was Yvonne, Geoff's lively, dear wife, and their four sons, all of whom I soon got on well with in my rough-and-ready English.

The youngest of these went off to get pencil and paper and awkwardly scribbled down a question: Was I looking forward to seeing kangaroos tomorrow morning? It was astonishing how quickly he had assessed my situation.

Very early next morning we were awakened by the house shaking. Our beds trembled slightly, and then we remembered Geoff telling us that possums created this cannonlike "thunder" when they jumped from the trees onto the corrugated-steel roof. From there they crept under the roof, where they, as nocturnal animals, spent the daylight hours. Every night, soon after dusk, they would wait in the trees in front of the kitchen door for their carrots, apples, and toast, but they were not tame enough to touch.

Again in the very early morning, Geoff drove us out to the edge of the bush. The first rays of the sun began peeping through the trees and illuminating the tender green leaves and the light brown coats of the kangaroos, who now began congregating from every direction. As Geoff went up to them, they hopped toward him. They would not let themselves be stroked but readily took food from our hands. Some of them had young in their pouches. One male, the size of a man, more shy than dangerous, took the bread we offered him. When they realized that our food resources were at an end, they turned once again to graze. Then Geoff clapped his hands, and instantly all of the animals vanished into the bush except for the male, who turned back for a moment to catch a last glimpse of us.

For more than a week I would wander alone in the mornings and evenings on the hospital grounds, where kangaroos grazed either singly or in groups at the edge of the bush. When the animals had retreated to the bush during the day and were invisible, I would walk around the area and admire the supremely attractive environment enclosing about twenty pavilions. The idyllic scene was enlivened by a number of different kinds of birds, including parrots, rosellas, and parakeets in the most spectacular colors, all of them in abundance, together with an occasional laughing kookaburra. Lake Macquarie, which bordered the grounds, was inhabited by Australian black swans as well as thousands of ducks. At water's edge, perched on branches or on nearby rocks, were cormorants, waiting for the lake to provide a meal for them or stretching their wings to dry in the sun. Swallows shot here and there just above the surface of the water, while seagulls sailed leisurely above them, accompanied by the heavy, regular beating of pelican wings nearby. Moorhens, in brilliant blue and violet, cowered among the reeds of the streams off the lake, so well camouflaged that even the trained eye had difficulty in locating them. Close at hand was a wooden platform, where, if they were so inclined, patients could do a bit of fishing. This natural environment did much to soothe their nerves. They made use of the relaxed atmosphere around them, took long walks, or indulged in some kind of sport.

The impressions I acquired here made me think intently about my brother, Peter. I began imagining how Peter would benefit from these surroundings instead of having to stare at the bare, joyless white walls of his clinic in Switzerland.

Quite often we drove through the apparently infinite bush on roads that were like roller coasters and also made visits to the moors and large lakes with their small islands. Geoff mentioned that occasionally there were kangaroos there, too, as they sometimes swam over to them. One time we drove up to a large cave, where we found a large eagle's nest and, immediately next to it, the smaller nest of a songbird. It looked as though the builders of these two nests had been neighbors and had peacefully brought up their respective young. We stood quietly in the solitude of the cave, absorbed in our own thoughts.

When we eventually emerged into the daylight, it was as though one had been transported into dreamland. There, below us, was the unending green of the dominant eucalyptus forest, a broad, totally unpopulated expanse, and at the end of it, on the horizon, stood a chain of gray-violet hills. Elated by the scene, I gazed at the wonderful play of color in the heavens, something I had rarely seen in the northern hemisphere. The deep, almost violet-blue sky was dotted with a few fluffy clouds. I was deeply moved by the grandeur of this panorama.

Back in Sydney, we settled down in a small hotel in the Kings Cross area. From there I took the ferry on several occasions to spend the whole day at Taronga Zoo, where I got to know various species of kangaroos, including the wallaby, a dwarf kangaroo, and other marsupials. My mother accompanied me on a visit to Doctor Straham, the director of the zoo, and I gave him the letter of recommendation I had with me from Professor Hediger.

"I knew you'd come," he said. "Professor Hediger talked about you at a conference we attended in Nairobi."

I was speechless with pride and happiness. Mother, too, was delighted to hear this. Doctor Straham then took us on a tour of the zoo by car and also invited us, together with several prominent citizens, to the inauguration of the new Platypus House. There we were even escorted by a TV team. Unfortunately, we did not later appear on the news.

THE next port of call was the capital, Canberra. To our utter surprise and delight, Myky appeared at the airport to greet us. From there he took us on a short tour of the city and to the CSIRO. The scientists there, some of whom I knew by name, accompanied us through the many kangaroo sections and comprehensively informed us of what went on there. My mother was obliged to do the interpreting but got stuck from time to time on the technical terms for things where I could be of great help.

In the hallway of the experimental observation department, I met Doctor Frith, the departmental director. He was busy putting a young kangaroo into a gunnysack and signaled over his shoulder to me to go with him. Once in the laboratory, he placed the animal in a small cage together with some hay. This done, he then told us all about his activities. I still felt too inhibited to ask him questions but was very glad to be present to watch him conduct his own experiments, an experience that helped me greatly to understand the terminology of many a scientific periodical.

Myky was happy to learn more about my wishes and aspirations and therefore suggested a trip to Pebbly Beach on the east coast. Pebbly Beach! There was that name again! Over the years it had acquired an almost magical quality for me.

The journey took us through farmland, where sheep and cattle grazed, up and downhill through a bush landscape. From time to time, strong sunlight broke through banks of gray clouds. We stopped at a small place to buy provisions since fresh goods were not always available every day in the bush.

After what seemed a never-ending journey, we turned this way and that in downhill curves that unfolded a magnificent view of the countryside and the sea below. Not far from Bateman's Bay we joined the very uneven coast road, where the drive was truly bone jarring. Heavy, low clouds hung over the darkened bush, bathing it in an eerie light. It was as though the route between the innumerable crooked, broken trees, a veritable labyrinth of twisted, intertwined branches and bushes, would never come to an end. Many of these were overgrown with other plants, and some were covered with dead-black soot from earlier bush fires, and there were some that the fire had totally hollowed out. A wind. Rain.

At long last, the first indications of a glade appeared and shortly afterward a wooden sign saying: PEBBLY BEACH!

8

Pebbly Beach

A LITTLE below the path was a sandy bay with a few meadows in which one could see several huts with corrugated roofs. This minute, peaceful settlement of not more than a dozen huts was Pebbly Beach. Myky pulled up at a garden gate. The house behind was hardly detectable for the wild chaos of tall plants in front of it. A dog raced toward us, barking like mad and waving its tail, followed by a slim woman with short, sleek, graying hair. She sized us up through her glasses and welcomed us when Myky said who we were. Mrs. Schwallbach—for that was her name—ushered us into the kitchen, where we all sat down at a table while she prepared coffee for us. Tessy, the dark-brown dog, crept under the table and snuggled against my knee.

While we sipped the delightfully smelling coffee sweetened with honey, I looked around, fascinated by the interior of the house. The kitchen was a museum of well-preserved original antiques from kitchens of the past. The nineteenth-century, wood stove, for example, could have been my grandmother's. Here it served very well, as electricity was somewhat erratic and supplied by a small, oil-driven generator in a ramshackle building. Through a slit in the door, I glimpsed white crocheted curtains in the living room, for a moment suggesting the atmosphere of old-time Russian homes.

Pebbly Beach Bay, my favorite place.

It had begun to rain slightly. Dressed in a dark cape, boots, and a gamekeeper's hat, Mrs. Schwallbach stepped out into the rain to get kerosene for the fridge in the hut that we were to use. We followed. Halfway there, she stopped, clapped her hands, and shouted.

"Call roos! Call roos! Two girls are here!"

I looked around and was astounded. Before me were dozens of kangaroos standing with bowed backs under a large pine tree that was protecting them from the rain. I was in my element! The animals were perfectly willing to be stroked. Later my mother said that she had never in her life seen such a radiant expression as that on my face at that moment. I thought with melancholy of my father then and recalled our tiff at the breakfast table when he stiffly asserted that I would never come into direct contact with half-wild kangaroos.

I felt a strong rapport with Mrs. Schwallbach from the very first moment and not only because she, like me, was greatly attracted to these animals. It was much more a matter of her unusual personality,

Doris in dialogue with one kangaroo in 2008.

her charisma, and her sheer goodness that drew me to this woman, and I can say the same even today. All of these characteristics were contained in her smile, a smile that issued from her essentially friendly nature. Thus, I didn't take things too much to heart when, at times, we were not able to understand each other very well. We proceeded by writing everything.

In a nutshell, Pebbly Beach was to become an important part of my life. This small, unprepossessing settlement on the edge of the Pacific became a symbol of reflection and of inner, spiritual maturity, a place where my soul found peace. Just one stay there—and there were to be many more—or simply the thought of the place always helped me in some discreet, mysterious way to overcome many difficult situations, even those that at the time seemed hopeless. Pebbly Beach taught me to understand my deepest feelings and in this way strengthened my self-confidence. It helped me to understand the ideas I had of myself and others and so complement and extend them. Like this, I was constantly enabled to modify my conceptions of the world and bring them in line with new ones.

This unpretentious little place was a rarity even by Australian standards. The fact that it could have come into being at all was due to the dedication, the selfless, daily work, and the unerring purposefulness of Mrs. Schwallbach.

Our Hostess and Her Life

ONE day Mrs. Schwallbach took down heavy, leather-bound photo albums to show us pictures of quite a different life, one that had begun in Russia before the October Revolution. In them were pictures of Saint Petersburg and Moscow, as well as those of a life in the country. Among these pictorial reminiscences were photos of her first years in Australia, too, where she had lived since 1927. At that time she lived with her husband in Kings Cross, Sydney, and ran a coffeehouse there. And, of course, there were albums with many pictures of Pebbly Beach, which later became her permanent residence.

Driven by curiosity, the desire for adventure, and, above all, a joie de vivre, she and her husband had explored the east coast much in the manner of vagabonds until they discovered this delightful spot on the Pacific. There was nothing there except the remains of a deserted sawmill and the loading area annexed to it, all of which had been abandoned sometime during World War II.

These two adventurers effectively rediscovered Pebbly Beach in 1946. They rented the land and began building a vacation resort. They drove here in a truck loaded with their essentials all the way from Sydney, some sixteen long hours away. (Today, it's only about a five-hour drive.) The early days were hard; everything had to be done by hand, and their home could be reached only by following a narrow downhill path through the bush. They put up tents and furnished them with every kind of household utensil. Financially, they managed to hold their own by catching enormous amounts of fish and crustaceans that they then sold. On the rocky part of the coast were several natural pools of seawater where this seafood could be harvested. Wooden huts eventually succeeded the tents, which then served as warehouses, and later a hut was set up to store the daily supplies delivered from Bateman's Bay, a small township not far away. At this time, freshwater reserves were inadequate. To rectify this, a large, flat, slanted roof was erected on four posts in an open area to allow rainwater to flow through broad channels into a large storage tank. This structure served not only as a covered parking space for vehicles and a storage area for tools, building materials, and food troughs but also as a refuge for kangaroos when it rained. Two cows and several hens and ducks supplied the Schwallbachs with milk and eggs.

At first, as I mentioned earlier, the two of them lived in tents, but later, and with help from others, they built a roomy house at the edge of the bush. This house still stands. Not long after, several huts were erected, each on a low, concrete base about a meter above the ground

Pebbly Beach: kangaroo trio in the morning
eating grains from the old oil drum table.

and fitted with two water tanks and a shower. A wood-heated oven supplied warm water.

In those days, one didn't encounter kangaroos in this area. The wide strip of bush, which at one time was home to them, furnished hunters with their quarry, but as the animal stock was depleted, the area was designated a national park. Pebbly Beach was of course incorporated into it. Around 1958, the first kangaroos shyly reappeared at the edge of the settlement. Little by little, they awakened Mrs. Schwallbach's interest, and in order to attract them, she regularly put out food to win their trust. With patience and devotion, she was eventually able even to stroke them, but of course this took some time. In the years that followed, many, many more kangaroos streamed into the settlement, and from animals that were once wild and shy grew a colony that gradually became tame and trusting. Although Mrs. Schwallbach had little time herself for scientific observation of the kangaroos, she nevertheless knew a lot about them. At first, only young females appeared; they were followed some time later by mothers with young in their pouches and others in tow.[14]

Pebbly Beach became an attraction for a large number of local animals. A little later, the first red-necked wallabies appeared. These are extremely shy creatures, but they turned up each morning and evening and used the area as a playground—and still do. But that wallabies would go up to a beekeeper and help him with their hands—that was something quite new to me.

The Schwallbachs had allowed a beekeeper to set up his hives at the edge of the bush while the eucalyptus trees were in bloom. After extracting the honey with a centrifuge, he would pour the rest of the hot liquid into a metal vessel so that the wax would separate. As soon as the contents had hardened, he placed the upturned vessels on a long board. The wax was now on the ground, covered with a layer of leaves, flower buds, and other particles mixed with a little

14. "Others" refers to those young that do not climb back into the pouch but are still dependent on their mothers for approximately another eight months.

honey. So that the wax could be used again (for example, for making candles), this layer had to be very carefully scratched off—a time-consuming task. Then something astonishing happened. The wallabies came along and began sniffing at the upturned vessels; they then scratched the black layer off for themselves since apparently it was very tasty. From then on, they waited impatiently until the next vessel was ready for cleaning.

One day the beekeeper initiated Mrs. Schwallbach into this "secret," and when she saw with her own eyes how these little fellows were eagerly licking the vessels clean, she was quite impressed.

THE sudden death of her husband did not leave her as a lonely widow. There were the guests to see to and, not least, the animals. Her dog, Andy, for example, would bring in the cows from the meadow with his barking, but he was a bit chary of dealing with kangaroos. After Andy died, Cocky, a cockatoo, followed in his place. He literally tore up the floor and later met his end in the jaws of a fox. Then Tessy, another dog, came along and took up his duties but also formed a playful relationship with a kangaroo called Susie.

A World of Its Own

THE beautiful, partly bizarre diversity of the colorful aromatic plants at Pebbly Beach, the fruit trees and the lemon shrubs, as well as the many types of cactus plants, all surprised and delighted me. At our front door, which led straight into the kitchen, stood a garden table, which the kookaburras had appropriated as their very own landing strip. Sometimes these birds would fly as a fivesome together onto the "airfield" and then enjoy a little get-together. Standing at the front door, one could observe the currawongs, highly attractive, pitch-black birds with yellow eye rings. They romped on the lawn or swooped in free fall for some morsel thrown to them and then quarreled for right of ownership. Among them one could also find magpies in their smart, black-and-white plumage, as well as bee-eaters and red-blue crimson rosellas, a cheeky species of parrot.

There were times, too, when one could surprise a bowerbird in his dark, silk-blue plumage on a quick visit to the garden. Then there was the gray-and-white butcher bird that would place himself on a branch and peer into the kitchen to see who was inside.

This was like a signal for Mrs. Schwallbach, who, even in the middle of a conversation, would lift her head and listen. Then she would go to the table, on which was a very small glass bell over a plate, lift it gently, take out two small pieces of meat for the visitor, and go to the door. Without the slightest hesitation, the bird would fly straight to the morsels, flap his wings furiously, grab them from her fingers, and then make off as suddenly as he had come. Not far away, he would slice up the meat professionally with a few movements of his beak and swallow it. Impudent currawongs would frequently interfere with the other birds present.

The countryside around Pebbly Beach was magical in its remoteness. From a dense forest of eucalyptus trees and thickly populated bush spanning several square kilometers, the ground fell steeply from a plateau a good twenty meters to the rock-lined sandy beach below. The shoreline was dotted with a number of sea basins, which

Silk Bowerbird, a collector of blue items.

were constantly filled with tidal seawater and were home to star-fish, mussels, snails, and other crustaceans and also a few small fish. About three hundred meters farther on was a small lagoon, and from there one came across another stretch of rock that had been worn smooth by the sea. Here one stumbled upon a heavy post rammed into the ground that had been used many years before as a bollard for ferryboats. From this point, one could take the wet, slippery path over many a sharp stone to the cape beyond, which offered a magnificent view of the crashing waves.

The name "Pebbly Beach" comes from the huge pebbles that cover large areas of the beach. The place is still small, and at that time it was unlikely to have been found on a map. "If only we had come here right away!" I exclaimed.

It would not be long now before we would have to take the plane home. Mother blamed herself for suppressing my earlier enthusiasm for this truly magical place. We thanked Myky warmly for his great generosity and hospitality. After all, it was he who first mentioned Pebbly Beach on his initial visit to Basel and sparked my fervent interest in it, almost, it would seem, as though I had listened to an exotic fairy tale. Without him, I would have been far less likely to be able to fulfill my desire to watch kangaroos in the wild. It was very difficult, you see, to find a suitable region to observe half-tame kangaroos. Added to this, of course, was the fact that here was a harmonious symbiosis of human beings and animals, and this alone made Pebbly Beach something of a rare phenomenon.

I pleaded with mother to extend our stay, so the next day Mother, accompanied by a few of Mrs. Schwallbach's friends, drove to one of the few outlying post offices in the bush. From there, she was able to change the booking. Thus, instead of five days at Pebbly Beach, we were able to spend a very happy eleven days there despite the rain. For me, even eleven days was still much too short, of course. On the other hand, the loneliness of the place (by now practically all the vacation guests had gone) was a little difficult for my mother to bear. Here in June, the winter had begun, but this locality had never seen any snow. The leaves of the eucalyptus trees remained green. No leaves fell, but the bark peeled, and this burned well. The high humidity even at 46°F increased the feeling of cold, and our fingers became stiff.

I started further observations right away and used every minute for them regardless of the weather. Every day followed the same routine: I got up at dawn (about 6:30 a.m.), went outside to draw water from the tank, and returned to the WC and shower cabin. During this time, kangaroos flocked almost to the front door. Our good-mornings began with strokes all around. They put their noses to mine for an exchange of breath, an act on their part that made it easy to accept me. After this, I distributed bread and they were satisfied.

When I was fully dressed, I went outside again and, in passing, enjoyed the bluish-red "crimson" rosellas, which had now gathered in the meadows. On looking closely, I discovered how they pulled out grass stalks with their claws and put them into their beaks. If I went out in the grass, they would fly up and remind me of colored garlands caught by a gust of wind.

Then I ran down to the sandbanks to see whether I could find a few kangaroos. On one occasion I noticed that, despite the cold morning, the animals had waded thigh deep into the water. The waves slapped their bellies. After about five minutes of this, all of them hopped out again. After breakfast around eight o'clock, I went to Mrs. Schwallbach's house, where she was feeding "her" kangaroos. She shoveled grain for them from a wooden box and let the lid of the bin slap down hard; this was the signal for feeding time. Instantly, the wallabies came storming down the bushy slope from every direction.

Each animal received a handful of grain, first the kangaroos and then the wallabies. They waited quite charmingly in a row, their heads in the same direction, with their front feet either on the ground or hanging loosely in front of them. Looking at them, one might think of English people courteously waiting in line for a bus!

Ducks and hens ran here and there, quacking and clucking, between the larger animals in the hope of finding a grain or two. Above, impertinent Australian magpies and currawongs dominated the scene. If I had bread with me, kangaroos would immediately surround me and scratch my arms or even my face for a morsel. It was as if to let me know that they would keep me captive until all the bread had been given away. It was a lot of trouble to extricate myself from their midst! On the other hand (and between you and me), it was actually a delightful experience.

Once, as I was giving a shy wallaby the rest of the bread I had with me, a kangaroo suddenly came between us and hit the wallaby so hard that it dropped the bread. In a flash, a currawong shot down from above and seized the bread in his strong, sharp beak—and off he went, never to be seen again!

During the day, while doing my observations or taking pictures or perhaps writing up notes, I would sit either in the middle of a group of kangaroos in the bush or in the meadows near the beach. According to my calculations, there were about sixty so-called eastern gray giant kangaroos in the neighborhood of Pebbly Beach and about fifteen of the really shy red-necked wallabies.

WHEN mother felt a bit lonely without me, she would call on Mrs. Schwallbach, and the two women would drink a cup of coffee together or spend time with a pretty wallaby with whom she had made friends, an association that gave me special pleasure. The animal had an especially fine brown-orange coat and beautiful black face and ear markings. Its eyelids were like velvet, and it was the only one of its kind that was not especially shy. Mother was almost able to stroke it and talked to it in Swiss dialect, which was a certain sign of her homesickness.

Lunch was at noon, and immediately afterward I joined the animals, having hardly a moment to take my mother to the sea or walk with her in the bush, so infatuated was I with my kangaroos. One day, though, she took me a long way into the woods. "Shhhh!" she hissed softly, suddenly pointing in one direction. She had discovered a lyrebird. In the mating season, the male opens his fanlike tail and at the same time sings exuberantly.[15]

---

15. One seldom comes across this bird, whose song is described as fascinating. Unfortunately for me, I wasn't able to hear it because of my deafness.

These days, the wind never stopped blowing. Night and day, there was always movement, if not wind proper, then a light breeze. If the wind came off the sea, then the fluffy cumulus clouds on the horizon would soon multiply and cover the entire sky within half an hour. The rain would just tip out of the sky. After a few hours of this, the wind would pick up from the opposite direction and blow everything back over the sea until the sky was polished blue again. Unfortunately, this didn't last long, and in the space of a day the weather might change several times. The colors of the horizon, the blues, pinks, and yellows that painted the sky, sometimes changed very quickly. If I wanted to select a subject and find the right light conditions for photographing it, I usually had to get a move on! Uninterrupted rain kept me at home "under house arrest," as it were, and these occasions always pleased my mother.

Every afternoon at about five, I would pack up my things and reluctantly leave the kangaroos to their own devices. On the way home I collected a few twigs and some bark to start a fire for cooking. Once inside the warm hut, I would sit down and pleasantly concern myself with my drawings. One evening, my mother tapped the table gently. I felt this light movement, stood up, and went over to the window. A full moon stood in the night sky, throwing its light over the still ocean. A gold and silver thread of glittering light twinkled and played on the water. This was the magic of an Australian night, and we were enthralled!

Despite the restrictions placed on my activities by the weather, I nevertheless managed to carry out my ethological observations fairly satisfactorily. Compared with those that could be made at a zoo and in the field, the results were quite productive. Summing up, one can say that differing environmental conditions play an important role in animal behavior. For instance, in the field, there is much less physical contact between the animals. Female kangaroos form groups of thirty and in some exceptional cases even more. The distance between these groups varies from fifty to two hundred meters.

IN CONTRAST to kangaroo behavior in the zoo, where I had observed young animals that had already left their mother's pouch, here they would jump into it again without warning in order to drink. I had never come across this phenomenon in the wild. Outside, there was always a kind of "ceremonial greeting" between mother and young and even a moment or two of play before the younger animal decided to nurse. The reduced flight distance offered by these half-wild kangaroos allowed me to observe them firsthand.[16]

And then we were on our way home. The powerful throbbing of the engines shook my insides. I had discovered my second home, which was slowly sinking now behind an orange-yellow-red horizon. We flew into the night; the darkness outside began to envelop us, and I felt uneasy about returning to Switzerland, a country that had perhaps become foreign to me. How would I react now to the delightful, honest-to-goodness forests and well-ordered fields and meadows of my homeland, where all that was wild and bizarre was completely missing? In Australia, my second home, it was precisely the wild and bizarre that so attracted me. And above all, what would I do in a country that was not home to wild kangaroos?

16. Flight distance has to do with the tameness of animals toward humans either for feeding or for touching. Big, half-wild kangaroos are less fearful and need smaller distances of trust than wallabies, for example. In the case of truly wild kangaroos, who have flight distances of several hundred meters, observing them at first would have been quite difficult.

9

Jacqueline

YOU will have already realized that I view kangaroos as individual beings. Every one of them has its own peculiarities and indeed its own unmistakable character. Because of her strong, special relationship to me, Dora can be described as something exceptional, but Jacqueline, too, of whom I'll say more in a moment, was in her own way quite a girl!

On the very first evening of our arrival in Pebbly Beach, I made my first contact with a group of kangaroos. I was able to move freely among them and soon sought to stroke them, but most of them looked at me warily and edged away from my hand by leaning to one side. The alien appearance of one of these animals immediately caught my eye. It was a female whose color stood out from the usual gray in this group of giant kangaroos. It was the color of the red fox, with a silver-blue shimmer, a rare, magical contrast if ever there was one! The head, too, was something of an anomaly. The eyes were slanted, an appearance that fascinated me.

Stretching from the animal's mouth to the posterior corner of its eye was a stripe of beautiful white. In turn, the external ear was larger than that observed in the large gray kangaroos. Its tail, limbs, and the anterior from the chin to the belly were beige, whereas the back legs and the front paws were black.

I was immediately so attracted to this animal that I let my hand glide over its coat—and how wonderful—she seemed to enjoy my caress. I fell in love with her at that very moment.

My mother took it for a male as it was so much bigger than the others, and because she was not so well informed about kangaroos, I had to explain to her that this particular animal was one of the species *macropus rufus,* a female red kangaroo referred to by Australians as a "blue flyer" since, thanks to its lightness (despite its large size), it was able to hop with such elegance that its movement simulated flight.

For some time we wondered how the "blue flyer" came to Pebbly Beach at all. Although it was an alien here, it was nevertheless tolerated. At dinner I asked Mrs. Schwallbach about the origin of these animals. Thanks to my mother's translation, I am able to recount in rough outline the long story she related.

A Stranger among the Same Species

ONCE, somewhere in Australia's semidesert, a mother kangaroo was shot dead. The orphaned baby was later found by a family, who successfully brought it up. However, it wasn't long before the house proved too small for the young kangaroo, and so it eventually turned up at the Schwallbachs' home.

This beautiful little creature—it had been nicknamed Jacqueline—showed no particular signs of fear, but even then Mrs. Schwallbach wanted it to get used to its new home gradually. Accordingly, she locked it up in the henhouse for three days and three nights. This hut had a small exit. No one was allowed to go near the animal during this time. Mrs. Schwallbach took this opportunity to secretly observe the kangaroo. On the fourth night, she opened the door. From then on, the kangaroo was allowed out at night but had to remain inside the henhouse during the day. This procedure was adopted in order to cultivate a sense of security in Jacqueline. Only when she had become thoroughly familiar with her surroundings and felt completely at home was she given full freedom to wander around outside. Each morning she ate her food from the same bowl as Tessy, the dog. Before long, she was reacting to her name and came hopping when Mrs. Schwallbach called her.

Jacqueline quickly grew into an unbridled young animal, much more boisterous than the gray females of her species. Again and again, vacation guests complained about her ripping their washing from the line, and Jacqueline was scolded for wildly pulling the line like a naughty child. To divert her attention from the guests' clean laundry, she was given her very own "washing line," decorated with rags and shreds of old clothing, which she could attack to her heart's content. But this was not her only hobby. None of the kangaroos disturbed the splendid flowers in the garden—except Jacqueline. No plant, whether in a pot or a bed, was safe. A fence was erected to protect the flowers—and it worked.

Jacqueline had her own "personal circuit," as it were, and would zoom along it with an exuberance and ever-increasing enthusiasm, covering the ground in huge, elegant jumps so that her course more resembled flight than a run. She seemed never to tire, and certainly the name "flyer" was a well-earned one.

Drawing by me: Jacqueline plays with hens. They did not find it funny at all.

The hens and ducks that populated Pebbly Beach belonged to the overall picturesqueness. If it rained for a long time, they would stay with Jacqueline in the open space that served as a storage area. One day Mrs. Schwallbach surprised Jacqueline at play with the hens. Jacqueline touched each feathered representative very gently with both forepaws and stroked it delicately. And did that produce a fluttering and a quacking in this bird community! The ducks didn't want to be left out and let themselves be similarly attended to—a scene that must have been hilarious!

Jacqueline and I

THE day of my first contact with Jacqueline, now in her twelfth year and a fine specimen of her species, was also the first day of a wonderful friendship. It all began with my setting up the camera on its tripod in order to photograph a group of kangaroos. I had scattered a little bread so as to be able to document their quarrelsome behavior while feeding. Jacqueline, who had watched all this from afar, raced wildly over to me, held my arm tightly while she searched for something to eat. A little annoyed by her rough manners, I gave her something and then returned to concentrating on the others. But then I felt her claws digging into me, and I pushed her resolutely to one side. This didn't deter her. For a moment, she stood as still as stone but then continued to beg until there was no more bread. From that day on, I never went out to observe kangaroos with food on me.

If I were to spread some plastic sheeting on the damp ground next to her and then sit on it, she seemed undisturbed, and soon a kind of greeting ceremony evolved between us. As soon as she caught sight of me, she would stop grazing, come a bit nearer, and then wait patiently until I went up to her. This ritual was carried out several times a day.

On one occasion—I was writing up my observations—Jacqueline came up to me and sat in a squatting position about half a meter away. I noticed a deep wound on the underside of her tail. She licked it constantly, and as she did so, she looked at me fixedly as if she wanted to tell me about her injury.

Practically without exception, Jacqueline kept to a rigid daily routine. She was always present at the morning and evening feeding times. When the mornings were warm and dry, she didn't remain long with the other "Schwallbach kangaroos." Instead, she left for other pastures near the beach, where she would lie around and graze with another colony of kangaroos until the afternoon. Then she came back to her home territory. Although, as a giant red kangaroo, she enjoyed her time among the gray giants, I nevertheless noted that she was an alien. If, for example, she discovered a place to eat where there were plenty of plants or a shady spot where she could rest, the others did not follow her. Conversely, if the other "grays" made a discovery, she always followed suit—in flight, too. I often observed her to be alone and far from the other grays. From time to time, she sought the company of friendly human beings. Of these, Mrs. Schwallbach of course assumed first place, but because of the inherent dangers of the kitchen, she was seldom allowed inside the house. She also became much attached to me, to the point that I sometimes had the feeling that a "reincarnated" human being was seeking to contact me.

Like all of the "red giants," stemming as they do from the very dry regions of Australia, she disliked rain. Her coat was thin in comparison with that of the gray kangaroos. When they once stood wet through in front of my door in heavy rain, I grabbed the opportunity to have a good look at their coats. I discovered that immediately below the topcoat was a water-resistant, woolly undercoat that prevented the dampness from penetrating to the body. Jacqueline did not have this protective layer. For all this and oddly enough, she was the only kangaroo that had managed to remain dry!

However, I suspected what she was up to. Jacqueline favored dry, sheltered places such as the area where the huts and water tanks were located. These stood on stilts and thus provided a roof. She could also remain dry by standing under the storage area. Once I had moved to share a dry, sheltered place with her in the garden, but instead of playfully snuggling up to me, she held her nose high in royal impatience. When the dark rain clouds eventually gave way to a clear sky, she hurried out into the green open spaces. There were other times when she was suddenly surprised by heavy showers. If, on these occasions, she happened to be a long way from cover, she would speedily make for the nearest tree. However, if this particular tree didn't offer enough shelter, she would then limber up like an athlete before a race and catapult herself from there with a few enormous but elegant jumps to the storage area shelter! I always had to laugh on watching this performance. And, just in passing, I had never seen Jacqueline bathe in the ocean like the other kangaroos.

One sunny morning I came across Jacqueline at the edge of the bush. She saw me coming and raced downhill to greet me—and then stopped above the embankment as though to play a trick on me. She waited there until I caught up with her. I gave her some bread—and then she started in! At that moment I was forcefully reminded of what Mrs. Schwallbach had once said about having received a hefty kick on the thigh from Miss Jacqueline's two hind legs, for which, in return, she had received a painful box on the ears and never attempted that kind of thing again! However, the need in Jacqueline's case was apparently so strong that she had selected me as her next victim. To be sure, it wasn't that she had something against me but that actions like these count as part of kangaroo boxing tactics, a playful gag that is not without its dangers for human beings.

Jacqueline placed herself directly in front of me. In accordance with kangaroo ritual, I stroked her chest and arms, a gesture she apparently enjoyed. After a while, though, she raised the upper half of her body so as to make herself taller than she actually was. I immediately recognized this as a signal of what might follow. Nonetheless, I remained calm, and gradually we resumed our familiar ritual: I continued to stroke her, which she still seemed to enjoy. Then, using both forepaws, she grabbed my arms and pulled herself up to her full height and more by standing on tiptoe, using her tail as support until her snout was level with my nose. In strange excitement, she rubbed her snout on my shoulders and began to gnaw the sleeves of my jacket. Precisely at that moment I felt a dull thumping made by her back feet, which, in retrospect, was a kind of preface to a kick, and this was exactly what she had cooked up for me! Like lightning, I pushed her back with both my hands against her chest and swiftly got a few meters out of her way. She stood there at her full height and looked at me, nonplussed. She appeared to be unable to grasp the notion that someone might prefer not to be the recipient of such a "loving" kick.

The next day I dared to go a step nearer. In so doing, I improved my posture so that I wouldn't be thrown backward by another kick. I placed one foot behind me (to support me like a tail) and at the same time held my nose in the air. This is the posture a belligerent male kangaroo takes in order to protect his eyes from a rival's stiff blows. As far as I was concerned, I had to look after my glasses on top! Then we went into a clinch, I with the palms of my hands, fingers spread, and Jacqueline with her forepaws. This went on until she felt the game was over. It ended abruptly, and for her, the matter was settled. I wasn't able to entice her to keep playing and would have to await another opportunity.

A short while after this encounter, Jacqueline, in fact, did get her first opportunity to give me a quick kick. It was not to be the last painful experience of "cordial" kicks. Interestingly, it was always the females that awarded me these very personal injuries, which are in no way to be conceived as a desire to do harm. Apparently, in the matter of sport, kangaroos keep the sexes apart.

These "sporting" intimacies were frequently associated with bruises to the thigh.[17] Anyway, I could easily put up with a few black-and-blue marks and regarded them with equanimity; indeed, they privately evoked a certain pride in me since I regarded them as a token of comradely familiarity.

Moving Moments

ON ONE of those few days of sunshine before the departure from Pebbly Beach, I maneuvered Jacqueline to a place where I could

---

17. Normally, a kangaroo reaches the thighs only when it attacks with its hind feet.

photograph her since I didn't want to leave without taking a few pictures of her. Today was an opportunity to do so, and she allowed me to steer her into position. After a while, she began to look around as if searching for me, then she hopped toward me and kept very close. I reflected for a moment, and then I realized that the next day we would be heading back to Switzerland. The thought weighed heavily on my heart. It seemed as if Jacqueline recognized my sadness at that moment. All of a sudden I wondered what she would do without me, but such concern was childish. The question would be better directed toward me. Had I not developed such an attachment to this exclusively animal microcosm, it would now not be so difficult for me to return to the ways of the world at large. As a result of my bond with this "kangaroo kingdom," I felt at times as though I had been possessed by the mind of a kangaroo! Jacqueline, for her part, seemed partly human, an impression that was only strengthened by her sparkling, slanted eyes. To the extent that I had humanized the kangaroos, I felt, too, that I had become an animal in part, so strangely had I adapted to their way of life—or so I imagined.

I was near to tears. Then Jacqueline touched me gently as was her custom when she wanted to play. Again she held my arm, and again she gnawed at my jacket excitedly. We were slapping each other on the shoulders and arms when she suddenly broke off, looked out to sea with her paw on my arm as though she was intently listening to something. We stood there for what seemed an eternity. It was a moving moment. Jacqueline let my arm go. I lowered myself until our eyes were opposite each other's. With a heavy heart, I looked up to the sunlit trunks of the eucalyptus trees. I slowly moved my face nearer to hers to carry out our ritual of touching noses. I gently pressed my nose against hers, but she didn't react. Instead, she remained immobile as a veil of cloud passed across the sun. Jacqueline lay down. I placed the tripod and the camera in a suitable position, switched it to "self-portrait," and settled next to her. Not long after this, Jacqueline stood up, walked lazily a few meters away, and lay down in the grass for her "siesta." I saw her once more at evening feeding time.

The next morning, our farewell went by very quickly. Although I was in tears, they were not so much tears of sadness at departure as tears of gratitude for the opportunity I had been granted to experience such deep fellow feeling. My thoughts are with her.

Once back in Switzerland, I was watching TV and witnessed the landing on the moon, an event that so utterly fascinated me that it soon appeared in my dreams. In one, I am starting off for space from Pebbly Beach, a crowd of surprised kangaroos around me. The rocket is a large, hollow eucalyptus tree.[18] There is no fire, no smoke, and no noise. I rise into the sky without a sound. Far below I can make out Jacqueline and the other animals on the deep-green meadow near the beach, and tears well up in my eyes. All the other animals disappear to a minute, red point, and then that, too, disappears. The horizon bends more and more until the earth appears as a globe, and the farther away I travel, the brighter the stars become all around me. Return is no longer conceivable. I am already flying over the moon, and the most delicate moment has come for me to prepare for my mission: boarding the moon ferry. Terror seizes me as I realize that I've forgotten how to exit from the rocket since I've been so absorbed with Jacqueline . . .

Then, on another night, a different dream liberates me: I'm living in my old house in Riehen, together with my parents and Jacqueline, who is free to jump about in the huge yard. Every day I spend gloriously happy hours with her, utterly free of care, picking cherries and raspberries and other fruit for her until one day my mother takes me to task for spending all my time with Jacqueline instead of sitting sensibly at the typewriter. I burst into tears and run to my father, who comforts me, and we go into the yard, where all three of us enjoy our time together.

EVERY letter I received from Pebbly Beach was very special and made my heart beat faster. Mrs. Schwallbach reported most colorfully on all that the animals had been doing. The details were partly

18. Actually, these tree trunks are often hollow.

amusing, partly routine, but also contained the incredible and certain moments of sadness. And of course, she spoke of my Jacqueline:

> Jacqueline is as lively as ever . . . your favorite stuck her nose into the casserole full of hen food and just wouldn't let go! . . . Jacqueline is getting older and doesn't jump about like a mad thing anymore; she doesn't chase the ducks and hens anymore either. She's getting older. . . . Jacky ran to the big container behind the storage area; she gets her large portion of grain there . . . and I enticed her to come along. She followed. Then I opened the garden gate to feed my good old Tessy, who's ill and has hardly any appetite. I gave him some bone marrow, but he turned his nose up at it. But as soon as Jacqueline began to eat it, he put his nose into the bowl as well and so both of them ate happily from the same bowl as they used to do ten years ago when they were young. It was a charming scene because it seemed that neither of them had forgotten those days.

I OFTEN dreamed of Jacqueline, and sometimes, too, she was present in my daydreams. In this way, she accompanied me on my long walks through Switzerland's woods and was even with me as I traveled by streetcar—a very special kind of "stowaway."

At times I gave way to bouts of temper when I felt that someone had let me down or, in my opinion, had not sufficiently recognized how hard I had tried to make up for a mistake. In situations like these I sought comfort in thinking about Jacqueline. This kind of exaggerated mental "correspondence" with Jacqueline is critically illuminated in the following dream:

Out of a sense of shame for my misunderstanding and frequently for my inaccurate interpretation of others' conduct, I fall down dead on the spot. In the blackness that then surrounds me I can yet detect a bright yellow in the distance and the turquoise blue of heaven.

I fly far beyond the horizon and directly toward a bizarre "upper world." Once there, I land on a rocky plateau, where I discover a young stranger. Cautiously, I move toward him, and he looks at me in a friendly way and then asks what I'm doing here. I hesitate for a moment before saying, "I haven't heard anything from Pebbly Beach for so long that I fear Jacqueline has died. Now I'm going to see for myself." The young man looks at me accusingly and replies, "Why don't you seek the love of God?"

As soon as I woke up, I felt deeply ashamed. It was as though I had made a god of Jacqueline. Finally, a happy dream:

Sad and alone, I find myself walking among a crowd of people through Basel. Then, suddenly, Jacqueline! She squeezes out of the crowd and hops straight over to me. I greet her with tears of joy, and the people around us are happy because we are happy.

A Sad Return

IN SEPTEMBER 1974 I returned to Australia just in time for spring. I found myself back at Pebbly Beach, this time with Kathrin, a young lady from a village in the Berner Oberland. As my new traveling companion, Kathrin proved to be a big help with oral communication and with my scientific research. Instead of my very careful mother, I preferred someone who gave me more free time and space for my work. Like an excited child, I imagined that Jacqueline would display the same joy that I felt at seeing each other again, but of course, these were only my own feelings projected upon my kangaroo friend.

As soon as I had hurriedly unpacked my things, I went off in search of her. It was rainy and cool, so I finally discovered my "darling" as expected in the dry area of the storage sheds. I squatted down before her—and then boundless disappointment! She looked at me blankly, showed not the slightest sign of greeting, and hopped away.

Although, as formerly, she often stood at the open door of the hut and I saw her each day, the old camaraderie of the past was no more. When we encountered one another, her expression remained quite empty for the most part, and if I tried to stroke her, her head would begin to tremble, and then she would tear out grass by the roots to show her irritation and try to avoid me.

It was a strange attitude and a form of odd behavior that I had never experienced with any of the other kangaroos. Jacqueline no longer gnawed at my clothes, let alone treat me to a few joyful kicks! Instead, I received one or two heavy blows from her forepaws, especially when she wanted to get rid of me. From this moment on, it was clear that the distance between us could not be bridged. I felt desolate.

"You see, Jacqueline is not a person, and neither is she a dog that runs up to a someone, wagging its tail and barking like mad to greet him or her," said Kathrin in an attempt to shake me out of my discouragement.

I just could not admit to myself that Jacqueline, at sixteen years of age, had simply grown old. Her once beautiful coat of fox-red had now become a dullish gray mixture. For most of the day, she lay on the lawn, seldom came to feed, and rarely went down to the meadow by the sea. She had retired into her loneliness. She still allowed me to feel her pouch, which did not look particularly healthy anymore, and I discovered a lump inside it. The idea of surgically removing it was out of the question, although she still had considerable strength despite her advanced age, and she occasionally proved this. At breakfast, the same scene as always took place between us. Jacqueline made it plain that she wanted something—in other words, she begged for food. Sometimes, indeed, she had the cheek to take something good from the table in front of our very eyes. I deterred her with a light, friendly slap, to which she responded by shaking her head in a trembling manner and stood there as though made of stone. I then jumped up, jerked my hands under her armpits, and tried to push her to one side with all the strength I could muster. But she stayed put.

During the hot summer months, Jacqueline resided in her own delightful "palace" at the edge of the bush. This area consisted of six large clearings she had made for herself, each of which was one to two meters long and about thirty centimeters deep. These days she had the air of a spoiled old lady who had reserved several comfortable beds for herself. The decision as to exactly which of these beds she favored for her siesta depended on where the sun stood in the sky, the corresponding shade available, and the temperature at the time. If it became too hot or too cool, she simply changed places. Jacqueline's preparations for the bed she would use involved an odd ritual. She would hop slowly into one of the clearings and then stand motionless in it for a while, her tail hanging somehow unnaturally behind her, but pushed through her back legs and bent to the front. She would then scratch the dirt until tail and feet were covered with a bit of cool earth. Next, she would rub her nose vigorously, sit on her haunches, her tail between her stretched legs, and set about cleaning herself. In so doing, she also licked her pouch clean.[19] Finally, tired out by this strenuous procedure, she would roll over on her side and doze until the sun's rays told her that it was time to stand up and move to a new bed.

I HAD long been back in Switzerland when a letter arrived from Mrs. Schwallbach. I almost broke into tears on reading it:

> Jacqueline suffered badly from arthritis, so that hopping became more and more difficult for her. The vet came and examined her, and I gave her some of my tablets. These were laid between slices of bread, and she ate them. A few days later, she refused food altogether. I covered her with blankets during the night, when she had retired to the garden to sleep, but these kept slipping off her when she changed position. The ground was a little uneven and therefore uncomfortable, and so she tossed and turned in considerable pain. It has been the hardest winter I can remember, and at night it was terribly cold. Finally, I rang the vet again. It was obvious that Jacqueline was suffering dreadfully, and the doctor put an end to her misery.

I was almost glad that our once intimate relationship had clearly ebbed on my last visit; otherwise, my sadness would have been

---

19. According to Mrs. Schwallbach, no male belonging to the group of gray kangaroos ever showed sexual interest in her. They regarded her as an alien.

much greater. It was in any case difficult enough to get over her passing.

I can still easily visualize her wonderful coat, the reddish back, and the thin white of her cheek stripes with their black dots. The enthusiasm I felt for these colors was not simply a reminiscence of Jacqueline and "the past that is no more." These elements also inspired me to include them in my artistic work and so give my wonderful memories creative expression.

10

Moving like a Kangaroo

AFTER the unpleasant cold of an Australian spring, in September 1974 Pebbly Beach became warm and sunny about midday, and this was an opportunity for us to go outside and picnic in front of the hut. Geoff and Kathrin prepared something to eat in the kitchen, while I kept watch outside. This was necessary since there were currawongs and magpies in every direction that were addicted to snacks and were ever ready to swoop and steal.

We took our places around the richly laid table in sunshine that now beat down, but at that moment—heavens above!—we were suddenly surrounded by about fifteen kangaroos. Several of them sniffed the coffee, assessed the cheese, and tried the toast while others poked us in the back with their snouts. Unwillingly, we got up, tapped and slapped at their noses and chins, and shoved them out of the way, but did that help? Not at all! None of them took the hint. Since Kathrin and Geoff couldn't think of any other way to repulse them, I went into the usual "attack" position. I spread my arms and fingers and sprang at the next animal to slap it soundly on the hips. Geoff and Kathrin did the same, but even that didn't help much. Hardly were the animals driven in different directions when they were back in formation—this time, with the hens and ducks as allies!

Happily, this brazen attack was a one-time event. It seemed that our defense strategies had impressed them, as from now on they left us in peace at mealtimes. At my request, we refrained from feeding the animals altogether at such times. This allowed us to eat without being disturbed, and, just as important, they no longer regarded me as a food supplier but as "one of them," and this indeed was of particular importance for my scientific work.

Ten years earlier, during one of my visits to the zoo in Zurich, something unusual had happened. I was crouching down in one of the outside pens among the large gray kangaroos when one of the senior males hopped over to me, seemingly with nothing particular in mind. Aware of the danger of attack, I remained still. With studied slowness, I turned away from him, bent my back a little, and looked over my shoulder once or twice in his direction. He remained quite still, watching me. My mother photographed this scene without really knowing what was going on.

A few days later, I showed the pictures to guests and tried to explain my behavior. For some reason that I failed to understand, they were amused at my explanations. When they had all gone home, I turned to my mother and asked what all the good cheer was about. "Well," she replied, "they think that you enjoy behaving like a kangaroo yourself!" I was annoyed at this. Of course, I felt a bit embarrassed, so I tried to explain the situation to her, but she could not appreciate the earnestness of the situation and said that I was talking nonsense. What I was doing had nothing to do with animal psychology, she maintained. Nevertheless, I didn't let it go at that and persisted in asserting that one had to adapt to an animal's behavior and that in this one had to mimic its movements as much as possible. Failure to do so would make it impossible to spend time with the creature. However, it was only when I had explained that I had behaved like a female kangaroo in order not to be attacked by the male that the light went on. Understanding this, my mother was from that moment convinced of my scientific acumen and later proudly informed others of this.

WHILE in Australia's open spaces, I had an opportunity from the very first to broaden and improve my understanding of species-related attitudes as far as kangaroos were concerned.[20] In order to live with them better, I corrected my bodily postures every day, indeed, sometimes from hour to hour. It was not an easy business to maintain the correct pose. Having thought about the matter and with conscious determination, I tried to transform my human behavior into kangaroo behavior. I did not want to disturb the atmosphere prevailing within a group of kangaroos, so I would push my body forward with my head down when walking and keep my head down even when standing. Our normal, upright posture irritates kangaroos. They immediately sense a stranger in their midst. If, for example, I were to stand up too quickly, all of the animals would immediately prick up their ears, a sure sign of some kind of danger. (As far as I was concerned, I was always on the alert when a kangaroo swiftly and unexpectedly raised itself to its full height.)

AT THE beginning of my field observations, I plunged into the life of the kangaroo. By this I mean that the distance between the animals and me was reduced to an absolute minimum, a relationship that also enabled me to touch them. With the exception of the young animal that had gotten used to life outside the pouch, animals in the open field never came into bodily contact with one another. This didn't apply to their life in a zoo, however, and it was this situation that enabled me to sit in the middle of a group of kangaroos and observe them as they were either lying or standing well away from one another.

It was often possible for me, for example, to sit between widely scattered groups of lying or standing animals. On these occasions I never had anything edible on me, neither bread nor apples, since this would have nullified my studies of animals in their natural habitat. The visual and olfactory signals reaching the kangaroos would have abruptly changed the situation and focused their attention on me.

20. This includes the so-called kangaroo body language.

When I had concluded my observations or taken a longer break, I could stroke them and indulge in closer contact, and that was something they loved. This can be understood as a beneficial substitute for their personal hygiene activity.[21] If kangaroos groom each other alternately in this way, then it is almost exclusively an activity that takes place between mother and baby and is practically unknown between adult animals.

The kangaroos were interested not only in being fed but also in receiving this kind of "fur care." If I stroked an animal on its chest, it would raise its chin slightly and move its head back and forth in sensual bliss. If I were to lay my arm directly on its chest, the kangaroo would then "capture" it with both forepaws crossed and turned inward, trapping it so firmly that it was sometimes difficult to free myself from its grip. This gave me the feeling of an intimate relationship.

Invitation to Play

EVEN as a child I had always felt a strong desire to play with cats and dogs, and it was always a great pleasure to grab the thick, warm fleece of a sheep in an alpine field. My mother, on the other hand, looked rather askance at this, as she felt that it might induce an unpredictable panic among the other sheep, but here in Pebbly Beach one of the kangaroos invited me to play with it, and I didn't want to miss the opportunity.

The half-wild female kangaroo Berta belonged to a colony of animals that lived in a remote corner in the hills. They occasionally came down to graze in the meadow near the sea. Most of the animals in this group were very shy, and very few allowed themselves to be touched.

Berta was easily recognized by the scar left by a scratch on the bridge of her snout. Whenever I moved among the kangaroos in the

---

21. Here, the habit of combing an animal's coat with the teeth is meant. Licking in this case is a much rarer occurrence.

meadow, she would accompany me "at arm's length," as it were, keeping a good three meters between us. Apparently, she did not want to come into direct contact with me. With her, the tendency to flee was very strong, and it was only when I had a bit of bread in my hand that this inclination could be temporarily overcome. On such occasions, she would audaciously grab my arm, at the same time being very careful not to allow me to touch her. She had often seen me playing with Jacqueline, and somehow she wanted to come into closer contact with me. Her shyness, however, maintained the upper hand. This contradictory attitude resulted in the development of a special kind of "catch-me-if-you-can," a game that almost always took the same course.

She would come almost within arm's reach and would then wait until I made a move. If I then put out my hand toward her, she would hop in a half circle, light as a feather, and then wait behind my back until it was my turn to move and face her again. This went on ad infinitum.

One day I was involved with Jacqueline and paid no attention to Berta. However, this need to wait so long for a rival was just too much for her, and perhaps it was jealousy that reared its ugly head. With great leaps, she hopped toward me and pushed Jacqueline away from me with both forepaws. Jacqueline, however, returned the compliment.

Hardly a day went by without Berta demanding to play our favorite game. She would come up to me, only to back off immediately and wait for my advance.[22] Now and again, there were a few modifications to our game, depending on the way we moved. If I turned around toward her, we then continued to stand out of reach of one another. If I then took a step forward, Berta would lean sideways to make an *S* with her body. In so doing, she held her head in an odd way as if she were saying "Would you mind very much if I cuddled up to you?" Up to this day, I've never experienced a similar ritual.

---

22. Later, I was reminded of the fact that dogs often behave in a very similar way.

April–May 1982. Each morning at half past seven, the pleasantest task of my stay began: feeding the kangaroos. On my way to the rotting old wooden hut, I was already followed by a herd of animals, perhaps all forty of the Schwallbach colony. It was only with some difficulty that I was able to push my way through them to the door. Once there, I could hardly open the door for the press. As well as I was able, I pushed the animals aside and scrambled inside, bolting the door behind me. In the half-light of the old hut, I could feel the hubbub outside. I mixed the food for them—a good-quality grain that they liked very much. The tumult beyond the door increased. It was as though I was dealing with a horde of hungry predators. I appeared outside the door, the bucket of food held high. I used my free hand to smack down any animal that ventured to put a paw over the lip of the bucket. Laboriously, I pushed my way through the throng and managed to spill only a little grain while doing so. It was my custom to distribute their food at a different place each day in order to keep the grass from being trampled. Once the kangaroos were eating happily, I had time to go around with my empty bucket to check on their health and their young.

Pebbly Beach, November 1984

ONE afternoon I set out with my tables and writing equipment to take a look at the kangaroo colony inhabiting higher ground, referred to as Jack's Hill. I wanted to spend a couple of hours observing their eating habits there. I found the animals grazing in broad meadows dotted with clumps of trees, fields that sloped down to the sandy beach below. It was a wonderfully idyllic scene, and not a soul was in sight. I walked carefully among the animals and selected one of them as the subject of my observations. I was concerned at the time with how much of a certain species of plant a kangaroo consumes. There was a strong wind, and it wasn't long before thick clouds began to race across the sky, obscuring the sun. I had hardly begun working when the first heavy drops of rain began splattering down. I shoved the papers under my windbreaker to protect them, and the very next moment it began to pour. I was a long way from home. The kangaroos shot off to a nearby hut that stood on stilts. I joined them and crept into the low shelter. And there I sat in the closest contact with these kangaroos, all of us waiting for the rain to stop.

It was then that a strange feeling overwhelmed me. From one second to the other, I was no longer able to distinguish reality from dream. It was as though my whole life had broadened out before me and consisted of nothing else than kangaroo dreams! The experience lasted for a fraction of a second, and yet it seemed an eternity. I experienced neither happiness nor confusion. It simply happened.

I have remembered this experience and often asked myself whether my life has not consisted of a long series of dreams, dreams that I have had at home in my room somewhere in Switzerland or in Australia or experienced while in the European countryside, dreams in which I have lived with these animals. After all, were they not the inspiration?

11

A Community of Individuals

THE forests and steppes of East, West, and South Australia are often plagued by heavy rainfall. Even the very dense foliage in some regions fails to offer sufficient protection against the torrential downpours, such as those in 1974.

Kangaroos deal with bad weather in their own way: With their heads down, backs bent low and snouts almost touching the ground, they stand as still as statues. The ingenious structure of their coats protects them from physical harm, and thanks to the thick wool of their undercoats, their skin always remains dry. The pile of their coats, which is a characteristic of kangaroos, plays a particularly important role in this. It divides at about the middle of the back, at a vertebra, and runs from here to the lower part of the head. From the middle of the bent back (the peak, so to speak), the water flows down the animal's flanks, over the arms and legs and even via the tail. Water on the upper part of the back, on the other hand, finds its way from the back of the neck to the forehead. At this point, however, the passage of the water is checked by a crest, formed by the direction of pile running toward the head, which is met by pile running in the opposite direction from the snout. The result is that, instead of running over the bridge of the nose, water now runs off and down the temples.[23] The crest, which runs from one side of the head to the other, is called the "forehead line." This line is highly differentiated as to position and pattern and accounts for each kangaroo having its own unmistakable identity.

"Look! That's Lulu with her two children, an adult and a little one! Over there you can see the two kangaroo mothers, Dusja and New Girl, with their offspring and a grandchild. Next to them, Valja!" Mrs. Schwallbach enthusiastically pointed out several of the members of her large kangaroo family.

Looking at all these kangaroos, I felt a bit daunted. How could one possibly get to know each of them with such ease? Of course, at the zoo in Basel I had been able to identify "my" kangaroos among all the others, but there were only about ten in all; here, the kangaroos she affectionately referred to as the "Schwallbach Mob" were about three times that number!

And, indeed, it took me a long time to identify each one, and because there were so many, I had to find a new way of recognizing them, so I began using the folds on their foreheads as a distinguishing feature. This method worked, and after considerable hard work, they gradually became familiar. Not only was I able distinguish each animal at first glance but, using the same technique, I also came to recognize the members of other kangaroo colonies to some extent.

Once, as I set off with my mother to search for the Schwallbach Mob, which had to all intents and purposes vanished from the scene, we came across the Bat Mob. (These were names I created for identification purposes while carrying out my studies.) Seeing them, my mother immediately assumed that we had discovered the missing animals, only to be corrected by my telling her that none of these animals belonged to the Schwallbach group. She opened her mouth

---

23. This remarkable fact concerning the different directions of the pile, which serves as an efficient "surplus water drainage system," provides evidence in support of the argument that climatic conditions have remained constant for a considerable time and that the kangaroo has managed to adapt to them.

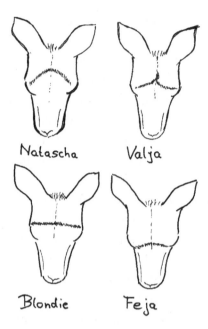

Natascha   Valja

Blondie   Feja

My kangaroo studies: Various forehead drawings show
how different animals can be identified by their foreheads.

wide and looked at me, knowing nothing as yet of my forehead-code
trick of quickly identifying them.

Once Mrs. Schwallbach came up to me, lifted the hair above my
forehead, looked at me intently, and said, "Aha, so that's Doris!"
Those were happy days at Pebbly Beach!

Along with the forehead code there were of course other recognition methods based on kangaroo physiognomy. Dusja, for example,
had a very broad nose; New Girl had harelike, plush cheeks and
deep-set eyes. Matilda's eyes, on the other hand, were very small.
Lulu, with sixteen years on her back, the oldest of the mob, had
many a scar on the bridge of her snout.

In addition, the color and pattern of the coat could vary in
small ways. Doris, the kangaroo that Mrs. Schwallbach named after
me, was dark brown, whereas another kangaroo, called Marilyn
Monroe, was silver gray. Between these two extremes were numerous color nuances. However, it's generally pointless to rely on color

discrepancies to identify an animal since these can vary according to the light or the weather.

The easily visible ear notches, which nature has given them, are often a very helpful means of recognition. It was in this way that I learned to recognize faces during my stays at Pebbly Beach. Since my last visit, other animals had joined the group and young animals had grown to adulthood. Half-wild kangaroos typically live for about sixteen years, which is a relatively short life span. For me, this meant that every time I visited Australia, and to my regret, "good old friends" had passed away during my absence, but I was always glad to see new faces that would become attractive objects of study.

It was of course very important for me to accurately recognize individual animals; otherwise, proper research would not have been possible. Precise recognition enabled me to investigate each animal's habits—its patterns of eating, sleeping, and relaxing and its sexual life—as well as group dynamics.

Every animal is different from every other in the way it conducts itself; one could almost speak of its "character" in this respect. As soon as one gets to know an animal somewhat, one quickly recognizes that they are as differentiated as we human beings are. Then it becomes obvious that they have varied "temperaments" as well. There is the "pleasure addict," for example, and the "joker," the "self-pitying type," the one who desires harmony in all things, the "boaster," and the "troublemaker," as well as the "jealous" and the "lazy, easygoing" types.

If we ignore the strict standards of behavioral science for a moment and attribute human characteristics to animals, then things can be quite entertaining. For example, when Tanja was stroked, she threw her arms into the air as an expression of great joy. Practically every morning, Hedy climbed onto the corrugated iron roof that normally covered the piles of wood. When she wanted to lie down, she just let herself fall with a thump onto the steel, which frightened all the other kangaroos. This "shock ritual" apparently delighted her when she realized that the others were always good for a jolt.

Our Baby and her adolescent daughter, Blondie, remained in intimate contact with one another long after Blondie left the pouch and long after the suckling period. They stayed together when grazing, wandering around, and resting; they were always close to one another and attended to each other's personal hygiene, which was an exception to the rule. Miss Grumpy, an old, odd, dark-brown kangaroo who was often at loggerheads with her companions, growled vigorously (I could feel this) as soon as I laid my hand on her back.[24]

And they can learn as well. My observations showed that many a kangaroo could develop remarkable capacities by using their forepaws. One kangaroo, for example, hopped toward me with a raised arm to one side in order to aim a precise blow at the bread in my hand. At the Basel Zoo, as another example, was a kangaroo called Trudy, who, similar to the ingenuity of a chimpanzee, would use her forepaws to angle for grass through the bars of the cage. I also recall a dominant male kangaroo of the Basel kangaroo group that would take the strong twigs of a maple branch and bend them cleverly with his forepaws, holding them while he ate the leaves. If he was unable to reach a branch easily, he would hop as high as he could, grab the branch, and land with it in his paws. It reminded me of human beings picking apples or cherries.

The forepaws of a kangaroo and the hands of a human being or an ape are constructed differently. A kangaroo foot is thickly covered in hair on the upper side, but the underfoot is soft. The five-digit paw is equipped with long, thick, sharp claws. None of these five digits can be compared with the human thumb, so, in the act of gripping, all five digits have to curl at the same time. Unlike humans, kangaroos cannot grab a branch in a pincer movement.

The question of what skills kangaroos are capable of acquiring induced me to carry out a few experiments while at Pebbly Beach. I wanted to find out whether they would be able to use their forepaws

---

24. I remember quite well as a child being called "Miss Grumpy" by my parents, as I had the habit of growling if I happened to be dissatisfied with something. "You're behaving like a grumpy old thing," they would say at these times and tell me that kangaroos never grumbled and were always very still. How wrong they were! Kangaroos can make all kinds of noises.

to retrieve a piece of bread from a hole. For this purpose, I chose a sturdy box with an edge measuring about sixty centimeters and a depth the exact length of the arm of a kangaroo. It was possible, therefore, for the kangaroo to touch the bottom of the box with its paw. I cut a hole in the middle of the lid that was not so big that the animal could stick its nose into the box. To ensure that the box could not be moved by shoving, I attached it with cord to a stout piece of wood and put heavy stones at each corner of its interior. I then placed the box in the field not far from our hut and scattered breadcrumbs around the hole. I waited excitedly with the camera at the ready to see what would happen.

For a long time nothing happened. Kathy and Wulli, two kangaroos who were lying close, showed no interest at all in this new contraption. At long last, Blondie came by to sniff it. It took a very long time before she finally realized that bread was scattered around the box and began to eat it. I quickly grabbed other pieces of bread, showed them to her, and then let them fall into the hole. All this was done before her very eyes. Seeming to realize immediately what had happened, she began at once to search for the bits of bread. First she sniffed at the hole and then searched for the bread in the immediate vicinity of the box, scratched at the earth, and finally returned to the hole in the box. She repeated this process several times without further inspiration. After about five minutes, she lost all interest in finding the bread and turned to grazing.

I interpreted this result as a personal failure. Apparently, I had overestimated kangaroo intelligence. But at the very moment I decided to call off the experiment, the unexpected happened. Blondie returned with Lulu, a wise old kangaroo. The latter kicked Blondie away from the box so that she could have it all to herself. She smelled the box with great interest and dug around it with her paws until, accidentally, she put one of her front paws into the hole. She scratched energetically a little longer. The box loosened slightly at the bottom. Encouraged, Lulu grabbed the box from the side and turned it over. Then she searched the bottom carefully and discovered the delicious prize inside.

Cheered by this, I carried out further experiments in the days that followed, but every day resulted in failure. On the other hand, there was much to laugh about. On one occasion, for example, a whole herd of kangaroos gathered around the box and vehemently quarreled with one another.

Then one day Mrs. Schwallbach appeared with a beanstalk and reported an astonishing incident that she had witnessed. The vegetable gardens were securely enclosed on all sides by stout wire fencing. However, a wallaby had appeared, put his forepaws through the fence, selected a beanstalk, and cleaned out all the delicate beans from their pods!

KANGAROOS possess a certain awareness of guilt, which I witnessed one day during Mrs. Schwallbach's morning kangaroo feeding. The kangaroos were busily competing for place, standing on their tails and their hind toes, snarling and hissing at each other, dancing around Mrs. Schwallbach for advantage, grasping at her arms and shoulders, and ripping and seizing the pieces of bread from her hands with their teeth. She smacked and pushed the roughest of these away. But none of the animals was willing to give up. They remained standing and drew themselves up to their full height until their noses were almost touching Mrs. Schwallbach's face. The mêlée continued until Mrs. Schwallbach scolded them all and tapped them on their noses. As she tried to extricate herself from this hungry multitude, a female kicked her. Slightly annoyed, Mrs. Schwallbach turned sharply and smacked the offending animal smartly on the cheek. The gesture went home to Our Baby, a light-colored female. Her head shaking, she placed herself directly in front of Mrs. Schwallbach in a way that suggested that she was sorry for what she had done. Her attitude was as clear as day. Mrs. Schwallbach accepted her "apology," nodded in a friendly way, and stroked the animal. Reconciliation had been established.

12

The Bosses

THE appearance of the large, imposing males on the scene was always a fascinating moment for me, but, quite apart from that, it was also enrichment as far as my studies were concerned. The very presence of these "giants" could virtually throw Pebbly Beach into an uproar. Their arrival precipitated a good deal of movement and disturbance in their groups, especially when the males went forth to take a look at the females. They regarded human beings with more or less indifference as long as they felt undisturbed in their activities. However, as soon as they were occupied with sampling some delicacy, they could be very pushy or even threatening, and then it was advisable to keep out of their way.

At first I was very wary of them and rarely in their company. However, after a time I came to realize that they were peaceable. Thanks to my experience with animals and especially my knowledge of their body language, I was finally in a position even to dispense with Mrs. Schwallbach's well-meant admonitions and spent quite a lot of relaxed time with them.

When I returned to my quarters from an early morning walk, which would take me through the bush and over the beach to the sea, the sun would appear in the deep-blue sky, warming the cool morning air. The huge, dark-green tops of the eucalyptus trees shimmered in the sunshine. They were like abstract pictures, standing as they did, with various "strokes" for tree trunks set against a pale green to gray background. The trees shone brightly and changed from a brilliant yellow one moment to a strong brown the next. A herd of kangaroos was grazing in the meadows surrounding the white huts, still wet with dew.

The hut dwellers and vacation guests at the site were already up and about and had begun making their cooking fires. From every direction, clouds of smoke, laden with the delicious smell of toast, floated in the air. My empty stomach began to rumble. Kathrin, my traveling companion, was just about to turn the toast and lay fresh twigs on the fire. I laughed and rubbed my hands in pleasant anticipation of the breakfast to come. Suddenly my eyes opened wide in shock. Next to Kathrin was a large, dark muscular body. It was Papochka, one of our three giants, and he was eyeing Kathrin curiously. Evidently, like me, he had been drawn to the spot by the delicious smell of toast. I snatched my camera and secretly filmed the scene at the fireplace. In so doing, I didn't bother to turn the toast, although it was my job to watch it. I could only manage to watch this large, impressive animal, half in fear and half in fascination and prepare for flight at any moment. However, the great male stood there without making a fuss as I turned my attention to the toast again. The slices, however, were more than a trifle well done. From this time on, if we wanted to warn someone about burning the toast, we'd say, "Watch out! There's another toast à la Papochka on the way!"

The animal received its name, by the way, from Mrs. Schwallbach. It comes from Russian and means something like "Our Little Father Boss," a fitting title for one of the largest and most feared kangaroos along Pebbly Beach.

George with the Flapping Ears

GEORGE was second in the hierarchy of bosses at Pebbly Beach. He had deeply cloven ears that fluttered like two rags in a strong wind. Kathrin and I called him Flappy rather disrespectfully. "It's a good thing that George isn't a human being," Kathrin remarked once, "so it's not too much of a disadvantage for him!" However, how could one be absolutely sure?

It had poured rain all night long, and the following morning Mrs. Schwallbach had gone to our "minipowerhouse," a small generator[25] next to a number of oil cans in a tiny shed. She wanted to check it and refill the fuel canisters, but she was in for an unpleasant surprise: Flappy had sought shelter from the rain there and made himself comfortably at home. Mrs. Schwallbach didn't dare enter the hut while he was there because of the danger that he might attack. She tried several times to draw him to the door with bread as an enticement. But all was to no avail; George just did not enjoy getting wet, and this meant that we would have no electricity as long as the rain kept up. Jokingly, I asked Mrs. Schwallbach whether he'd be a good assistant in getting the generator going again.

Cuddly, Our Don Juan

WE WERE sitting in the wonderful morning sun at a breakfast table set with good things when Cuddly came near, stretched his neck over the table, and took his time carefully sniffing everything. As a consequence, the saliva ran from his mouth, almost ruining the whole spread. It amused us, of course, but on the other hand it was pretty unappetizing!

The name "Cuddly" had been thought up by Mrs. Schwallbach. He was rather small and thin, and his body was not particularly muscular for a male. However, in the matter of sexuality, he surpassed the other two males, who were considerably larger and stronger. For my studies on the sexual behavior of kangaroos and their courtship rituals in particular, Cuddly was a godsend.

In many aspects, he was what one might describe as a "lady's man." Within a few hours, for example, he would present himself as a suitor at various places, and for this activity, he behaved in a characteristic manner. This peculiarity I had noticed nowhere else, neither in the wild nor at any zoo. On physical contact with a female

25. This little apparatus supplied the whole settlement with electricity, but it was so weak that it was hard to read by lamplight in the hut.

mate, which consisted of light tapping and scratching, saliva would run from his mouth as though at the prospect of the forthcoming sexual activity. Apparently for him, foreplay was a real hors d'œuvre.

When a Harem Disappears during Sleep

DURING my first stay at Pebbly Beach, I never got to see a male kangaroo among the female groups. Mrs. Schwallbach told me that the males emerged from the bush for only a short time every three to four weeks at the most and that they were far shyer than their female counterparts. On my second visit, I most definitely wanted to study the males. And my wish was fulfilled. Hardly a day passed that I didn't encounter the "bosses"!

One morning Kathrin reported that "somebody" was at the open parking place. I was off at once and discovered George, who was lying at the back on the rough wooden floor. He lay there quite peacefully in the middle of the Schwallbach kangaroos, his arms crossed over his chest. Nothing of any interest happened, so after a time I grew bored and left. From there I went off into the "Pat Zone," where a woman named Pat lived with her daughters in a wood house near the forest. Since she fed the kangaroos regularly as well, I was also able to do research on the "Pat Mob." There my eyes opened wide: In a garden open to all of the kangaroos lay Papochka, dozing. For me, this was something entirely new, that is, to come across two bosses in such a short time. This is why I anxiously anticipated the moment when the two antagonists would meet up with one another. What would happen? The excitement mounted. At the moment, the two of them were about a hundred meters apart, practically out of view of each other.

Nothing happened for the whole of the morning. The two bosses dozed comfortably, grazed with the females, and inspected one or another for her readiness to mate. Finally, the scene changed some time during the afternoon. At some point, George had left his area in the Schwallbach zone and was grazing alone on the beach meadow, which was actually in the Pat Zone. Farther up and still removed from George's view, Papochka continued to sleep peacefully. For this reason, he didn't notice that he was gradually being abandoned by the Pat kangaroos and left to his own devices.

I quickly left my spot and ran down to the beach meadow, where I settled about twenty meters away from the Pat Group. After a short while, George appeared and, after greeting a few of the females, began grazing with them. This meant that he had now taken over the leadership of this group. Papochka, who was still lying behind the bush, had succeeded in sleeping during the departure of his harem! The question was, what would he do when he finally woke up and realized his appalling loss?

Another half hour went by. Then George interrupted his grazing, went over to a female, and carried out an intensive smelling operation.[26] Apart from this, nothing untoward occurred.

No sooner had I decided to bring my notes to an end for the day than panic broke out among the members of the Pat Group. Papochka was there! He stood squarely facing his rival, and both animals had drawn themselves up to their full height and stood with their knees and bellies almost touching. Then, suddenly, they both leaned back and punched each other hard and fast with their front paws. The females rushed away in every direction, and I, too, took flight. For one horrible moment I imagined that the two warriors might both descend on me!

Happily, my panic was short lived, and I recovered sufficiently to return to the sparring ground. Once there again, I found the scene practically unchanged. The two contenders had moved their altercation a little farther away; standing motionlessly a few meters apart, they were catching their breath for a moment. They were no longer standing upright but stooped, supported on their front feet, staring intently at each other with terrible eyes. Then the picture suddenly changed. Both of them appeared to have lost interest in each other.

---

26. During this procedure the male lowers his snout so far that the stream of the female's urine actually touches his nose. He then examines the stream as well as the puddle made by the urine. If the urine indicates that the female is ready for copulation, then mating takes place within the next few hours.

George began to graze, but Papochka came a little nearer to his side. And what did George do? He spun on his heel, placed his fore-paws on the ground once again, and simply turned his back on his opponent. At this moment, Papochka seemed to realize that he had lost the battle and had to relinquish his power. He looked briefly at George before finally disappearing. George pursued him for a short distance, and then the two of them came to a halt and began to graze again. Finally, they hopped away from the area and vanished into the bush, Papochka in the lead. What did they do there? Perhaps they carried on fighting. I dreaded the very idea, and later that night I dreamed that the bush suffered a terrific earthquake and that trees and bushes were ripped out of the ground, roots and all, and had crashed to the ground.

Termites on Their Wedding Flight and an "Outdoor Sauna"

LOOKING back to one of my most unusual days at Pebbly Beach, I recall one as "the day of the outdoor sauna" because of the extreme humidity. Quite early in the morning, there were already heavy clouds in the sky, and the damp atmosphere was unbearable. We sweated until our clothes literally stuck to us, and yet we had to spend several hours a day in this hothouse and simply put up with it. As it happened, our energy was unaffected, and we managed to get along.

It was precisely on such an oppressive, sultry day that the ter-mites decided to vacate their two-meter-high, conical hill dwelling and migrate in huge swarms to gather for their "wedding flight." Thereafter, the air was filled with these tiny, flying insects.

Kathrin and I sat outside our hut on the terrace, eating our mid-day meal. I brushed my hand through my wild, bushy hair, which was already full of termites and quite sticky. Regardless of whether I was so predisposed, these small insects filled me with loathing. They landed everywhere—on our heads, on the exposed parts of our bodies, and, of course, all over our clothes, and I found myself extracting them one by one from my hair. With great self-restraint, I carried on eating as I watched the pale yellow, swirling clouds around me, convinced at the same time that there was nothing in this world I could do about their party.

But then I sat back, shocked to the core. Directly in front of me stood a huge figure under a tree. It was George. I almost choked; next to him was Papochka, stretching himself up to his full height! It had begun to rain. Hurriedly, I slipped inside for the camera, which I set up on its tripod under the awning of the hut and in the hope that there would soon be contention between the two, but things remained perfectly calm.

After a while, Papochka vanished. Later I found him grazing peacefully alongside a number of Schwallbach kangaroos at the foot of the meadow embankment. I kept to one side in the interest of safety.

It continued to rain uninterruptedly, but that didn't really disturb me—even when the raindrops smeared my notes. What irritated me much more were these flying termites, whizzing around me by the hundreds and even creeping into my blouse, where they tickled me and prevented me from concentrating. Luckily, these insects didn't belong to the stinging variety, but the experience was nonetheless unpleasant.

I lay there on the lookout, full of anticipation, never letting Papochka out of my sight for a second, and—lo and behold—something rather eerie occurred. Without interrupting his grazing, he came leisurely but directly toward me along the embankment and was apparently quite unconcerned about anything—until he spotted me.

I fixed him with my eye. Did he regard me as a rival, and, if so, how would his aggression show itself? I began to feel rather uncomfortable. Papochka scratched in the grass and, without warning, pulled himself up to his full height. He remained quite still in this posture for several seconds, after which he rubbed his chest with the spread digits of his forepaws and threw back his head as far as possible until his snout was pointing skyward. Then he let himself fall forward again and began once more to scratch vigorously in the grass. In the meantime, his penis had become visible. He lowered his body toward the ground even more, rubbed his chest, his chin, and his throat, moving his muscular arms to and fro, following these movements with his head. Again he scratched in the grass and rubbed his chest with small clumps of it, which he held in his front paws. This sequence was repeated a number of times—and then he hopped directly toward me!

I rushed out of his way as quickly as possible and managed to find shelter under the base of a hut standing on stilts. When I emerged a few minutes later, Papochka had disappeared—much to my relief.

No Boxing Match and No Fisticuffs

WHEN I was younger, I once saw two male kangaroos taking part in a friendly fight for quite a long time at the Basel Zoo. "Just look at these two fellows boxing!" I remember exclaiming to my companion at the time. He, however, cut in by saying, "No, no, one doesn't refer to them as 'boxing' but as 'hitting' each other. The reason is that the animals hit each other only with the palms of their hands!" And of course he was right.

Even while seeing them hitting each other for the very first time, I had noticed that the males more often slapped each other with the flat of their front paws on the shoulders, chest, and upper arms, whereas they tipped their heads back for the most part in order to protect their ears and eyes. Nonetheless, I had also resorted to the familiar term "boxing."[27] Every time I've asked my acquaintances in fun to fight with me as kangaroos do, they have used their fists. Whenever this happened, I stopped the game and explained that kangaroos go about their play quite differently. I then demonstrated the proper technique, which is not easy to imitate correctly. Looking at the business carefully, in the first place it is impossible

27. This general misunderstanding has led to repulsive, tasteless circus performances where the animals are fitted with boxing gloves and encouraged to go at one another.

for a kangaroo to make a fist of his forepaw. Even clearer are the differences between the stances of a human boxer and a fighting kangaroo. The former lowers his head, whereas the latter throws its head well back when it fights.

At Pebbly Beach in those days lived a young male kangaroo that had been orphaned and been brought up by hand. As a consequence, he was very accustomed to human beings and liked a good fight with both human visitors and those of his own kind. This meant that I was eligible for such an encounter, too. When, on one occasion, he failed to bring a battle with me to an end, I decided to do it for him and took a step or two backward and then slowly and carefully— and hopefully with dignity—squatted. I had observed this move in a number of fights and wanted to demonstrate to this fellow that now there was a break or even that the battle was at an end. However, the signal was to no avail. He came over and gave me a blow with his sharp claws. The punch landed dangerously near one eye, which bled immediately.

Very Special Romances

ONE evening the sky was filled with scattered clouds that almost obscured the setting sun, and when the strong, full colors of the surrounding countryside on the edge of the bush began to lose some of their luster, the kangaroos appeared against this background as silver-brown shadows. It was in this gentle, evening atmosphere that I was witness to the courtship of our Don Juan, Cuddly, as he made advances to the females, Natasha and Feja. It was quite a remarkable sight.

Cuddly spent a long time snuffling Natasha's head and neck, showed considerable interest in her pouch, and touched the small face that peeped out of it with the tip of his snout. However, this was a bit too much for Natasha. Irritated by it all, she hit Cuddly on the nose. But this did not put him off for a moment, and he carried on with his investigations until Natasha rejected his attentions and jumped away.

Thus snubbed, the prospective suitor then turned to Feja. She retired slowly, pursued by Cuddly, who rubbed her tail with both front paws and sniffed at the mound of her anus. Feja stood stock-still. Cuddly went around her and then stood directly in front of her. Then Feja pulled herself half upright. By way of greeting, they touched one another with their noses for a quite a while. Animal behavior records describe this as "a significant exchange of breath." During this activity, there were also notable movements of the mouth, combined with tongue movements to give sound, as mentioned before.[28] In between, Feja raised her forepaws and leaned against Cuddly's flank. After her tender gesture, the two animals promenaded around with each other and continued to graze together for as long as one could make them out against the silver strip of the horizon.

Cuddly's love life was much more varied than that of the majority of the kangaroo males. On another occasion, he carried on a whole series of "tender gestures" with one of his chosen partners when he suddenly hopped a few meters away toward a few high bunches of grass and sniffed at these for a long time before brushing his chest against them in a peculiar rhythmical manner. He repeated this ritual several times before returning to his mate.

Then he stayed near his partner, who held her head low, whereas he carried his high without glancing at her but instead "stroked" the air in front of him like a blind man. At the same time he scratched at the ground with both forefeet instead of rubbing the tail of the female. As a last gesture, after he had gone through all the motions of this "blind" fondling, he looked his partner in the eye and began stroking her on the head and the upper part of her body.

There was also impressive love play between Papochka and New Girl. At first they stood side by side in a half-bent position, their heads facing each other. Papochka scratched the upper part of New Girl's chest with his forepaw while making sexual advances to her by using his mouth and simultaneously issuing the clicking sounds

---

28. These clicking sounds associated with the mating season, I was told, can be heard a good twenty meters away.

associated with mating. Then they stood squarely in front of one another and engaged in mutual stroking with light, tapping movements. While this was going on, New Girl clung to Papochka's chest with one of her front paws, nibbling at his chest while he stood there, his head thrown right back in delight.

I was once in a position to observe them both rubbing each other's chest rhythmically, their heads held well back, but charmingly following the movement to and fro. It was a fascinating spectacle!

The Mountain Fastness of the Chiefs

THE territory of the kangaroo chiefs was very large and extended from Pebbly Beach to a range of hills. The really large males rarely turned up at the settlements. When they did come, they were mostly alone or in twos and threes. Because they did not have a strong sense of territorial acquisition, they often infringed on the rules of who was allowed to go where. They frequently ranged, for example, over large areas while on the lookout for fertile females and went from one kangaroo colony to the next. Just where they went or stayed when they were not in Pebbly Beach remained a mystery to me for a long time.

One day an acquaintance invited us along on a trip into the mountains, where, he maintained, a large number of huge, well-nourished male chiefs lived. We set off in the early evening while it was still light, and at dusk we arrived at the hills. From there we had a superb view of the sea. The gentle, yellowish-blue of the horizon melded slowly into a darker blue above, where the stars twinkled brilliantly. The sea was a greenish-blue and black and threaded with a soft, silvery glitter. The crashing waves beat the sand with broad lines of foam, which lay for a second or two in shining luster before disappearing. Eventually, night fell. I trod delicately, almost reverently, on the soft, overgrown stones and let my glance ride effortlessly over the water. It was as if I had been transported from the real world into a fairy-tale one. Right in front of me, for example, the hundreds of flowers on the bushes were illuminated by a strange, unearthly light as though they were lit up just for me!

The darkness was settling rapidly, and the last of the light lit up the few strips on the horizon; the hills with their rich vegetation were hardly discernible, and yet black figures seemed to be moving there: yes! It was them indeed—a horde of seniors enjoying their nocturnal meal.

13

Manuela

ONE morning I was just getting ready for my daily routine of observation, when a young man who seemed to be on an urgent errand suddenly appeared. Since he didn't appear inclined to let me know what the problem was, I sent him off to Mrs. Schwallbach. A few minutes later, he returned with both her and Kathrin, and I learned that he had run over a kangaroo in the bush and required our help. There was no more discussion, and we set off without further delay.

We soon found ourselves on a long tour through the bush on a clay-colored road that turned this way and that like a snake. Overhead, the sky shone through in an intense blue from the tops of the trees as they flew past us. The sun's rays radiated here and there through branches and twigs to the bush below, forming a pattern of sharp thorns that strongly reminded one of abstract paintings. The route itself was very bad, and we passengers were tossed about like so many tin cans. But all that was nothing compared to the concern I felt for the kangaroo, which was probably pretty badly injured. How could we transport it? I asked myself. Most likely it was a wild animal and for that reason extremely shy. Would I be in a position to give it first aid? I'd never been in this kind of situation before. One thing was quite clear: We would have to get the animal back on its feet.

My excitement threw me back into a dream world, to the time when I had last come across an injured kangaroo. I felt an inner emptiness, and this confused me.

The vehicle braked abruptly, and we soon discovered the injured animal in the ditch. It was a fully grown female; I knelt down next to it and felt its body. Its arms and hind legs were already cold, the eyes lusterless and dull. I felt the animal's chest near the heart[29] to try to find a heartbeat, but without avail. The animal had probably died of shock. Then I felt the creature's pouch, and there I felt something move!

"It's alive!" I cried, and the others ran over to me. Carefully I lifted the baby from the pouch, which had already seen quite a bit of dirt. The baby was naked, rosy, and blind, about fifteen centimeters long, and at this moment quite defenseless against the merciless sun and the cold wind, so I quickly wrapped it in a piece of linen, and we drove home.

When Mrs. Schwallbach set eyes on the baby, she simply shook her head. She had brought up a whole series of young animals in her time. It would not have much chance of survival, she said, but we agreed that I would nevertheless try to help it pull through. Perhaps my wishes for its survival were unrealistic, but this tiny, helpless creature clung so much to my heartstrings that I couldn't regard myself as anything but its "mother." (Indeed, in my fantasy I saw this little one as a "gray goose" waddling after me as if I were Konrad Lorenz.)

We began assembling everything that was necessary for the care of a baby kangaroo: small bowls, drop measurers, a small cooking pot, milk, a flask, and a small woolen pouch. Mrs. Schwallbach gave us a clothes hanger, an old blouse, and a dressing gown and showed us how to make a proper pouch out of it.

I was able to wash the small creature in our hut, and this I did very gently with a damp cloth, later placing it in the woolen bag. After that, we had to think about preparing the baby's formula. The milk had to be diluted with water and boiled with a pinch of salt. Then it had to cool to the right temperature before it could be fed to the baby.

29. In kangaroos, the heart is found not on one side, as in human beings, but in the middle. It is situated directly at the thoracic vertebrae, and thanks to this feature, it is particularly protected from shaking when the animals hops.

In the area of its mouth, I discovered the very small hairs that functioned as its sensory organs. The ears remained flat on the head, and its eyes were still firmly closed. I dropped small amounts of milk onto the mouth in the expectation that it would open, but only a very small, round opening came to view. I tried very carefully to put liquid into this tiny hole but wasn't successful. An hour later I tried again but still had no success. Somewhat desperate, I decided to allow the little animal about half a day's rest and kept it warm so that it could get used to its new, unusual circumstances.

In the meantime, the pouch substitute was ready. We hung it on the wall, not far from the stove, and placed the small creature in the wool sack with a hot water bottle underneath and heated stones wrapped in a cloth. We estimated the temperature in the woolen bag to be 95°F, which should exactly correspond to the mother's pouch temperature, but this was not easy to maintain. On our next attempt at feeding we at last had some success; the small thing took about ten drops without trying to grasp the teat of the doll-sized flask I was then using. Its pouch was already slightly recognizable, and we called our new resident Manuela (this was a name, by the way, that I had always wanted for myself). Kathrin and I then celebrated our small triumph with a Coca-Cola.

Manuela had to be fed every two hours, so I had little opportunity to sleep, especially the first night. Every two hours I brought Manuela in her sack to my bed and allowed her to drink greedily from the pipette, or drop measurer. However, my concern for Manuela's survival brought on nightmares, and I even dreamed that I was parading her around town as a proud, fully developed kangaroo and that this created quite a stir.

Morning arrived, and Manuela was still alive, but she drank noticeably less during the day than at night. I made a list of the amounts she drank and how much she discharged as waste products each day. Ideally, I would have liked to bind Manuela in her sack around my body in order to give her my own warmth.

Manuela and my foster parentage were the talk of the settlement, and I was asked again and again about her health. Children were especially interested and wanted to peep into the pouch, and we had our work cut out to prevent them from doing this. Kathrin used to remind me that very few people were privileged ever to get to see inside the pouch of a kangaroo.

Kathrin helped me with the feeding in the nights that followed. On one occasion, Manuela held the teat so firmly in her mouth that Kathrin had a hard time removing it. After every feeding, I massaged Manuela's belly with a damp fingertip in order to facilitate excretion. It was rather a difficult job cleaning her after feeding and keeping her in the woolen sack, as she was extremely wriggly and continually twisted and turned, kicking out her limbs and tail. She also threw out her forepaws and hind feet against our hands and scraped her fully developed, sharp (though still white) claws over her closed eyelids, a habit that caused us a lot of concern.

On the other hand, it was comical to watch her resist us by waving both forefeet above her head, much as a stubborn human child does when it positively doesn't want any more to drink. In addition, there was nothing we could do in the matter of cleaning other than to remove Manuela completely and clean the interior of the sack with a wet cloth or replace it with a new one. Manuela's liveliness and her intact digestive system were indications that our "upbringing" was bearing fruit. I was so convinced of this that, in my euphoria, I overlooked something vital. On the fourth day, Manuela's skin took on a bluish color, and she assumed a shriveled aspect. It was as though she were wilting, but we didn't take sufficient notice of these signs in time to save her.

It was late afternoon. I had just returned from my observations and had packed my notes on a few exciting kangaroo "battles" in my rucksack. I was ready to feed Manuela when I noticed with a shock that Kathrin was coming toward me with a torrent of accusations. I had not informed her, she said, of Manuela's bad condition. The truth was that not only had I not noticed anything but also that I was also too inhibited and too self-conscious to let the others advise me on how to care for Manuela. Thus, my shock was mixed with shame.

Outside, a frosty wind was blowing. It had come from the Antarctic, so it hadn't been easy to maintain the necessary warmth in the hut. We had all worked hard to collect enough fuel to not only keep the hut warm but also have enough heat to sterilize the feeding apparatus. As far as I was concerned, everything seemed a question of the right and the need to take better care of Manuela.

Then it was feeding time again. My heart beat rapidly, and with great trepidation I got up and warmed fresh milk. With a trembling hand I felt the small body. Manuela was alive! I laid her in her little sack in my lap and gave her something to drink. Practically swallowing the teat, Manuela drank more than she ever had before. In fact, she emptied the flask. We were both amused and relieved to watch Manuela's "drunkenness" without suspecting what would then happen. Her insatiable hunger was actually one last attempt to cling to life, and shortly afterward life left Manuela once and for all. Feeling the truth of this, I froze inwardly. The faces with their questions and concern were all focused on me. Manuela was dead.

We disbanded in silence. Kathrin cried. Then we found an empty carton and wrapped the small corpse in soft flannel, surrounded it with wadding, wrapped the whole in white cloth, and buried the carton in the bush in the early morning. The death of this small being followed us wherever we went. In some strange way this tiny creature had brought light into our thoughts and feelings.

Manuela survived for a full three days and nine hours after the road accident and, according to the CSIRO, was about three months old at the time of her death.

14

Of Mothers and Children

AT ABOUT six months a pouch baby shows itself for the first time. Initially, only the back feet or the tip of the tail makes an appearance, but then a pink-colored head with large, bright eyes appears and is followed by the baby's arms. It is during this phase that the first fine, dark hair begins to form on the pink skin. After this, it is a good month before the animal leaves the pouch for the first time.

One morning on my rounds, I came across Mathilde, a kangaroo mother with her as-yet very lightly haired baby. It stood in front of her on wobbly legs, and it was evident that it had left the pouch too early. The mother tried everything to entice the baby back into her pouch and finally succeeded only after much effort. When the baby escaped a second time, she followed it immediately, approached it from the front, and made nasal contact with it. At this, the little one put up no further resistance and sprang right back into the pouch.

Because of my observations of such techniques employed by kangaroo mothers, it was clear to me that offspring at this stage are not able to properly recognize their moms. It is possible that the little ones interpret the brisk movements directed toward them as hostile gestures and see the mother at this moment as an "enemy" and thus fear them.

Usually, they recognize their mothers entirely by their breath, a sense of recognition that is established as the mother cleans the pouch. In other words, Mathilde had consciously given up trying to catch her young by other means and had resorted to contact with her nose.

Kathy, another kangaroo mother, initiated her seven-month-old baby's first important attempts to leave the pouch by her intensive body care, that is, by scratching her chest, belly, and flanks. The young fellow inside, who had so far only occasionally peeped out of the pouch, now began leaning out a bit more. My intuition told me that the final exit wasn't too far ahead. I proved right! Kathy continued scratching herself everywhere, including the area near the opening of the pouch. The young male inside began fidgeting until he managed to lean his arms and head against Kathy's chest. His hind legs and tail now appeared, and with great effort he started easing himself out of the pouch; it was only the ring muscles on the pouch that held him back. And then, suddenly he was free of them. Once outside, he took a few, wobbly steps—and returned hastily to the pouch.

September is the season for exits such as these, which usually take place in the early hours of the morning. Rain, wet meadows, and dew-soaked grass don't seem to make any difference to these sprightly youngsters. Rarely do any of them exit from the pouch at midday. If at all, then the exit activities resume in the evening.

I myself was busy every day with my early morning observations. The general physical hygiene of the younger animals, the development of their feeding habits, and even their excursions and games were my main focus. The results showed a surprising variety in the behavior of the kangaroo mothers in association with their young. It was interesting to see, for example, how the mothers encouraged their young in numerous ways to leave the pouch. Licking the small head, the eyes, ears, mouth, or even their stretched-out back legs sometimes worked. The kangaroo mother might even spread her forepaws over the pouch opening in order to encourage an exit.

Once I observed Kathy busily licking the mouth of her pouch— when the young occupant suddenly tumbled out. Within seconds, it recovered, then combed and scratched itself with its forepaws before sticking its head briefly back inside Kathy's pouch as if to make certain that it was really outside. Then it hopped about for a moment or two and returned to the pouch, only to fall out the next instant! But again, just as though the young animal were equipped with a steel spring, it righted itself again. Kathy, clearly infected by this playful mood, grabbed her offspring and nibbled so vigorously at its fur that the small animal fell over. Like a jack-in-the-box, it was back on its feet and then stood before Kathy on its hind legs with its small head thrown well back—all without falling over. The whole sequence was strongly reminiscent of an old-time slapstick film.

As soon as the young are outside for any length of time, a new phase begins. They press their mothers to nurse them or allow them to seek refuge in the pouch again. I remember a scene that seemed impossible at the time since such behavior was unusual for kangaroos. A small kangaroo had crept out of Mathilde's pouch while she was dozing and began hopping wildly around her head. It hit at and grabbed her neck until Mathilde turned and waved her front legs in the air so that she could play tag with the youngster. Finally, she pulled the young creature toward her firmly and licked and nibbled its fur just as an ape mother would.

The young animals' favorite "toys" are their mothers' ears. They keep trying to grab them until they succeed, and then they chew on them, so kangaroo mothers' ears often have a number of nicks and notches. If the mother shakes her youngster off, it will sometimes try to either press her head with its body or forepaws or even hit her head frequently with its back legs, especially when the mother is lying down. At such times, it is not possible for the young to climb into the pouch. It often has to wait, but it nonetheless persists in trying to crawl back in by widening the mouth of the pouch by force. If the young choose to use their sharp paws, their efforts to get into the pouch are far from comfortable for the mother. The result is that the mouth of the pouch and the upper part of the interior all too often look like a tattered old shopping bag! This doesn't seem to bother the mothers a great deal, though, since they remain lying patiently for the most part and sometimes don't even open their eyes. Indeed, they are a picture of maternal patience and calm.

The young are also inventive. It is not unusual for them to hit the mother on the head, chest, and neck until she simply gets up. This is just what they wanted. As soon as she gets to her feet, the little one hops into her pouch.

Valja, Gämsli, and the Poisonous Black Snake

THERE was a twelve-hour day of observation before us. It was to begin at six in the morning and end at six in the evening. Kathrin and I were to take turns every hour. My objective was to determine exactly when the kangaroo baby was truly free of the pouch after two months of alternately getting in and out of it. This moment occurs when the mother refuses to admit the young back into the pouch. She can also facilitate this by voluntarily slackening the ring muscles so that the baby kangaroos just tip out of the pouch.

I was already on my feet at six a.m., quickly swigged a Coca-Cola, and went off to search for Valja, the kangaroo mother, whom I had selected for my observations. I had named her young male offspring Gämsli (which in Swiss German refers to a young chamois) because he always climbed the steep embankment at a terrific speed without showing any sign of exhaustion.

At the beginning of my activities, Valja was standing high up on the embankment, while Gämsli climbed up and down the slope, light as a feather as usual, and then back to his mother to poke his head into her pouch for breakfast, as was his custom. But suddenly Valja interrupted this process and hopped away. Gämsli followed her. I followed them both somewhat breathlessly since they were much faster.

Now Gämsli greeted another youngster and exchanged snout contact with him but was hastily driven away by the other mother. Much perturbed, he found refuge in Valja's pouch. Here he stayed for a good half hour, and during this time he hung his head and his four limbs out so far that they almost dragged along the ground.

From this elevated vantage point, he condescended to nibble at the juicy green grass available to him, when he was suddenly and unceremoniously tipped out of the pouch. However, he managed to land on his feet and began cleaning himself like mad, at the same time making grotesque movements. At that very moment, Kathrin appeared to relieve me.

It was now seven in the morning. As I saw from Kathrin's notes, Gämsli had vanished into the pouch for half an hour as there was a lot going on outside. As usual he grazed from this position. Finally, Valja had had enough of this heavy weight, bent forward, and licked the young animal in her pouch until he emerged.

Eight o'clock. "Shhh!" Kathrin put her forefinger to her lips. "Breakfast!" I replied quietly and looked immediately in the direction of the two kangaroos. I managed to suppress a loud laugh only with difficulty. Gämsli had lifted himself up to his full height, and, while placing his forepaws on his mother's neck, he was tenderly putting his nose against hers.

The heat now forced us to find more shady places, so I was obliged to give up my observation post. Playful Gämsli allowed himself no rest. He tried the foliage, the grasses, and small pieces of wood, hopped toward bushes and plants in order to stretch to his full height in front of them and then hit them with his forefeet like a small maniac in a fight. The rough ground tickled him, and flies danced round his head. He ran around madly, slipping around as though electrified until he fell off a piece of wood with a bump that brought him to his senses. He shook his head as though he couldn't grasp what had happened. I laughed until the tears ran down my cheeks.

After the animals had retired to their siesta, there was peace in the camp. Only Gämsli disturbed the atmosphere and insisted on tearing around as usual.

Ten a.m. Now it was my turn to relieve Kathrin at her post. I was shocked to find that all of the kangaroos had rushed off into the bush. Kathrin had run after them but could not catch up with them. Somewhat downcast, she returned to tell me that a certain

Jack Higgins had driven by with his water tank and that the appalling racket had made the kangaroos panic. In the ensuing confusion, Gämsli had followed another mother called Dusja. She had, of course, noticed and had turned on him, kicking him with her hind feet. This behavior brought Kathrin into the fray, and she, in turn, gave Dusja a slap or two.

It was all over with our intended twelve-hour period of observation! We combed the bush but failed to find even one animal belonging to the Schwallbach group. Then Kathrin came across a bent "pipe" about as thick as an arm, which, to her surprise, turned out to be a pitch-black poisonous snake with beautiful, shiny, scaly skin. She looked at it for a while, her knees knocking, and then dashed back to tell me what she'd discovered.

The weather turned ugly and heavy rain set in. I was obliged to wait for one and a half hours before it started to clear up, and then I went back to our original places. Three kangaroos appeared, among them Valja—with an empty pouch! It was clear that she was anxious since she stopped grazing several times and looked around in every direction. I watched her mouth, which told me that she was calling her young one. Later Kathrin said that her calls indeed were very loud and that they could not be missed.

While this was going on, Valja kept looking attentively toward a group of kangaroos that was approaching. She kept her eye on the bush and continued to call and wait. Several kangaroos came along, but little Gämsli was not among them. All of them were grazing, and only Valja ate very little. It was obvious that she was worried.

What happened next was to provide me with a few valuable findings and also supply a culminating point to the day. It seemed that Valja suddenly had an insight as to where her child might be. Very carefully, she began searching the pouches of the other mothers! She first sniffed at Mathilde and received a few blows for her trouble, but this only increased her anxiety, and she continued her investigations now almost feverishly. Finally, New Girl was up for inspection. On snout contact it looked almost as if Valja wanted to ask permission first to look into her pouch, and this was granted. But here, too, she had no success. Valja's distress took on new dimensions. She slapped her tail up and down intensely. She called without interruption and more urgently than before, looking all the while in every direction. I felt her desperation, too. All kinds of wild ideas raced through my head as to what could have happened. I imagined, for example, that our comical little friend Gämsli, who had become such a part of our lives, was now being processed by the intestines of some snake or other!

After an hour or so the sun came out again, and I ran over to Valja—and who did I see slumbering away in her pouch as though nothing had happened? To my utter relief and delight it was the incorrigible Gämsli sleeping peacefully. What a relief!

In Mother Earth's Pouch

IT WAS still light one hot December evening as I wandered here and there along Pebbly Beach until I came to a group of young kangaroos that included Our Baby and two young, half-grown animals. Among this group was a delicate young animal without a mother. It happened to be a quite beautiful young female with thick, light fur that was rubbed off on both sides at the back. This was a sure sign that her pouch time was not yet at an end.[30] The mother was nowhere in evidence, and I wanted to find out how long the young animal could go on without a parent. In the process of distancing themselves from their mother, the young animals undertake longer and longer excursions, while the mothers withdraw more and more.

As the young animal did not want to put up with being alone any longer, it timidly approached another mother. In this case, it chose Our Baby, who immediately raised her arms and swept the youngster out of her way. The younger animal drew itself up and listened. As the desired mother's milk was not forthcoming, it turned instead to eating grass. While grazing, it would frequently lift its head to listen intently in every direction. In short, it was the picture of a typically

---

30. The movement of the young in the pouch causes this loss of fur.

confused young animal. Finally, it hurried straight back to Our Baby, but she moved away. However, the small animal knew nothing else to do but to repeat the process. Perhaps its persistence would eventually flag.

I was convinced that the younger animal knew for certain that Our Baby was not its real mother, but its needs pushed this fact into the background. Every attempt to secure a relationship with Our Baby, however, resulted in failure, and it finally gave up. The young female rushed down the embankment and looked all around, only to run up again in frustration. And so it went—up and down, up and down. In order not to lose sight of this distressed creature, I ran with it as fast as my legs could carry me.

When would its mother turn up? Almost one and a half hours went by; the sun had not yet set. The young animal was now standing at the edge of the bush, and to judge from the movements of its head and jaws, it was complaining bitterly. I had to battle against my compassion for it. How would this neglected creature get through the first night without the surrounding warmth of the pouch?

Somewhere in the damp meadow, the animal found a small hollow, where it lay down, exhausted. It seemed that here, at last, it had found Mother Earth's pouch, but hardly thirty seconds had gone by when this resting place seemed too large. The young female tossed and turned, remained lying there for a while, got up, and then renewed its search.

This situation so much softened my heart toward the creature that I set off myself in search of its mother—and it wasn't long before I found her. It was Kathy, with her much-distended pouch. I tempted her toward me with a little bread, and she followed. Luckily, at that moment, the little one also turned up on the scene. Its back uplifted, it stood for a moment and looked at its real mother. Then it hopped straight toward her, grabbed her pouch with its forepaws, and drank mightily. Then it climbed back into the longed-for security and comfort of Kathy's pouch.

15

It's Certainly Not Deathly Quiet!

I USED to jot down my observations rapidly, using a few abbreviations and personally invented "hieroglyphics." The speed was determined by the "whims" of my observed objects. I did my best but still lost important details, and many times, while writing something down, I even lost sight of the animal I was observing. I would have dearly liked to record the way my friend Kathrin did when reproducing bird sounds, for example. However, as far as I was concerned, would the spoken words be understood so that the text could be transferred to paper? Anyway, it was worth trying. Kathrin showed me how to use the apparatus and assured me that I would soon have a lot of fun using it.

My next important observations were coming up. I excitedly put the microphone to my mouth, my finger on the "release" key. Then we were ready. I pressed the key and the thing started up. It was astonishing how quickly my speech accorded with the movements of the kangaroos: If they were slow, for example, I spoke slowly; if their actions were fast, then I spoke more quickly.

"One twelve [time]—Cuddly has changed his position from the sun to the shade . . . otherwise nothing new . . . Papochka hops toward Natasha and sniffs at her." And so on. For the moment, nothing of interest until "Two twenty-five—Cuddly hops . . . to Natasha; Papochka remains where he is. Cuddly stands. Wait now . . . he's hopping again, touches and scratches Natasha's tail. She hops away and disappears."

Looking at the meadow outside the hut, I saw the ducks coming and going untiringly, the hens flapping and quarrelling, and the currawongs flying this way and that or waddling between the grazing kangaroos.

"Two thirty—Papochka and Natasha have flat ears, and both are standing. Natasha gone—Papochka hops after her between the storage place and the stacks of wood—down—now they're standing opposite one another. Natasha hits Papochka with one of her paws... Now he's chasing her."

I nearly filled the tape with my talk. Late in the evening, Kathrin pressed her ear to the apparatus while she let the tapes run. The ball pen danced in her hand. Impatiently, I walked up and down, looked over toward her somewhat concernedly, and poked the fire. Were my words really so difficult to understand? Suddenly Kathrin laughed and I looked up inquiringly. Suppressing her laughter, she told me that there was so much adventitious sound on the tape, such as the quacking of ducks, the cackling of hens, the screeching of currawongs, and the roaring of the sea, that my voice was sometimes almost inaudible.

It was clear to me that these other noises were not the sole problem for the listener but also the monotony of my performance, which is a characteristic of those who cannot hear. I therefore decided not to make any more tapes for the moment. However, Kathrin urged me not to give up but to concentrate more on clearer articulation. Her loving encouragement inspired me, and so it was that Kathrin became a friend as well as a teacher with regard to correct pronunciation. Sometimes she came with me on my observation trips and was always there to remind me to speak quietly, calmly, and slowly. In the "fury of the battle," so to speak, I tended to fall back into the bad habit of speaking too quickly and excitedly. The more I learned to speak in a disciplined way on tape, the more comprehensive and comprehensible were my findings.

Moreover, I found another use for the recorder. I would hold the microphone directly in front of the mouths of begging kangaroos during their morning feed. Or I would pluck up enough courage to approach one of the senior males just as he was making sexual advances to a female. In this way I collected quite a number of rutting and mating sounds, and, although I could not hear them, I nevertheless sensed their vibrations on the machine. This fascinated me.

I used to practice snarling with Kathrin and in so doing would touch her neck, something I had done in the old days with Auntie on first taking up my speech lessons. Finally, I was more or less able to imitate the sound, and of this I was mighty proud.

I was now in a position to "read" the various sounds kangaroos make by watching their mouth movements. Among them were not only the various mating sounds, threatening sounds, and sounds indicating submission but also sounds made by kangaroo mothers to call their young. Our lessons in imitation of these sounds went so far that Kathrin used to listen carefully to me in order to test me and see whether I made the sound correctly. There were, of course, problems associated with snarling and purring sounds because these were for the most part not "readable" for me. However, I could feel these sounds clearly whenever I was able to place my hand on the animal's back.

Kathrin was of the opinion that I should speak more on tape about the games the young kangaroos play when they emerge from the pouch. But the truth was that I was much more in my element when we were studying the mating season and the tense feelings among the males at that time. I loved it when a situation bristled with energy and the desire to attack, whereas my partner preferred attractiveness and charm, two very different aspects that on this trip wonderfully complemented each other. The impressive, bloodless tactics carried out by the senior males at this time were for me somehow symbols of my own battle for recognition and independence. However, I should add that these represented not only my own vital endeavors to that end but also those that other people with disabilities were obliged to carry out to obtain equal social rights.

Hearing with the Body

I HAVE already said something about "hearing despite a hearing disability." Although I am not able to detect tones and sounds directly, I am nevertheless able to discern certain vibrations very clearly. It is as though I have "ears" all over my body: in my skin, hands, and feet, especially the soles of the feet. As soon as a motor begins to roar or throb, for example, I am able to sense it. The same is true for slight cracks and bangs, whose vibrations in the air I am able to perceive on my skin. Voices, on the other hand, whether produced by humans or animals, I can apprehend only tactilely, and I can't detect them via air vibrations. If I put my hand on the throat or the chest of someone who is speaking, for example, or pick up a second resonating body, like an empty carton or a plastic canister, I can sense the voices in this way.

However, in the bush, where the air is full of birdsong and the various sounds of other local fauna, it was always deathly quiet, and for this reason I grew anxious if I stayed there for too long on my own. But as soon as I found myself within the precincts of Pebbly Beach and felt the company of the kangaroos, I was again perfectly at home. They gave me security and orientation and substituted for my lack of hearing—but how?

Thanks to the ever-watchful nature of animals, it was always possible for me to "hear" with my eyes. Kangaroos can move their ears in the most delicate ways when detecting sounds and even move them independently of one another. For this reason, they can hear the environment in the round, but I, too, can receive a lot of important information. For example, when these animals stretch their necks, I immediately perceive the degree of their excitement. In this way, they help me to orient myself in the field and detect impending danger in time and thus avoid it.

16

All Kinds of
Remarkable Things

ONE morning in 1982, when it is very early and I am still half-asleep, I am outside in front of my hut at Pebbly Beach, watching the wonderful play of colors in the morning sky. All around me, it is still pitch black. Only far away in the east above the horizon at the cape at Pebbly Beach is there a hint of light. For a few moments, the world seems to be signaling the first and the last day, the ancient and the newly born at the same time. The world shows itself in an odd gray, a color that stands out among all other colors. The brightness increases—dawn advances.

Then the sky is quickly covered with the finest shreds of cloud and haze and turns first light yellow, then a grayish blue, from which a bright lilac and the first pink shimmers issue. The pink intensifies and quickly becomes red and fiery, spreading slowly, mixing with yellow, orange, pink, and lilac to give a rapidly brightening blue. The cape's deepest black silhouettes are sharply etched against this unfolding beauty, and here and there the tufts of treetops testify to the presence of a river landscape, which still lies in the dawn's shadow.

There is not a second during which this kaleidoscope of color is motionless; again and again a new mixture is created. Red can become orange; orange can become pink; and a stimulating purple can also coalesce into gray or flame into red.

The play of form is no less fascinating than the colors. Clouds of all kinds, wisps of cloud and shreds of fog all take part in this ever-changing pageant of constant growth, enlargement, shrinkage, breakage, dissolution and disappearance, disengagement and coalition—truly a wonderful coming and going, brightening and darkening, conjunction and cleavage. It is as though the heavens are being painted by an invisible Divine Painter, one who knows of the eternal passage of coming into being and passing away.

I walk down to the beach. The fresh dew soaks my gym shoes, and my feet become a trifle cold, my hands clammy. Nevertheless, my good cheer knows no bounds! It is an uplifting feeling to meet the day with such joyful devotion.

The manifold interaction of color is also playing in the waters of the lagoon, the puddles, and the ebbing waves on the beach, where it glitters briefly before being engulfed by the sand. Soon these colors will encroach upon the bush itself, and shortly it is so light that the play of color pales to nonentity. Only an illuminating yellow and a few, orange-colored layers of cloud remain. But a small spot near the cape grows steadily brighter. A spot of light breaks over the horizon and becomes larger and larger. The sun is back and casts its light far and wide until the bush comes to life within seconds to reveal its twigs and branches, leaves and trunks in a gentle pink.

High above, on Jack's Hill, a large, old eucalyptus tree stretches its branches against the western sky, and at this moment it is bathed in pastel pink. But this is only a forerunner. A few minutes later, it is enveloped by the sun's first rays and blazes into red as though ignited. It is a moment of shocking beauty, and I am moved.

It is not long before the sun has mounted the horizon, and the green of the meadows, the foliage of the trees, the blue of the sky, where a few white clouds play for a while, the rusty red of the eucalyptus stems, the bright beige of the sand, not to mention the undulating gray-blue of the sea all announce the coming of a new day.

In the trees all around me are merry, laughing birds busily puffing out their plumage as though it were so much woolly stuffing. Kangaroos emerge from the bush into the morning light. The air is growing warm. The meadows are alive with the red, blue, and green-yellow garlands of parrots that fly here and there in constant movement as though cheerfully greeting the morn. Now it is here to stay: The day begins!

Stones That Inspire

ON THIS particular visit to Australia, my traveling companion was a younger woman named Bettina rather than my mother. Not only did Bettina have a scientific background and a deep interest in nature and in kangaroos, but she had also mastered the Lormen (or Lorm) manual alphabet.[31] The latter was especially important as I had been losing more and more of my sight since contracting a case of the measles at the age of fifty-four.

About twenty meters behind our hut at Pebbly Beach was a narrow, steep path that led somewhat precariously down to the sea. On several occasions I took my life in my hands by traversing it, but not far away was a place that, for me, harbored secrets. It was said that there was once a stone toilet here, used long ago by Aboriginals and then abandoned. Truth be told, I felt a certain disinclination to delve further into the subject on my own.

---

31. The Lormen technique originated in the Czech Republic and is relatively widespread in Europe. On the other hand, it is generally unknown in English-speaking countries since communication there is based on gesticulative language used by those who are deaf and blind and those who can see.

In communicating by Lormen, beginners often use a Lorm glove, on which one can see the alphabet. The fingers and the palms of these are stitched with lines, circles, points, and letters. The receiver of a message pulls on the glove and allows the sender, who is unfamiliar with Lorm communication (e.g., a salesperson, doctor, nurse, or police officer), to write. This means that the sender strokes or taps a message into the open hand. The receiver feels or sees this act of "speaking" and can read what is being said from the hand. If both partners are familiar with the Lormen technique, communication is very rapid and can take place without a glove.

This sign language is named after Hieronymus Lorm (1821–1902), who, as the child of a rich Jewish merchant family, came into contact with many intellectuals and creative artists of his day. When, at the age of sixteen, he suddenly became deaf and in later years blind as well, he, together with his family and friends, managed to develop this Lormen method for better understanding between them. Added to this, Hieronymus Lorm was also a great poet, a philosopher, and a literary critic. In 1873 the University of Tübingen awarded him an honorary doctorate for his work.

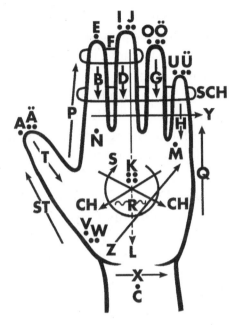

Lorm Deafblind Manual Alphabet. This is the method that friends and helpers use to speak with me since I am no longer able to lipread.

Nevertheless, a spot not far from there glued my attention to the ground for hours on end: pebbles—millions of pebbles, smoothed and rounded by waves that had given the place its name. If one lay down during the day on the sun-warmed pebbles, the experience would be a most pleasant one since one would feel not only the warmth but also the smoothness and soft roundness of these stones.

Just like children, we found it difficult to pause in our search for the most beautiful and the most perfect examples. Pebble after pebble was lifted from the ground and assessed, and often the very next stone was even more beautiful than the last one. At times we dug up to our elbows in this hard but smooth mine of pebbles. We often came across brownish stones that had a pattern of lines and, less commonly, stones with white or blue nicks in them; in these, very delicate opals were to be found. I asked myself again and again how far below the ground these beds of pebbles extended.

This wonder-world of stones awakened deep feelings within me, and at times I felt that nature itself was speaking to me through them. If I lost myself in the search for them, it was as though I had touched a distant chord from long, long ago, a time when the souls of human beings and the souls of animals could still communicate with each another, as is told in the stories handed down by the Aboriginals.[32] Thus it is that these silent witnesses to long-forgotten times always convey a certain magic to me when I tread on them.

Where Do the Certainty and Strength Suddenly Come From?

ONE afternoon Bettina said she would like to go fishing at the end of the cape. I had a few hours free while the kangaroos enjoyed their siesta and took my camera with me down to the beach. From there, I went on over the flat, stony banks, carefully balancing myself, and at the same time taking care not to get my sneakers wet. "That was pretty good going, what you did there!" Bettina called to me as she saw me coming. At first I didn't quite understand what she meant by this remark, probably because I blocked it inwardly. I had a fear of accusations, but when she repeated the compliment, I was greatly cheered since I knew that she was voicing her respect for my courage in overcoming my innate difficulty in balancing.

From that day on, I often set off on my own to meet Bettina or the others. This was not without its dangers, as I was frequently obliged to scramble over two rocks around the cape that were at least three meters high.

After many weeks of dryness, the weather suddenly turned oppressively humid. And then the rain just fell out of the sky! I often looked out of the window at the kangaroos on the beach, and the moment the rain let up, I was off to see how the land lay. There they all were indeed, standing at the edge of the sea!

32. However, this time is not regarded by the original inhabitants as "past" as we understand the word but as something peculiar to the present.

Overjoyed to see them, I ran back to the hut and called Bettina to come with me, grabbed my camera, and stumbled in haste along the steep path to the sandy beach. Bettina had in the meantime caught up with me, and once we were down at the shore, she said that I should hurry over to the other end of the bank, where there were other kangaroos near the rocks.

I ran as fast as I could over the damp sand and arrived in time to see one or two of the animals from the Jack Group plunging into the sea. As quickly as I could, I took a picture of this.

One evening I told Bettina that, because of my balance problems, which were the result of Usher's syndrome, as I mentioned earlier, I still didn't trust myself outside when it was quite dark. On hearing this, she encouraged me to try. I did so, and thanks to her pep talk, felt very good and full of self-confidence. With easy self-assurance, I walked through the darkness, flashing the beam of my little flashlight in every direction. From time to time, its shaft of light encompassed grazing kangaroos, and I enjoyed this entirely new experience of watching them.

It wasn't long before I reached the now deserted beach meadow, and I turned the flashlight off and looked at the sky. Neither stars nor moon were visible because of the low clouds. There was nothing around me but pitch-black night, and I suddenly began to feel a bit creepy. I decided to use the flashlight to find my way back to the hut and report with pride on my excursion to Bettina. I then asked her to disregard whatever future reservations I might have with regard to my independence. Where possible, she was simply to ignore them. She not only agreed but also urged me to look my fears squarely in the face whenever I could. I never enjoyed so much personal confidence as with Bettina, and there were times when she seemed like a good fairy.

Do Kangaroos Swim?

"CAN kangaroos swim?" I once asked my father when I was a child. He laughed and replied, "Oh yes, I know they can swim well, but only of course when their pouches are properly zipped up!" I didn't like his joke much, but the question of what happened to a young kangaroo when his mother had to flee through water troubled me for a long time.

One afternoon I was standing on the beach meadow just as a group of kangaroos disappeared in the direction of the lagoon for no apparent reason. I was a bit annoyed at this but not for long. A few hours later I met Kathrin, who told me that she had been able to watch three kangaroos from Jack's Hill swim across the lagoon, which was a good three meters wide. One of them, she added, was a mother with child, and she was convinced that the young one had survived. However, I was somewhat skeptical.

I had read a number of articles on whether, in the case of severe flooding, kangaroos can swim in order to save themselves. There were also TV shows on the subject. In addition, I had received an interesting tip from my pen friend, Geoff, who had once taken us touring through the bush and shown us the magnificently wild waterways of the Macquarie Lakes in eastern New South Wales. He told us that kangaroos often used to swim over to the islands, which were rich in vegetation. On another occasion, I was assured by a ranger on the island of Rotamah that he had personally seen a kangaroo swim from the island to the mainland several times, a stretch of a good kilometer.

However, I finally came across much more precise information. Kathrin and I were invited to a scientific film presentation on kangaroos' spectacular swimming movements. Especially fascinating was the behavior of two red giants that had never been introduced to water and were brought to a swimming pool in which it was possible only to swim. They were hardly in the pool when they began to hop! However, after only a few seconds they modified their behavior. They began swimming. To do so, they used their forepaws and hind legs alternately, much as dogs and horses do, to propel themselves forward, and their tails were used horizontally (waved sideways) as a fish or a lizard would do.

EVERY morning and afternoon I walked along the short, sandy section of Pebbly Beach on the lookout for fresh evidence of kangaroo tracks that led straight into the sea. I wanted to collect data in order to find out exactly how often and in what weather conditions kangaroos go into the water. I had often noticed, for example, that they did not hesitate to take an ice-cold bath in the early morning. On the other hand, I had never observed an animal wading far out to sea. Put humorously, one could say that "Mr. and Mrs. Kangaroo were not too disposed to put their feet into water that would reach higher than their ankles or the tips of their tails."

Late one afternoon I was to witness an amusing scene. Two animals from the Schwallbach Mob, then grazing in the beach meadow, hopped down the embankment directly toward the sea, where they dipped their hind legs and tails into the water. After a while they were joined by six other animals, who went in even deeper, so that the waves reached their abdomens. Valja, the most courageous of kangaroo mothers, was among them, and the waves wet her pouch and the baby peering out of it! Almost all of them stood parallel to the bank or a little at an angle, and they all looked toward the swell, waiting for the next wave. When this was rolling toward them, they took a quick leap backward onto land and then waited for the next wave. They seemed to find this game as delightful as we humans do.

ONE morning while in the middle of the kangaroos, I noted a rare bird that had a green-blue, mosaic plumage. At first I thought it was a kind of parrot, but Mrs. Schwallbach told me that this strange visitor was nothing other than a young, male satin bowerbird. At the moment, he was molting, a long process that consisted of several rather bizarre stages. During these, the colors of his plumage changed. The fact that the older feathers are either plucked or scratched out by these birds was something I had never observed before. Did the satin bowerbird do this all in secrecy? Whatever the case may be, after the brown feathers, green feathers follow, and then azure-blue ones, and then, at the end of this metamorphosis, come those dark, silky blue feathers.

Mrs. Schwallbach's Death

IN MARCH 1988 I happened to be staying again at Pebbly Beach with Bettina and her family, but on this occasion the visit was to be marked by sadness. A few months before my arrival, I had been notified of Mrs. Schwallbach's passing on December 1, 1987. She had been the founder of this little settlement that I loved so much. The happiness of revisiting the place was therefore tinged with sorrow. It was difficult to imagine the place without her, for she had brought life into the settlement, and her absence depressed me.

A couple named Stuart and Yvonne had taken over Mrs. Schwallbach's home and operations. Although it might sound a trifle disrespectful, it was Mrs. Schwallbach's welcoming coffee that I very much missed—despite Stuart's and Yvonne's cordial greetings. These two had long since been managing the business and organizational side of the settlement and counted among my friends. As for Mrs. Schwallbach's house, this stood locked and empty. On the now deserted terrace was the decaying body of a Rosella parrot, and on glancing through the window I once more caught a glimpse of the furnishings I knew so well and felt a pang of unhappiness. But one detail comforted me: the flamingo flowers that were growing everywhere in the garden and were among the first species I saw here. She had planted them. It was as though her soul were living on in their splendid beauty. The thought comforted me. Later the place was to become a kind of memorial for guests and visitors, and I tried to immortalize it in one of my aquarelles.

Mrs. Schwallbach had suffered from lung cancer. In the last three months of her illness, her life had become an agony. When the condition was diagnosed as incurable, she had been brought back from the hospital to Pebbly Beach. In the years prior to her illness, her physical independence had been much restricted, and this was one of the reasons that our correspondence had finally come to a halt. Then, one day and just as the public health care assistant had left the room, Mrs. Schwallbach departed from this world.

No one went into her deserted house for ten years, probably because all those who had known and loved Mrs. Schwallbach felt that her spirit was still in the place. Even Stuart's dog was disinclined to go inside the house for some reason. Stuart firmly requested that I not set foot in it, either.

IN 2007 Ursi, my new travel companion since 2005, and I visited Mrs. Schwallbach's grave. We were surprised at its size and not less by the fact that it had been wholly covered by stones from Pebbly Beach. The entry to the grave itself had, as is usually the case, been hermetically sealed, but the area around it and the paths separating it from the other graves were covered with wild flowers and herbs and incidentally offered passing kangaroos nourishment, as we could see from their tracks everywhere. Sure in the knowledge that Mrs. Schwallbach would have been glad to know that her favorite animals visited this place, I left the spot feeling happy.

17

Dreams

WITHOUT exaggeration, I can say that dreaming itself and my own particular dreams (which also include my daydreams) carry considerable significance. On the one hand, they are a form of reflection on what has happened during the day. For me, these occur not only in numerous variations but also in the most remarkable figures and with the oddest embellishments. Every dream presents reality in another light. In this way I learn to comprehend my life ever anew. On the other hand, many of my dreams offer what I occasionally miss in real life. Among these are wonderful encounters with people and animals, an exhilarating freedom of movement, many different roles that allow me to have enchanting, surprising adventures and to always enjoy crystal clear, unimpeded vision. Added to this, I try to note whether those dreams that often repeat themselves change from time to time. It is just at the moment they change that certain personal developments can take place, which can be very interesting. Those dreams, which herald forthcoming events or supply one with knowledge in advance, make dreaming so important for me.

I try to preserve what has been dreamed as freshly and vividly in my mind as possible, so that I can keep the way open for new inspirations. For this reason, I've never been really interested in the classical interpretation of dreams. I feel that such explanations are rather narrow and seem to be intent on destroying the dream world. It is this that I particularly want to prevent. Is it not possible, for example that the symbols occurring in dreams change in the same way as the words we use?

Anyway, my own dream ego has changed over time. So it is that in becoming older I have apparently been obliged to pay tribute to my dreams. I don't hop through my dream landscape as I once did, for example, and should I do so, then I soon get out of breath and have to puff and pant, especially when I find myself in flight or having to climb mountains. One thing is sure: My dream-eye has remained as clear as ever it was. Perhaps our dream-body is just as vulnerable and transient as the physical body, and perhaps it is only our soul, which "observes"—even beyond the grave.

One phenomenon that has accompanied me throughout life still troubles me: When I dream, I never have the feeling that I'm in a dream, so that when I wake up, I always have the inevitable conviction that I've been deceived, and from this follows deep disappointment. Just like a wild kangaroo!

Very often between my twentieth and fortieth birthdays I dreamed that, like a kangaroo with feet together, body bent forward, and arms hanging down, I would bound over fences and brooks, springing high over the fields and even over the heads of my astonished friends! Those were wonderful dreams indeed, dreams in which the thrill of speed and the feeling of infinite freedom were united. Although I possessed the faculties of a kangaroo in those dreams, I wasn't a proper kangaroo but a kind of humanized one. These dreams, despite their impressive "reality," never gave me the feeling that I could actually perform such feats in broad daylight. Even with the most intensive training, it is in any case quite impossible for a human being to imitate this coordinated hopping movement.

Sometimes I ask myself whether I am the only person in this world who dreams about kangaroos so much. It's quite likely. Now and again I have asked people who have a lot to do with kangaroos, either privately or professionally. None of those I asked dreamed so frequently and so intensively about these animals as I do. The only exception to this is perhaps my colleague, Vreni; the longer she worked on her dissertation on kangaroo behavior, the more she dreamed about these animals.

If I chance to meet kangaroos in my dreams, I talk to them quite naturally and informally. And I encounter them everywhere when I dream about them, whether I am walking through the country or in town. Moreover, if in my dream I chance to come across them face to face, it's always a surprise. How do I react on such occasions?

I touch them very gently, one after the other, and thoroughly inspect their heads. None of the animals is put off by this; on the contrary, they come closer to me and nuzzle up to me with their soft noses and begin to nod as if to greet me or begin to shiver slightly. Sometimes an animal will lift a forepaw to scratch me gently. All these manifestations arouse a feeling of deep attachment in me. Then one of them will look me in the eye and distinctly move his lips to speak to me. "Who are you?" What do you want from us?" Soon the others try to take part in the conversation. It is truly marvelous how clearly I can read what they say from their snouts! I answer them faithfully in my own way, and very soon we are all enjoying the pleasantest of chats.

Then one of them will press his claws into my arm, but I feel no pain. At the same moment and directly in front of me, these animals are transformed into human beings, so now I have a whole row of unknown human faces right before me. However, I can identify one face. It is the kangaroo that had pressed my arm and spoken to me shortly before. It is the face of a very stubborn individual from a home for elderly Jewish people, a woman who appears to enjoy disrupting my creative professional activity. As soon as I recognize her, I feel so miserable that I leave the group of kangaroo-people there and then. No creation without them . . .

When I was not yet thirty, that is to say, before the coming of crewed spaceflight, I dreamed the following:

I am completely alone on the planet Mars. Far and wide, there is nothing but a carmine-red desert, a desolate wilderness of stones and craters. My utter loneliness is hard to bear. I feel oppressed and sad. How long can I survive here without the company of another living creature, and how long without nourishment? Then I have a liberating brainwave. I will simply fill this dead planet with life! I spread my arms and declare Mars to be my appropriated territory. I immediately fall into a trance and begin to meditate. "I hereby bestow fertility upon the planet!" I go on to moderate the sun's unmercifully strong rays beating down and burning on this heavenly body and create an atmosphere in which there is not only water vapor but also clouds and rain—and cold. I create all this in silence and quite alone through the power of my thoughts. Good, clean, dark soil comes into being within a day and brings forth all that is green from this stony waste. Many lakes, both great and small, are also formed.

The next day is reserved for the creation of animals. From sand, mud, and stone I first create the kangaroo, which I find to be an easy task. Then, from the same material, I create mammals, birds, fish, and reptiles. Proud and happy beyond words, I survey my creation and look forward to my first day of rest. When that day comes and I am about to lie down for a delightful rest amid my kangaroos, I become aware on all sides of an immense, intolerable roaring. Overcome with apprehension, I discern a human form coming toward me in the distance and soon recognize who it is. A feeling of shame grips my being. It is God in the form of an ageless old man with a long, white beard and dressed in a dark gown. He eyes me indignantly and takes me to task for my arrogance and presumptuousness. He punishes me by turning all my animals—including the kangaroos—into ugly, black, piglike monstrosities! In pain and helplessness I watch all this happening before my eyes and finally find myself lying among all these tarry, formless abortions. How happy I am to wake up on our Mother Earth!

The Creation and its subsequent array of created things seem to count among my favorite dream motifs, and both are related to my artistic activity. This, of course, doesn't always have to accord with the dimensions of our solar system. No indeed. In my dreams I can use my gift of "bringing into being" on a much smaller scale. For example, I have dreamed of being at home, where there are several large sacks full of clay:

I open the nearest one and use the contents to make model kangaroo figures that reach to about knee height. I work very quickly, so the living room and bedroom are soon full of such figures, and in so doing I find myself barely able to weave my way through them. Then, all of a sudden and in the strangest of ways, the figures, instead of hardening and drying, begin to transform themselves. A fine down begins to form on their clay surfaces and gradually covers every inch of their bodies. This soft hair becomes firmer and denser and begins more and more to resemble a coat of fur or a hide. Although a little earlier, the eyes had been little more than suggestions, the clay then opens to reveal liquid, dark, polished eyes! And that's not all. The mass of clay solidifies, rendering the figures soft and smooth. On the undersides of the feet and paws and elsewhere on these figures I notice blood vessels, and soon blood is circulating in them.

As I watch, a delicate stirring quickens the once stiff, resistant clay figures, and the sculptures begin to move. Their movements remind me of live animals. These magical beings dance around me and are only too willing to be stroked and petted. Like a magician, I stand in their midst, surrounded by the creatures I've brought into being. I am filled with an incommunicable joy. Oh, but then I have to rush off to buy food for my darlings. When I wake up, I find myself in my three-bedroom suite. Alone. I need a while to come to myself—and fall back into sadness.

I don't always need to play an active role in my dreams:

I am at the zoo in Jerusalem and come across a templelike place; I go through a well-lit corridor and discover a huge fenced-off compound and wonder what kind of animals live there—when I catch sight of a large group of kangaroos and lions. It seems rather odd to me, even incredible, that the two are kept apart only by a light yellow, velvet curtain. How can that be? A number of rabbis approach me with measured steps. Their faces are earnest, their attitudes pious, and while solemnly sizing me up, they gesture that I should answer my own question as to how kangaroos get along with lions. Sternly, they order me to pull the curtain. Trembling and almost paralyzed by fear, I do as I'm told. Imagine my relief and surprise when I see that the kangaroos are not at all disconcerted by the sight of the lions and that the lions show no signs of aggression. I am beholding a scene of peaceful coexistence between herbivores and carnivores. A miracle indeed!

The rabbis praise my courage with affectionate gestures. Now I am allowed to go into the compound.

Magic and All Things Mysterious

WHILE I was training as a weaver, in my free time I used to visit the Basel Zoo, where I met Dora, the female kangaroo. She was often in my thoughts during lessons. The reason for this was probably the fact that my fellow pupils didn't always allow me to take part in their talks. However, to be ignored because of my deafness was something I hated. I often flew into a rage because of this, and then I must have looked like a witch. In other words, I was biased and for the most part did not realize that the others were in fact really quite nice and kind to me. I was the pushy one. These encounters, I believe, precipitated the following dream.

A frightening darkness hangs over the cave entrance just a few meters away. Only a little light weakly filtering through the gaps between the dripping rocks illuminates the surroundings. I am curious but also a little fearful as I penetrate the cave's interior, walking along until I reach a gallery as large as a railway station concourse. Here and there, red, blue, violet, and orange-colored flames leap up and transform the room into a pulsing cloud of color. A secret rite begins to take place in the large, wide niches along the rock wall. Witchlike figures with sinister faces appear and come toward me. Fear grips me, and I can feel myself shuddering. These appallingly strange specters now surround me. Since there is no escape, I stand there rigidly, as if transformed to stone. After what seems an infinite period of terror, I feel a light touch on my arm from behind. I turn in horror only to discover, to my unutterable relief and joy, my great friend, Dora. Here is my dearest, my faithful kangaroo friend! At once the fiends around me withdraw to their holes in the wall. Dora is holding a large basket full of shuttles, reels, colored yarn, and even a weaving comb. Nodding slightly, she greets me most warmly. Overjoyed, I return her greeting: "Dearest Dora, it's so nice of you to bring all that I wished to enable me to start weaving tomorrow." My fears dissipated.

Happily, I take the basket from her, and Dora vanishes. I'm alone again but fortunately not for long. From the niches and folds in the wall the demons reappear, but this time they are laughing gaily, and I notice that they are my school friends, who now decide to dance. I, too, feel like dancing. I place the basket carefully in a corner and take part in the merriment. All of us lift our feet together in happy abandon!

In this dream my school situation was reversed: All the other students were witches, not me. Then, after Dora's appearance, they were all loving and friendly again. Moreover, when I felt like an outcast, I always turned to Dora, who seemed to have a soft spot for me.

Walpurgis Night on Ice

MANY of my dreams are characterized by the child's belief that after death the soul wafts from heavenly heights to a rock cave that is inhabited by the souls of kangaroos. The cave is by a lake, and there I meet all my dead loved ones again and, of course, my friend Dora, too. This is a scene that has never lost any of its vibrancy:

I find myself in a small wooden hut. While there, I put on my skates and go outside to the frozen lake nearby. Its surface seems to be firm and for the most part like a sheet of glass. At certain points, though, it is clearly very thin and brittle, so there is real danger of falling in and drowning. Nonetheless, I whirl and skate over the shining surface without fear. The ice even puts up with a few wild jumps!

As I glance over to the bank a little later, however, I see things that make me freeze with horror. The entire environment looks exactly like the kind of wild and gloomy landscape that I associate with Walpurgis Night. The sun has crept behind heavy, black clouds, and on the side of the lake directly opposite me, a huge mass of craggy, light-gray rock has risen into the sky. It seems to be made of broad, irregular courses of chalk or perhaps of fine, shining crystals running from top to bottom. Below, at the foot of this towering peak, is the entrance to a cave that is as large as the entryway to a cathedral. In the darkness beyond, very small strips of light are visible, and in the distance between the lake bank and the rock is an open space in which one can see a wooden hand loom. An ugly old witch sits at it, weaving uninterruptedly. I feel the violent, abrupt movements of her hands at the loom as if they were actual blows to my body. Every time I skid past her, this old woman grins at me with repulsive encouragement. But I ignore her and swirl on until I'm seized by fear and come to a halt.[33] There are threatening vibrations under my skates. It seems as if the whole earth has begun to tremble. A blue apparition, wrapped in a white halo, begins emerging from a hole in the ice. Is this perhaps the soul of someone who once drowned here? It floats over to the shore and from there drifts directly into the cave, where it is almost swallowed up by the darkness within. What remains is a fine line of light that, like a will o'wisp, twitches and twists. While I watch, beneath my feet there is a mighty earthquake that shakes the massive rock and all the landscape around. I am so affected by this ghostly vision that I quiver from head to foot.

Nickel Men, or They Danced for Me like Kangaroos

DREAMS always magically convey me into the earth's interior, into caves and underground dungeons. There, all kinds of eerie things have happened to me, but among them also uncanny and yet wonderful, delightful things:

I am standing on the balcony of our mountain chalet. The sun shines down superbly. Taking in the view, I look down at the river valley below and then halfway up the Eiger, where the green alpine meadows come to an end. Above them, broad, steep mountain rock, which is partially covered with snow, towers against the sky. At this moment I devoutly wish to be able to climb this great peak without difficulty. But how?

Then, to my great surprise, I notice a narrow wooden bridge stretching directly from my balcony to the mountain. It is supported by bizarrely wrought wooden scaffolding and seems a very risky affair. Daringly, I make my way over this bridge and reach a point halfway up the Eiger. There the bridge ends at a bleak tunnel entrance. Fearlessly, I enter what

---

33. In reality, I was at best a mediocre skater, but ice skating proved to be good training in countering my balancing problems.

appears to be a very deep cave. However, a moment later, I feel scared. Around a curve, I can see a tiny light in the distance. Relieved, I breathe normally again and walk briskly in this direction.

On approaching, I come across a sparsely lit hall of huge dimensions. What I now see is at once dreadful but at the same time has something remarkably fascinating and beautiful about it. Innumerable naked, muscular men inhabit this stone cathedral. Their bodies are of dully shining nickel that are flecked with silver-white. Their bodies are by no means stiff like nickel but, on the contrary, smooth and supple. These "nickel men" now form up into long rows in front of me. Their faces, which possess the most expressive features, are all turned in my direction. Then, as if by order, they all begin stamping powerfully and rhythmically. After a short time, they change their forceful movements to a graceful, perfectly timed dance. It is quite clear that they wish to greet me with their charming reception since they are all facing me. My earlier fears have flown, but I nevertheless keep a respectful distance from them.

For what then happens I have only one word, and that is "magic." I feel a strong, magnetic energy passing through me as these nickel men begin to read my innermost being. My life, my soul—indeed everything—is revealed to them, exposed like the leaves of an open book. Without objection, I allow them to do so. Even stranger than my lack of resistance is the fact that I can discern where each of these nickel men is as he observes the details of my interior. I am even in a position to help them by leading them in the right direction. And then, as though these nickel men wanted to do me a particular favor, they all begin jumping about like kangaroos!

Transfixed, I remain for some time longer in the semidarkness, having found a niche for myself, and continue to observe this remarkable display. The spectacle as a whole is in twilight, barely lit by many small flames that seem to spring from cracks in the cave wall. I am deeply happy. If the truth were known, I would never want to leave this place.

I recall a buckle made of dull nickel that once decorated a belt of mine, something I greatly prized. In addition, I also possessed small kangaroo figures of this material. As a child, I liked this metal. Moreover, there were many aboriginal dances that delighted me, and certain features of these closely resembled the hopping of kangaroos.

This dream has remained with me to this day in all its detail because of the exhilarating pleasure it provided. Apart from the mysterious inhabitants of this underground church, the dream also shows how long the smallest of past details remain unconsciously stored in the memory. They have long since vanished from the conscious memory of daily life, seemingly forever, but they remain in places that one could aptly call an "underground," similar to that of the cave in the dream—until, of course, they come streaming back at night in order to take their places in quite another visual presentation.

18

Kangaroos Overcome the Iron Curtain

ONE morning in August 1967, while my mother and I were vacationing in Zermatt, I received a letter from a mysterious sender, someone I did not know who lived in Dresden in East Germany (the German Democratic Republic, or GDR).

Frau Christel Göcking
Dresden Zoological Gardens
Dresden, 9th Aug. 1967

Dear Mrs. Herrmann,

Please excuse this unsolicited letter to you, but I was particularly interested in the article you wrote recently in the journal called the Zoological Garden. Your report on the pouch cleaning in the case of the large, gray kangaroo interested me especially, as I am concerned with looking after kangaroos here at the Dresden Zoo. I was therefore especially interested in your remarks on animal behavior. Although we don't possess any "gray giants" here, we nevertheless have red giants, Derby and mountain kangaroos. The animal behavior that you describe is very similar to that of the so-called red giants. I don't know, of course, whether you are interested in an exchange of information on this.

I would very much like to hear from you. May I ask what your profession is? Do you carry on continuous experiments? Are you a specialist in the "gray giant"?

May I look forward to hearing from you soon?

Yours sincerely,
Christel Göcking

I could not help but smile on reading this. I was charmed by the thought that behind this impenetrable wall to the east there were also kangaroos! Unexpected coincidence had brought me into contact with a person of similar interests. My mother had noticed the enthusiasm in my face and asked me what was in the letter. After she had read the letter for herself, she said with pride and a touch of irony that now I was a worldwide authority on kangaroos! I was no sooner back home than I sat down, elated, at the typewriter.

Riehen, 2nd September 1967

Dear Miss Göcking,
Many thanks for your letter of the 9th August. I am of course always delighted to find that others are interested in my work on kangaroos. I have been concerned for many years now with the "gray giants"; it is the only kind of kangaroo we have here in the Basel Zoo. As I have a lot of free time, I can visit the kangaroos there several times a week and invest a lot of time observing them. I often photograph them as well. Added to this, I am on very good terms with Professor Lang, the present zoo director, and spend time with him exchanging information on those issues and questions arising from my research.

. . . I would be enormously pleased to hear the voices of kangaroos, as I know that they aren't really the dumb animals they're made out to be. Although I myself can't hear, I know immediately when they produce certain sounds. This I can recognize not least from the movements they make with their mouths. . . . Less frequent are the d-d-d-sounds, which I can apprehend directly from observing their mouths, a process that I'm pretty well schooled in, as you may well imagine.

For some years now, I have kept up correspondence in English with friends in Australia, all of whom have a more or less direct relationship with kangaroos. . . .

Before I close, I would like to acquaint you with a few of my notable "kangaroo characters." There is, for example, my most faithful companion, Dora. . . . Of course, I'd be delighted to hear from you, especially when you wish to say a word or two about your "own" kangaroos. Let's keep in touch.

With many hearty greetings,

Yours,
Doris Herrmann

In this letter I introduced myself briefly and also mentioned that I had been born deaf and outlined my special relationship to kangaroos.

Dresden, 10th Sept., 1967

Dear Miss Hermann,

It's certain that I'll be able to learn a lot from you; that will be very useful in my work as an animal keeper at the zoo. The individual phases of pouch cleaning, for example, that you describe have been confirmed by my own observations of the horde of "red giants" we have here. . . . In the case of our tamest animal, Mecke, I was able to control the growth of the young animal anytime I liked. I was also able on several occasions to obtain mother's milk from her for laboratory analysis. She had an udder that was about as big as a fist and four teats, of which only one was functional and developed to about eight centimeters in length. Up to the end of the fourth month of her baby's development, the kangaroo mother did not allow other members of the group to inspect her pouch with any intensity, and she kept her distance.

In August last year, I took over the responsibility for the Antelope House, and also since this time I've concerned myself pretty intensively with kangaroos. [Here Christel provided a lively account of all the successful and unsuccessful attempts she had made to breed kangaroos.]

Unfortunately, there is precious little information about kangaroos. That to be found at the zoological library in Dresden is scanty. Despite the fact that it has a large library, I don't find much about kangaroos, and then most of it is in English, a language, alas, I don't know well enough.

In short, something about myself: I learned about poultry breeding in my home village not far from the GDR border. I engaged in this for about five years. After this, I went to Erfurt and took up a job there at the zoo looking after apes and monkeys. After two years there, I went to Dresden, where I've been for the last two years.

In my next letter, I asked a number of questions, among them whether "her" kangaroo has to be held down during an examination of its pouch and also whether it answers to its name. The reply followed quickly:

> Unfortunately, I have to tell you that our Mecke died suddenly. I was very sad about this. The cause of death was probably the inability to digest the autumn chestnuts fed to her recently. . . . I took her baby back home with me. However, despite the fact that the baby was kept warm all the time in a moist, artificial pouch, had body contact and a milk substitute, it survived for only three days. . . . In reply to your question: No, Mecke did not have to be held down. I always gave her a rusk and then looked into her pouch. When she was ready, she laid her forepaws on my back and waited until I had made my examination. She always came hopping toward me when I called her name, and the first thing she would do was to search my pants pockets for something to eat.

I wrote back and expressed my great sympathy:

> I'm so sorry that your beloved Mecke has gone from you. However, I'm sure that you'll be glad about the fact that you enjoy just as much confidence from the other kangaroos, which is shown when these allow you to examine their pouches without putting up a fuss!

At the beginning of our correspondence, the topics we touched upon were largely concerned with the red and gray "giants" (kangaroos) and their different forms of behavior at the zoo and in the wild. As to my question about the help she had given to the sick kangaroo mother, Christel replied:

> I carried out pouch cleaning as follows: In Mecke's case I pulled the tail through the back legs to the front and laid her almost on her back,

opened the pouch with one hand, and cleaned the interior of the pouch with the other. To do this I used a small sponge that I often wrung out in lukewarm water. During this, the baby was firmly attached to the teat, and so of course I had to go about the business very carefully: It was always necessary to remove the bits of muck that had attached themselves to its body and especially to its little head. Apart from this, I required the services of another keeper whom I could trust and who would assist me by holding Mecke's legs, which were inclined to fall to one side. This tendency made the work much more difficult. The cleaning was carried out twice a day and lasted about three or four minutes. It was not until a few days later that Mecke was able to carry out this work on her own again.

In December 1967 our correspondence took on a friendlier, more intimate tone. I recall once asking Christel how she managed to recognize "her own" kangaroos and distinguish between them.

How do I recognize them? The distinguishing features among my family of nine are very slight. They all have what might be called the "Chinese look," and this is most clearly represented in the case of Chini, a female who has striking facial features, but when one has to do with the animals every day, it is easier to recognize the small, individual differences. Among these is the color of their coats, which varies from one kangaroo to another. This can range from beige to light brown and all the way to light gray. The majority of them can be described as being of slim stature. Mompti, though, because of his powerful build and his longish fur, gives one the impression of being almost plump. This is true in the case of Wombat, for example, who received his name because of the peculiar shape of his head. Other physical characteristics such as abnormalities or exceptions giving one occasion to tell the animals apart are practically nonexistent—except for Mompti, who has a noticeable fold on one ear. On the other hand, there is a lot of difference when it comes to individual behavior. For example, the biggest male, called Quickly, is pretty quarrelsome, whereas the most easy-going are Omi, a female, and Sydney, the smallest of the males.

In March 1969 I flew to Australia for the first time with my mother. Christel was of two minds about this announcement. First, she wished me well on the way out and every success for my stay there, and yet, on the other hand, the visit pointed up her own situation all the more painfully and clearly:

> When are you off? How long will you be staying? That's a childhood dream of mine—just once to be able to travel there! Above all, it's the contact with kangaroos that has given me the strength to dream, but I fear it'll remain only a dream!

I found these words very touching. It seemed as though she had reconciled herself to the fact of being forever trapped behind the Iron Curtain. Despite this, her soul apparently lingered in far-off lands. It was for this reason that she gave her kangaroos names that reminded her of Australia: Sydney, Wombat, Murray . . .

. . . and another birth! Christel's account was as follows:

> "Hello! Hello! Professor Ullrich! Come quickly! We've got another birth!" The director of the Dresden Zoo slammed down the receiver and rushed outside. He hurried through the areas that were so well known to him and to the door of a particular stall, where I was impatiently waiting for him. "Quick! Here, sir! Here!" I called. We went into the building and were just in time to see a tiny kangaroo on its way to slip into its mother's pouch barely three minutes after birth. The director was amazed.

She went on:

> Here are one or two details on the course of a kangaroo birth. According to my experience, preparations take about an hour on average. The pregnant female settles into a sitting position, her tail to the front between her hind legs and cleans the pouch. In doing so, she changes her position several times, from sitting to lying or standing. Shortly before the onset of labor, the mucous parts are licked. The mother's licking process is also important for the newborn animal as it is in this way that the

allantois is removed. Immediately after this, the tiny creature begins to make its way to the pouch, and this without the mother taking any special notice of its efforts. Once in the pouch, the baby then takes advantage of one of the four teats at its disposal. In all the births that I've so far witnessed, the baby, thanks to its powerfully developed forepaws, can always access its way to the pouch entrance on its own by "crawling," an operation that usually takes about three minutes.

Apparently, things took a brisk course from that moment on at the Dresden Zoo, and every letter from Christel contained more exciting news: *"Something has happened again among the kangaroos—yes, you've got it—another birth! That's the tenth!"* she declared, full of pride. It was Wombat's turn this time, and it wasn't long before the eleventh followed. That was probably something for the records. Every time this occurred she wrote excitedly about the event, of "her birth," and it was easy to get the impression that she was talking about herself becoming a mother!

Yearning

Dear Doris, this week I received the last topic for my final examination for a master's degree in this profession. It has to do with feeding kangaroos in the wild and in captivity. I would like to ask you a question. Can you give me a few tips about the literature on this or recommend someone who is concerned with Australian plant life? Above all, I'm interested in plant analysis in which the percentage of protein, fat, carbohydrate, mineral ingredients, roughage, and vitamins is given. These details are particularly important to me.

Christel wrote this in 1970, and of course I sent her the material she needed. Then, quite peremptorily, the packet suddenly reappeared on my table, but this time it was scruffy and torn and had holes in it. Attached to it was a note that it could not be delivered over the border. I was overwhelmed by a feeling of powerlessness and also by a sinister awareness that I was being controlled by an unknown power. However, I assured myself that Christel would get through her examination successfully without my help. And this proved to be true. She passed the examination, and I was able to send my congratulations in March 1971. It was not until 2003 that I learned of things about which I'd hitherto known nothing, indeed had not even suspected. Christel wrote the following:

> In the case where a person qualifies himself or herself further in the GDR and is therefore eligible for promotion, that person is required to disclose all the written connections he or she has with friends or relatives abroad. As a result of this regulation, my husband, Kurt, was called upon to disclose all of his wife's correspondence after he had qualified as an engineer. After he had done so, I was summoned to hand over my correspondence with you, and in the case of noncompliance, he would not be allowed to assume the position of a senior engineer. Despite the fact that we informed the authorities that our exchange was exclusively about factual matters and was, moreover, wholly concerned with kangaroos, the state authorities remained obdurate. For them, the main objection was that this correspondence was conducted with the capitalistic West, to which, of course, Switzerland also belonged. As it happened, Kurt declined to take advantage of his potential professional promotion so as not to endanger our continued correspondence with each other. I, too, didn't want to be browbeaten by the political situation, and so it was that in this way my love for animals, both as a profession and as a hobby, continued to make me happy.

I think it doesn't take much imagination to realize how deeply this subsequent revelation on Christel's part affected me. Regardless of the difficulties surrounding her social and family life, Christel had managed to pass her examination with flying colors. Now I had a complete copy of Christel's diploma work for her master's degree in my hand. On reading it, a deep feeling of fellow sympathy arose in me. Here were two like-minded women, the one in the West and the other in the East, who had dedicated their energies to learning about kangaroos, two women whose common love of animals had created a bridge that spanned all borders.

Christel's life in fact took a different turn when, around 1975, she was obliged for family and health reasons to change her occupation and move from the Dresden Zoo to the city's "culture palace," but she still took time off to visit "her" animals at the zoo. At the conclusion of one of her letters, she wrote of her fear that I would not want to continue our correspondence because she no longer worked at the zoo.

In my reply, I sought to allay her doubts and told her of my interest in keeping up our friendly contact by letter and at the same time promised her that I would continue my part. Our exchanges, however, began to be a little irregular. They were in the main concerned with family matters and naturally—how could it have been otherwise?—with kangaroos. Our letters were a mixture of an exchange of experience with and rapturous enthusiasm for our beloved animals, but not only kangaroos. Other animals, too, occupied a place in our correspondence, together with comments on our respective family lives, all of it topped off with talk about the weather. It was an exchange that we both very much enjoyed, all the more so since our love for animals and the discussion of all its ins and outs enabled us to largely ignore the everyday economic and political difficulties with which Christel was doubtlessly confronted. This helped to divert her attention to our mutual interest. I would have dearly liked to interest Christel in the differing cultural and social aspects of the various countries I had traveled in, but I tactfully avoided these topics for obvious reasons. And as far as politics was concerned, I never uttered a single word, limiting myself almost exclusively to things botanical and zoological.

My suspicion that our letters were constantly subjected to control, a suspicion that was later justified—I kept to myself. The impression was actually confirmed by Christel herself, who informed me that my letters to her had evidently been opened and read without demurral by the authorities and that, when they arrived, it was clear that they had been tampered with. And all this without their ever having contained one political statement! Luckily for me, Christel's letters were practically all free from such scrutiny, but I was horrified by the very idea. This brought back memories of my mother's receiving censored letters from our relatives in Halberstadt (at that time in the Third Reich) and Holland.

At this time I felt as never before how close I had become to Christel over the years regardless of the possibility of our ever being able to meet in person. Our letters had become very lively; they were witness to how we viewed each other and formed a mosaic of our personal feelings, thoughts, conceptions, and activities.

Yet on second thought, I should have been a little more careful in my confident descriptions about how easy and uncomplicated it was for us to cross the Swiss border. I suffered from a bad conscience when I recalled that the great mass of the East German population had been forcibly robbed of this fundamental freedom. I knew, too, that any secret attempt to flee to the West could be undertaken only under pain of death. In the face of all this, our letters and parcels managed nevertheless to enjoy freedom of travel, and so were able to pass back and forth through the Iron Curtain without undue obstruction. In addition, I wished and hoped that one day Christel might come to Basel. Ten years had passed since our first exchange of letters. Would another ten follow without our ever meeting one another?

In 1982 I spent three months in Australia with my veterinary surgeon friend, Bettina. When I returned home, I had two large piles of mail on the kitchen table. I just let my baggage fall to the floor, grabbed an old stool, sat down at the table, and began hastily to open the envelopes. I read all the letters at once. I was disappointed to find none from Christel since I had written a long letter to her from the Australian bush. Then, shortly before Christmas, I received a long letter from her:

You've probably been waiting some time for a letter from me. In the evenings I feel the weakness in my body particularly strongly. And on top of this, there are the children and the homework they have to do, and I have to solve all their school tasks. [Her husband had left the family a short time before.] It can't go on like this.

Your report from Australia was, as always, of the greatest interest, and I was very pleased to hear about the birth of twin kangaroos. That's the second time I've heard of this. . . .

Here at the zoo, quite a lot of exciting things have happened. One of them, for example, has been the artificial raising of a female kangaroo. I spend half an hour each morning in the stall where the red giants are kept and have to watch out that I'm not attacked by a rather nervous male! I don't know whether I've already told you about our new Parma dwarf kangaroos (among them a female with a pouch baby)? I'm interested in knowing whether this young fellow will soon develop enough to peep out at the world!

I was enormously relieved to read all this and realized that all we had in common had not just flown to the winds! Things went on like this for many more years. Our correspondence was more or less irregular and was a reflection of our very different life rhythms. Once Christel reported that she had met a group of tourists from Basel. She had thought of me immediately and then closed by saying, "Perhaps, after all, we'll one day have an opportunity of seeing each other."

These words brought me almost to tears. I had the feeling that the communist world would remain inexorably rigid and closed to the outside world for an eternity. For me, there was nothing I could do but offer a little comfort here and there.

The "Wall" Is Demolished at Last

AS THE warm days of summer 1989 came to an end, the leaves slowly began to acquire autumn colors, and saffron decorated the meadows. Gaps at the Austrian/Hungarian border appeared, through which the Hungarian government permitted the first fugitives from the GDR to pass. The end of political division in Europe was in sight. I learned a lot about what was going on from TV and from the papers, all of which were reporting on the tense, political background, and was greatly interested in the course of events.

Nevertheless, I said not a word to anyone of my own interest in these developments.

By autumn, there was a veritable avalanche of refugees fleeing from Hungary over the border to Austria. Hardly a day went by without large demonstrations taking place in the German Democratic Republic. Hope was in the air. Waiting for Christel's reaction by letter to this unexpected political upheaval was a stiff exercise in patience for me. So it was for this reason that I decided that instead of turning on the TV every hour and following up the latest news on teletext, I would go outside for a walk in the cold November air in order to gather strength and confidence.

Was it possible that my dreams would come true and that I would really meet Christel one day? I constantly asked myself. I tried to make it clear in my mind why my thoughts always turned toward the Iron Curtain and Dresden. And always, the answer was clear— Christel had remained true during these long years of our correspondence, and, as a consequence, a deep, sincere friendship had arisen from our exchanges.

Only a few days later, the unexpected occurred and, like wildfire, was broadcast around the world. On the evening of November 9 the frontier between the GDR and the West was opened. The wall was no more!

Almost ten days after the collapse of the wall and several months since I had received anything from Christel, a letter arrived at last on November 20:

I would like first of all to apologize for the long silence and also thank you for your mail! There was always something to stop me from writing! As things are at present here, not a day goes by without another surprise. But a change had to come! We are so very proud of having reached our objectives, but there's much still to be done. As far as the new government is concerned, we feel we can rely on it and have confidence in its decisions. Many people are using the opportunity now to travel since the West is absolutely new to them. I would myself very much like to see other zoos and discover new countryside, so, if you

like, we could meet each other in the Federal Republic of Germany. At
any rate, I would be delighted to meet you in person!

My desire to meet Christel pressed upon me more and more, but
it was to be some time before we were to pave a way to each other
through the debris of the wall and its history. By the autumn of
1991, I could wait no longer. Together with Vera, my young, delightful traveling companion, I left Hanover by rental car to make the
journey to Dresden. It turned out to be a somewhat adventurous
trip, almost, one might say, an odyssey through countryside that was
completely unknown to me. We got lost several times, but somehow we finally arrived in Dresden. Two days after our arrival I met
Christel at last.

With my heart beating and with unsteady steps, I made my way
to the entrance of the Dresden Zoo, where we had agreed to meet.
And there she was, my dear Christel! It was some moments before
I was able to recognize her as I hadn't had a recent photo of her for
more than a decade. Despite the fact that she was now forty-seven
and here and there her face displayed a few wrinkles that were tes-
timony that her life had not always been easy, her bright blue eyes
and cheerful smile, her short blonde hair, a few strands of which
fell onto her forehead, all these still gave one an overall impression
of youth and beauty. At this very moment, the twenty-four years of
barbed wire and wall that had once prevented a meeting were at last
behind us! We looked at each other for a short moment and then
fell into each other's arms, half crying and half laughing. I could not
speak for joy. Slowly I managed to bring a few words to my lips—
and Christel understood me, although she had never been in contact
with anyone who could not hear. As for me, I quickly learned to lipread what she said.

Hand in hand with Christel, we all entered the zoo in the best
of spirits. I felt the warmheartedness and kindness that ema-
nated from Christel's rough farmer's hands. I was sure at that
moment that the bonds of our friendship would endure into the
future.

My friend Christel and I in 1993. It was our first trip together to Australia after the fall of the Berlin Wall.

I experienced our tour through the zoo as though in a dream. Christel took us to the parrots, too, as she was primarily responsible for this department.[34] She was especially fond of the macaws and other parrot species, but she still maintained her love for kangaroos. She took us to a beautiful field that was covered with all kinds of bushes. It was here that the red giants lived. My researcher's eye caught sight of something astonishing: Marching on top of the resting kangaroos were magpies, who were busily picking insects from their fur. It was a wonderful and colorful image: the green of the grass, the fox-red of the kangaroos, and the black-and-white of the magpies. Added to this was the alertness of the birds, contrasted with the tranquility of the red giants. Now I was at last with Christel and her kangaroos, and a feeling of joy ran through me.

34. Earlier I mentioned that Christel had, for family and health reasons, been compelled to leave her job at the Dresden Zoo. Later she returned to the zoo and was now working there as an international advisor.

Toward evening, we went to Christel's house on the edge of the town. It had been arranged that I would spend the rest of my time there with her before returning home. Time simply flew by.

Then the last day came, and we had planned to take a trip by car, which would soften the pain of departure—or so I hoped. There was to be a surprise at the end of this excursion.

We drove through undulating plains that were largely made up of meadowland. Only a few fields had been planted with corn or with other crops. Here and there one came across small villages and an occasional farm. The more we motored on, the more excited I began to feel. The weather became drab, and a mist barely allowed the sun's rays to shine through. From time to time it even rained. We stopped at a small village called Stürza and sat down to a midday meal. Then the journey continued through soft, green countryside. However, the scene was soon to change abruptly. Small forests and rough undergrowth began to dominate the landscape. We passed a billboard with the word "BASTION" on it and immediately behind this came upon a parking area. Here we got out of the car. What kind of wonder awaits us here? I asked myself. We then walked for what might have been fifteen minutes until we came to a remarkable view. For the first few seconds I was totally confused; I thought I'd been fitted with angel's wings and transported in the wink of an eye to Australia! It took me a few moments to recover. I burst out, "It looks exactly like the Australian 'Blue Mountains with Three Sisters,' not far from Sydney!" And in fact there in front of me, several grotesque-looking, humanlike figures ranged up from a deep, sparsely wooded sandstone gorge. I could hardly believe my eyes, but these outcrops of rock were remarkably similar to those I had seen in Australia. Christel seemed to read my thoughts, for she then told me that this particular area was referred to as "Saxony's Switzerland." Now I was really perplexed. Could I not have asked with the same justification why this place wasn't called "Saxony's Australia"?

The next day and in a happy mood, I set off on my return journey to Switzerland. We had agreed that we would see each other again in about six months—this time in Basel.

Together on Short Trips

AS WAS so often the case with me, whether I happened to be in Switzerland or in the Australian outback, I indulged myself in wild dreams. Every time I woke up, a feeling of happiness would overcome me, and I would immediately remember that Christel was here with me at home in Reinach and that she was slumbering peacefully and was certainly looking forward to having breakfast together.

The day after she arrived, we toured the area around Basel. While we were out and about, I noticed a certain pensiveness, if not absent-mindedness, in Christel. She seemed to be thinking of times past in the GDR, times that were not yet at an end. In a café I plucked up the courage to ask her gently about her past. She was hesitant at first, and then she told me that the hardest time she had ever known had begun in 1949. She was five years old when her beloved stepfather had lost his sight after a mine explosion. He spent many months in the hospital at Eisenach. Her mother had commuted every day between their home and the hospital to help care for him. During this unhappy time, Christel and her sister, Karin, lived with their grandparents, who owned a shoe shop. There were not enough beds in the home, so the two little children were obliged to sleep with their blankets on the shop counter.

When Christel had related this, we sat still for a long moment with our plates and half-empty glasses on the table. But then our being together took a positive turn, and we talked about things from our letters that had almost been forgotten. It was with a great feeling of relief that we could now talk freely about what had happened in the past.

From this time on, I met Christel two to three times a year, either in Reinach, Dresden, or somewhere else. We went on several excursions or short trips with one another. We walked together in the Berner Oberland, for example, over the alpine meadows and through the woods. It was the pure, natural life that we loved so much. We avoided the tourist traps at the spas, as this kind of thing got on our nerves. We adapted ourselves to our natural circumstances and regarded ourselves to some extent as "wild wanderers." Natural variety gave us great pleasure, and we were particularly attentive when it came to matters such as rare or endangered plants like the very small orchid that blossomed on the mountain slopes or the deep-blue gentian.

In late summer one year we were hiking together in one of the high valleys of Wallis, a canton of Switzerland. Christel had discovered some blackberries at the edge of the woods and heaped them up in my hand. Thinking nothing of it, I tipped them from my hand straight into my mouth, and it would have gone on like this had not Christel suddenly brushed the next "delivery" aside to prevent my eating the contents! Whatever had happened? I looked at my palm, and there sat a tiny green frog! Shocked and relieved at the same time, I put him down on the ground, thinking that we had both been lucky in narrowly escaping what some might have considered a "culinary delicacy"!

As for Christel, she combed the steep, harvested slopes for fresh, earthy potatoes until her bags were full. (Was this perhaps a flashback to postwar times and subsequent food shortages in the GDR? Was it that conditions then required people to continue to be practical?) Thanks to her knowledge of mushrooms, Christel found splendid edible boleti and the larch boletus, as well as other delicious varieties of mushrooms in the woods. Although in the past I had searched for mushrooms with my mother, these days my eyes could not help Christel much, so I reconciled myself to the job of carefully cutting a few mushrooms out of the ground that Christel had pointed out. In doing this, I was careful not to damage the roots. The nicest thing for me in this was the unmistakable aroma of plant and earth, which I breathed in deeply.

There were rainy days in Wallis, too, and on these, the water came down from above almost as though in the days of the Flood. I would give Christel English lessons in our vacation apartment, as we had planned a trip to Australia together in the near future. We went through the lessons together with gusto. The Rhône had risen sharply as a result of the continuous rain and was racing through the villages on its long route through the valley. A "lake" had formed in the large meadow in front of our house, which in the course of an afternoon advanced to the walls of the house and its basement apartments. Now and again, we looked out of the window, but our conversation turned on other things. Finally, we took a break, and Christel put her ear to the radio.

"In Brig [a small town in the lower Rhône Valley], a disaster alarm has been issued. The railway station and the city center are under water," she informed me. Not far from our own village, people had also hurriedly put up walls of sandbags.

The evening came and darkness quickly descended. The danger lurking outside began to encroach on our lively conversation about kangaroos. Other topics didn't manage to divert us, either. We remained quiet and were thumbing nervously through various magazines when all of a sudden the room was plunged into darkness! In a terrifying moment of panic I thought that total blindness had caught up with me and fumbled wildly for my flashlight. One can imagine my relief when, a moment later, I saw the light it put out. We rummaged around for all the candles we had, lit them, and began to prepare our cold evening meal. Before retiring, I locked the main door as usual, but Christel intervened, saying that it would be better to leave it unlocked since we might have to flee to the carpenter's family that lived upstairs. Thank God, this emergency didn't materialize; nonetheless, Christel's thoughtfulness greatly impressed me.

If only we were as vigilant as kangaroos, I thought. These animals show no panic either at the outbreak of bush fires or when the weather suddenly takes a turn for the worse but are always alert and ready to flee, knowing inwardly which route is the best and safest. This predetermined flight offers the optimal chance for survival. For us human beings, however, it is not always so easy in such extreme situations to let good sense prevail. Of course, kangaroos have no fear of material loss and consequently, feel no inhibitions as far as this is concerned, whereas we very often try to save the most trivial objects.

Despite the inclement weather that night, we nevertheless managed to sleep almost without being disturbed. By the following morning, the rain had abated, and from time to time the sun even peeped between the clouds. The water on the grass outside the house began to recede. We walked along the Rhône. Its banks were strewn with detritus of all kinds—uprooted trees and mud. We found dead trout and some that were even still alive. Christel carefully picked up the latter and threw them back into the river. When we eventually arrived home again, we were gratified to see that the electricity had been restored. Only the railway route from Brig remained blocked for a while longer.

Soon it was time to go home. Clever and prudent like kangaroos, we chose another route to get there. We drove in brilliant sunshine direct to Basel via the Gotthard Tunnel. From there, Christel went back to Dresden. However, this was not for long. A few months later, she was in Basel again, this time with a lot of luggage because we hoped to realize a plan that we'd long been forging: We wanted to travel to Australia together.

Island of Our Dreams

OUR destination was Rotamah Island, a small island on which I had carried out field studies of kangaroos before, and, like Pebbly Beach, I had come to love it as my second home. It was a petite paradise that I hoped Christel would find as delightful as I did, and indeed this hope was fulfilled. She could not hide her joyful anticipation. This paradise island with its opulent flora and fauna is about five kilometers long and just about one kilometer wide. To get there, one has to take a train from Melbourne and then a bus southeast to the coast, which has an abundance of islands and peninsulas. From the mainland one has to take a twenty-minute trip by water taxi. Once there, a young ranger pair welcomed us most warmly at a small wharf.

Accommodation was secured for us in a beautiful, white villa that served both as bird observation center and as a place for students and vacationers to stay. We picked a bedroom that I had slept in before and knew well. "There's my lovely bed, which I've especially reserved for you, so that when you wake up in the morning, you can see the kangaroos grazing right in front of the window!" I said to Christel enthusiastically. Later, on unpacking, I hit my head against the frame of the bunk beds, and Christel, who had noticed the collision, came up to me and said, "No, it's better if you sleep in your very own dream bed at the window. I don't want you to have any more bumps." So we changed places. It was precisely this unassuming modesty on her part that I secretly admired and which stood in such stark contrast to the enthusiasm she showed for this place and for nature in general.

In single file with Christel in front, we roamed this untouched landscape, which was to offer us captivating sights and impressions at every turn. Thanks to the intensive impressions of natural life around us during the next seven weeks, we must have counted among the very few people in the world for whom there was not a single day or even an hour of boredom. Often we would walk along the rows of banksias with their yellow, upright, cylindrical blooms standing in bright hundreds. As we went along, my arm frequently became entangled in one of these instead of being placed around Christel's neck, so similar were they! That is to say, the corn-shaped inflorescence and the short-haired, bright blonde head were easy to confuse. "Is it you, dear Christel, or is it a banksia?" I used to ask myself whenever we encountered these widely disseminated plants in Australia. Every time I thought of Christel's shock of hair in these latitudes and the banksias over there, I was overcome by a wonderful feeling of happiness that I had never experienced before!

Thinking back, I realize how right it had been to direct Christel's attention more strongly toward Australia. It was clear to me that this would be an indispensable aspect of life for us both. I recalled my mother warning me after a sleepless night a few weeks before our departure about my taking Christel to a country that was so completely alien to her. In all seriousness, she said, this could have the most adverse effect on her. For someone that had lived for forty years behind the wall and with all of its deprivations, it might be difficult to adjust to Western freedoms. In the heated debate that followed this remark, I finally convinced her that we were concerned here with a long-entertained wish of hers, which was about to be fulfilled.

After only a few days there, I began calling Christel the "white cockatoo," and this not only because of her pretty hair color but also because her greatest love was for parrots, then kangaroos, and then for great apes. What I was able to do in the way of mimicking in my contact with kangaroos, Christel used as a method in her contacts with them. She was a past master, for example, at imitating my spontaneous mispronunciations by using apelike lip movements, which made me burst into laughter. Nevertheless, "Cockatoo" was a much nicer and also a more suitable name for her. Caricatures of this type of parrot, which I enjoyed drawing, soon filled our travel notes— much to Christel's delight.

An international quartet had come together in this white villa on Rotamah: It consisted of the young ranger, Thierry, from France and his Australian wife, Joanna; Christel, from former East Germany; and me, from Switzerland. Quite soon after our first meeting, long conversations began taking place between the two rangers and me, conversations that hardly came to an end. The two young people very quickly mastered the Lorm manual alphabet, which was important for our mutual understanding.

Thierry and Joanna also grew accustomed to my English articulation as well, which had no Australian accent! When it came to rather longer accounts, explanations, difficult specific terms, or the day's schedule, they wrote things down so that I could pass them on to Christel in German. Because of this personal form of communication, an atmosphere of trust and an almost familial relationship developed between us. The two rangers took us out on extensive boat trips and introduced us to various bird-breeding grounds that were situated on faraway, uninhabited islands. I was delighted that Christel was thrilled by these experiences and that she was eager to capture all that she saw with her video camera. In this way, we were able to observe certain rare types of duck and seagulls, birds that are found in only a few places in Australia. We were also allowed to catch a few songbirds for banding purposes. I quote from one of the letters Christel wrote to my mother:

> This week, a long, stovepipe-thick, black snake crossed our path. I was a bit shocked by this but soon recovered. Then Doris placed herself behind me in order to photograph the creature comfortably. I thought that otherwise nobody would believe us. Our two ranger friends were quite astonished when they saw the photos. They identified the snake as a particularly poisonous variety. Since then we've been a little more wary.

One sunny afternoon, we were just about to leave the villa via the garden gate when someone seized my arm in an iron grip and spun me round. Within a split second, my view collapsed into the grotesque, and I lost my orientation. I stood there stiffly, waiting until my view righted itself again. Then I looked around. Christel stroked me gently on the shoulder and communicated with her fingers: "Look, there in front of you!" I looked more closely, was shocked, and then breathed normally once more. It was a black snake again, but this time a smaller version and probably a younger one. It was likely that it was poisonous, a "porter at the gate" that I was just about to tread on! The truth was that I was within a hair's breadth of being bitten, had it not been for Christel's timely and determined grab at my shoulder.

On one of our excursions we came across an otherwise unusual species, but one that is often found on Rotamah. It turned out that from this fateful moment on Christel was going to fall in love with this creature: the so-called ant hedgehog, or spiny anteater, whose Latin name is echidna. When we encountered it, Christel signaled to me to stop. Carefully, she approached the animal, which was sleeping peacefully in the undergrowth. Then she called me over to photograph it. The animal lay there unperturbed when it was photographed in series from all sides. Even as Christel photographed its spines at a distance of only a few centimeters, it continued to slumber on! These were marvelously delightful moments. Here, under our very noses was an ant hedgehog that was totally oblivious to us and seemed to inhabit another world.

Christel was a avid handcrafter. She took roots that the sea had deposited on the shore and from this weirdly formed wood made decorative objects such as a possum, an owl, or a duck-billed platypus for Thierry and Johanna. She would craft them with so much skill that it was a pleasure to watch her at work. The two rangers were as pleased as I was. I was proud of Christel not only because of her skilful knowledge of handiwork but above all because she had adapted so easily to the Australian way of life and had managed so well to settle in here.

Christel had also managed during our acquaintance to master the manual alphabet form of communication, but, unfortunately, there were times when I was somewhat absentminded. One day, for instance, she grabbed my hand and drew my attention to the heavens. "Look up there at the rainbow! Ooooaaa!" A little confused, I interrupted her and looked up at the sky since nothing would have delighted me more after all these years than to see a rainbow on this continent. Up to now, the joy of seeing a rainbow had not been granted to me despite the fact that I had often been on the lookout with my camera to catch one after rain and immediate sunshine.

Christel brought me back to earth from my daydreams. She shook my hand vigorously and tried again to spell out the words on it. "Wait. I haven't finished. Watch now: a rainbow." But again I interrupted her, feeling that, as if by inner order, I had to look up at the sky. This happened several times. Christel could not get beyond the word "rainbow." Then, at last she managed to get to the end: LORIKEETS!

Aha! Now I understood and at the same moment looked at the two rainbow-colored parrots that were sitting on the eaves looking at me as if they wanted to double up with laughter at my obtuseness. I still smile at this amusing misunderstanding.

During our evening meals we sat with Thierry and Johanna in front of the large window facing the fields and the sea, and from here we enjoyed a wonderful view. At times on bright evenings more than forty kangaroos would be grazing in this field, and their antics often brought laughter to the table. On one such occasion I was witness for the first time in my life to a fight between three male kangaroos. Christel related this scene in a letter to my mother:

Yesterday evening there was a sporting event here. Two kangaroo males fought one another. To try to divert their antagonist's attention, they stopped now and then to clean or scratch their bodies, only to pitch in once more with a determined kick at the other's belly or thighs. Then a third young male came, placed himself in position, and hopped up to one of the protagonists with easy unconcern. Was he perhaps a "referee" that had detected an irregularity in the proceedings and wanted to put matters right? Certainly not, for a moment later this newcomer even dared to interfere with the course of battle. For this he received a couple of hearty clouts but despite this was successful in pushing one of the males to one side. The row between the older fellows continued until the younger male tried again to come between the rivals. To this end he sprang onto the back of one of the old males and clung to the upper part of his body like a leech! This proved to be just too much for the older animal, and he finally managed to free himself from his little aggressor. A moment or two after that, they were all peacefully grazing as though nothing had happened. It was a great show, and we all had a good laugh.

On another evening, we were treated to the spectacle of an unusual drama. Christel again:

For some days now, dolphins have been tumbling and frolicking about in high spirits near the wharf or sampling the rich fishing grounds there. Despite the rain, I went down to the place, my camera wrapped in a plastic bag, and after a while Doris joined me. I don't think she saw them coming, for no sooner were they out of the water than they dived back in. They came nearer to us than ever before though, and it seemed to me that they swam extra near to us for Doris's sake. Then thousands of cormorants flew over the water in a line on the lookout for fish—a truly wonderful sight like a natural ballet.

On one expedition we observed a bright-gray heron wheeling high above the treetops and finally coming to land on a patch of swampy ground. We were completely taken with this charming picture of ease and elegance. Not long after this incident, we were disturbed in our activities by an environmental patrol unit and were told by two friendly officials that poaching had to be stopped by employing regular patrolling. Christel did the interpreting.

From this moment on, we weren't alone in our activities but tried to make ourselves useful as voluntary assistants to the rangers and environmental protectionists. So when we discovered signs of suspicious behavior, for example, we would record them, noting the time and place. The offenses ranged from the theft of echidnas to the illegal killing of kangaroos.

Words like "boredom" or "loneliness" were foreign to us on Rotamah Island. Our days were full of things to do. We either proceeded upright through the countryside or went on all fours when necessary, especially when we were intent on creeping up on a situation or researching it, and our encounters with animals were numerous.

It was especially impressive, for example, for us to be surprised by the appearance of a group of emus that leisurely crossed our path as though this were the most natural thing in the world. But there were other fascinating impressions in the botanical world like that of an old tree trunk standing in water that was overgrown with succulent plants in the most fabulous colors. We would discover new plant-life scenes every day. Thanks to the natural beauty of this island, it was all too easy to feel transported to a kind of primordial environment. I used to ask myself whether we would perhaps stumble across the "Tree of Knowledge."

One day Christel related an urgent report that captured my whole attention. Somewhere here, she informed me, was a "kangaroo apple tree." "A what?" I replied. "A kangaroo apple tree!"[35] I nearly choked as I immediately imagined such a plant, whose fruit was certainly

---

35. *Solanum aviculare,* or "kangaroo apple," is a shrub that is found in southern Australia and in New Zealand. Its red fruit are as big as cherries.

under strict surveillance in this Australian paradise and protected from both touching and eating. However, I suggested that she and I gather all our photographic equipment and set off tomorrow to have a look at it. We wandered along for hours in the pitiless sunshine and were plagued by mosquitoes. The odd thing was that these little demons were more interested in my blood than in Christel's! These external afflictions in particular, as well as the impassable route we had taken, one littered with roots and daunting undergrowth, were clear signs that we were nearing the neighborhood of the Fall. Suddenly we were standing in front of this other Tree of Knowledge.

On first looking at it and first touching its stem, I was overcome by the uncanny feeling of being surrounded and outwitted by kangaroo spirits. I reached between the bright violet leaves for the many greenish yellow "apples," fruits that were no bigger than cherries. I had no sooner touched them than my "casting out of the Garden of Eden" followed under a cloud of minute, swarming "angels"—the mosquitoes. I clung tightly to Christel so as not to lose my balance. Then I staggered back to the sandy path. Had I in this way been redeemed from a possible "Fall"? Only in Sydney's botanical garden did I eventually have a chance to pluck one of these apples, from which a whole row of trees later flourished at my home in Switzerland. I dreamed that kangaroos swung from their branches!

The day of our final departure from Rotamah came ever nearer, and we enjoyed the last days and hours left to us more than ever. Above all, we were struck by the beauty of the sunsets. The heavens were reflected in the waves of the sea in the subtlest of colors, ranging from changing pastel tones of white and yellow to light blue and gray. The wharf was populated by charming rows of pigeons and ducks, and on the branches that ranged above the water swarms of cormorants were flapping their wings. Soon the sky would turn red, but as yet sunset had not arrived, these sunsets that I knew and loved so much. This was a natural pageant that I had experienced only in Australia. It took place in a powerful show of dramatic color, lighting up the sky with a magnificent display of stimulating yellow, orange, and fiery red, which then was transformed into a silky red-and-violet before giving way to the black of night.

Gradually the light diminished, and the last golden strands of veiled night grayed to a dark blue. We thought of the journey before us and were sad at having to take leave of our young rangers soon.

Then we said "adieu" to Rotamah Island and, after a diversion to Tasmania and Sydney, landed back in Europe on a cold February day. That same day, Christel traveled back to Dresden, both happy and sad, but we had the certainty that we would see each other again in a few months.

A Confession and an Atonement

CHRISTEL and I traveled a lot together in the years that followed. We also went to Italy, where we stayed while exploring Pompeii. This area was buried in lava after a volcanic eruption shortly before the birth of Christ. The town was finally freed of this rubble only at the beginning of the twentieth century. The remains of the city impressed us beyond measure, and we did not shy away from climbing Mount Vesuvius itself, that dreaded hill of destiny that wreaked such havoc on the town and still smokes in warning. Then we went off to England's Cornwall, in the southwestern region of the island, a romantic area full of legends about pirates and smugglers and also climatically favored by the Gulf Stream, which blesses the area with Mediterranean vegetation. This was partly transplanted from south European climes. We also had a look at the hot springs there and in which the Roman invaders are said to have taken their ease.

In 1998, in our tour group we became objects of the liveliest interest. How was it, our fellow travelers wanted to know, that a person with a disability and one without could get along with each other so harmoniously? We earned a degree of admiration, and they opened their mouths wide on learning from Christel that it was the kangaroos that had brought us together.

But there were other, "wilder" plans on our agenda. There was a trip to Tessin, in Switzerland, for example, for those who had vision and hearing difficulties. Christel also participated just for the fun of it and also to learn more about Switzerland. She took part in our crazy "pirate performances" with much love and affection. Not only her friendship with me but also her experiences with her blind father came in useful in interacting with people with disabilities, and she understood wonderfully well how to communicate with them by tactile response methods. In the pirate performances, for example, folks with disabilities, accompanied by their guides, all equipped with rubber suits, pushed off in small, inflatable dinghies like a host of excited frogs on a passage downstream in a mountain torrent.

IN THE autumn of 1999 we also flew to Israel, where we had a great time in a kibbutz. The kibbutz had a new Australian park in which, by the way, a few of our "top favorites" lived. We spent time with these trusting gray giants, who hardly moved when visitors almost stumbled over them! They didn't seem to mind being roughly "stroked" by small children, either.

Not far from this park was a grove of trees in which a spring poured its water into a lake and in which we often refreshed ourselves. In so doing, hundreds of small fish nuzzled our bodies; it was a delightful prickling sensation. In the evenings, we sat above the kibbutz among Roman ruins through which a small stream tinkled, a stream in which Muslim men and women carried out their ablutions still fully dressed. As long as it was still light, we watched the kingfishers diving headlong into the water and then making their way out again with their beaks full. On our way back, we plucked fresh, sweet dates from sawed-off branches that lay on the ground, and when it gradually got dark, we sat comfortably at a wooden table in the kibbutz after our evening meal and enjoyed dates and wine by candlelight.

It was already October and yet still warm like summer. It was Sukkoth, the Jewish harvest festival: I looked up at the starry sky in a meditative mood and felt even here in Israel's "Promised Land" how very much attached I was to my beloved kangaroos, indeed, just as I had wished it to be as a child. I was dreaming like this when

Christel took my hand and wrote on it: "Do you feel that once, a long time ago, you injured a kangaroo soul?"

This was a question that was no doubt well meant, but it was at once a difficult and an appalling one. I simply remained silent, staring fixedly at the night sky as though I might find an answer among the kangaroo ancestors. I had an awful attack of lack of self-confidence. Had I in fact done something wrong while I was in Australia? Perhaps inadvertently?

At last, Christel confided the following to me. "It was when we were on our way to Australia and stayed three days on Flinders Island in Tasmania. In the evening there were steaks on the menu. You looked at them carefully, sampled the meat, and said, 'We can eat that all right; that's not kangaroo meat, for sure!' There, one has to be careful since it's always available. I had looked at my portion intently and assured myself that it was neither pork nor beef. But it tasted delicious! When our group guide came along, I asked him what we'd eaten. 'Wallaby,' he said shortly. Wallaby! Oh no! I dared not tell you; otherwise, you would have been sick right away. For you, of course, it was an absolute taboo to eat your most beloved creatures, your 'ancestors,' as you call them."

It wasn't easy at that moment to control myself. I sat still and asked God to forgive me for this unintended misdemeanor. Christel stroked my hand lovingly. Bit by bit I regained my composure and ate a few more of the delightful dates. Then we toasted each other and silently emptied our glasses.

Guilt and forgiveness had balanced out in these few minutes. The fact that Christel had waited years before finding the right moment to reveal this to me was not only an act of the finest human sentiment but also immediately allowed my feeling of shame to reconcile itself with nature.

19

My Brother
and I

MY SOMEWHAT younger brother, Peter, who was also born
without hearing and, moreover, suffered from other disabilities,
should really have a chapter to himself. So far I have mentioned
him only here and there in passing and merely touched upon his
disabilities.

For forty long years and right up to the death of my mother I
was tortured by a scene in a dream. It was always the same situation, in which my brother played the main role and which
never failed to put me into a renewed state of panic. In tears, my
mother would remind me that I formerly had a younger brother,
Peter, who had wandered off into the forest, never to be seen
again.

Every time I was confronted with this scene in my dream, I
would be shocked to the core and would react to it almost as if paralyzed. My reaction in the dream was always the same: Stiff with fear,
I would stare at my mother, unable to find a single word of consolation for her. Just as if I were paralyzed, I would then see my brother
sinking helplessly into the earth and yet with a rapturous smile on
his lips, and then the ground would quickly be covered with layers
of colorful autumn leaves.

Was this uncanny dream an expression of a deeply lodged sense
of guilt? In the meantime, I am quite sure it was.

ONE day when I was eight years old, I went on a walk with my brother and Auntie through a deep, dark forest. It was spring, and the ground beneath the trees where the warm rays of the sun shone through was covered with many kinds of flowers. We were just going down an incline when Auntie suddenly said that she wanted to take another path so that she could pick a few flowers. I was to continue on down with my brother, and we would meet each other at the bottom.

I gently took my brother's hand, but he disengaged it from mine, turned around, and went back uphill. Afraid of losing sight of Auntie, I ran on and found her. She was annoyed: "Foolish girl! Why didn't you bring your brother? Where is he?"

I read what she was saying from her lips, and my heart skipped a beat. I was ashamed of myself. Despite this, I pulled myself together, took heart, and ran as well as I could straight back uphill. I can still well remember how my heart throbbed as I fought my way through a tangle of bushes, stumps, and branches, past twigs and glittering, entwined foliage, thinking only about how to find Peter!

Then I caught sight of him, struggling away in front of me up the hill, waving his arms cheerfully in the air above his head. Everything about him seemed to be full of bliss, and this was understandable, as I knew how he loved trees. I grabbed him rather roughly and turned him around the way he should go. This curt action left traces of shame in me; I felt that I had not done justice to Peter and that I had left him in the lurch.

Some decades later, I related the mysterious, recurring riddle of this painful dream to my mother and her companion, Fritz. I wanted to free myself at last from these feelings of guilt and add that this incident had held me in check ever since. So I told them everything that had inspired these feelings, including how I had once left Peter all alone in the forest. I asked them both to interpret the dream for me. "Peter is with us in body and soul and woven into our existence, but a small part of his mind has gone away—the means by which he can speak to us," Fritz replied with much sympathy.

My Brother Is Different

THERE was much truth in these words. At Peter's birth, a forceps delivery, he had lost blood, thereby affecting the brain, and, as a result, the speech center had been irreparably damaged.[36] If one had gone about the birth in a more sensible way, Peter would have certainly become a brotherly companion with whom I could have communicated. Nevertheless, Peter and I had learned to accept this outcome and communicated with one another tactilely. Sometimes I would communicate with Peter by drawing what I had experienced, and this always seemed to please him greatly.

Peter was born without hearing in August 1936. He soon developed into a fine lad and even as a small child was something of a madcap. He would often stand at the railing of his cot and stare out of the window for a long time with rapt attention. I had to summon up the courage to approach him because he was only too fond of pulling my curly hair, and this caused me considerable pain.

My brother's face was the reflection of his soul inasmuch as it mirrored all his joy, his troubles, his sadness, and his high spirits. Every day I would look into this mirror, and in this way I took part in Peter's changing moods. If I sat or lay next to him, my body pressed closely to his, I could actually feel the varying play of his sensations. If he were contented, for example, he would grunt or mumble to himself or even laugh, and I would feel these as vibrations. If, on the other hand, he felt uneasy about something or did not agree, he would deliver a special grunt. When he shouted or cried, I could feel a particular vibration issuing from him. If he felt especially happy, he would wave his hands about, and if he were sitting at the time, he would wave both his arms and legs in the air.

---

36. It was only much later that Peter was diagnosed as having Usher's syndrome. This inherited condition manifests as a combination of a slow, progressive deterioration of the retina—retinitis pigmentosa (RP)—and either early deafness, affecting the inner ear, or deafness at birth. The syndrome takes its name from Charles H. Usher, a British ophthalmologist, who in 1914 described the inherited, recessive nature of the disease.

If he were eating at such times, the joy would pass into the tips of his toes under the table. His happiness was always manifested by his bodily movements. Just as with those who have no disability, these physical expressions disappeared with the onset of puberty. His merry laugh and his grunt, though, have remained. A few of his characteristics apply both to the early days and to the present, and these very clearly show his state of mind: When he feels pleased, for example, his mouth assumes the roundness of a circle, as though he were about to deliver a kiss, and he claps his chest with the flat of his hand. If he hadn't seen our parents for some time, he would look at them while waving his arms and gurgling or laughing with joy. It's the same today when he sees his old friends again. This is his special way of expressing his joy. Generally speaking, there is no shaking of hands. When we wave to him on leaving, he waves to us warmly in return.

Throughout his life, Peter has been capable of expressing conventional thanks only with difficulty. His gratitude is usually expressed by gurgling or laughing. These are easy for me to register. In other cases he would grasp a present with both hands and put it to his nose in order to smell it. His "yes" to this was not a nod of the head but a purposeful grab at the gift. His "no" to what might be offered was a demonstrative repudiation, accompanied by a discontented grunting. However, there were exceptions. On one occasion, Mother told me of an incident in a bakery, in which eight-year-old Peter was standing before a large selection of cakes. When she offered him a piece of cake, he suddenly held up his index finger, waving it to and fro to indicate negation.

My brother expressed his anger and disappointment by hammering the wall, as well as his own body, with his hands or fists. Sometimes he waved his arms in the air to display these feelings. On one occasion I was making some handicrafts when Peter stormed in, locked the door behind him, and then smashed the wooden playhouse that he had earlier so perfectly put together. I went out to tell Mother what had happened. In doing so, I found out that Peter had damaged the heating system in some way, for which he had received a box on the ears. This kind of violent reaction was a way of admitting his guilt, a way of punishing himself. First, he secluded himself, and then, at the high point of his self-punishment, he destroyed his lovingly built house.

A Very Special Kind of Artist

THE strenuous, daily speech-therapy exercises that Auntie tried to do with Peter proved a failure. On the other hand, he displayed considerable practical intelligence. Just shy of four years of age, he was able to button and unbutton his clothing, and shortly afterward he was also able to dress and undress himself without assistance. Very well, but would he also be able to learn to tie his shoes? Yes, indeed! Untiring patience enabled him to learn how, and his success filled him with pride and happiness.

The most pleasurable pastime for him was drawing, using lead pencils or colored crayons. In this, he was as good as anyone of his age who did not have a disability. The fact was astonishing. Especially notable was his ability to observe things in great detail and then depict them on paper.

It turned out that what he had observed during walks or drives he could reproduce with astonishing accuracy. He was particularly attracted to the Gothic or Baroque windows he had seen in the city, for example. He simply loved these, viewed from different perspectives, whether open or closed. In the course of time, he went on to portraying the trees he encountered in our yard or in the woods around. Fascinated by their trunks, he would sit in front of them for long periods of time, observing their branches, later putting them all carefully on paper. It was particularly touching for those watching him when Peter would stand in front of a tree and then stretch out his arms to embrace it. Did he want to familiarize himself with the bark of the tree in order to gauge its thickness or firmness, or was he was responding to an inspiration in his soul, such as that native to natural peoples, an inspiration to show their affection for "plant life," as it were?

At nine years old, I am telling my brother Peter, who is six,
via the hearing tube how beautiful kangaroos are.

He was a master at depicting the intricate twig and branch forma-
tions at the top of the trees. This orchestration of leaves and branches,
this entwinement of here and there, this coming and going, this up
and down of the tree's growth had made a strong impression on him.
His favorite tree was a beech that had a thick, markedly bent first
branch. It stood in our yard, and Peter, who was an avid tree climber,
often used to go up it.

At nine years of age, my brother had a passion for light and shade.
His interest in these was enormous; one could almost say that he was
under some sort of spell in this regard. For him, the sun was of all
importance. Every day he would observe the movements of light and
shade from his room or while on walks. In this way, he taught himself
about the movement of the sun and, it seemed, became conscious of
the relationship between night and day. If, for example, the sun was

already low on the horizon, Peter would pull at us in a determined manner to persuade us to go home before evening came. When we were in the mountains, he never ever missed watching an impressive sunset.

Although he never owned a wristwatch and wasn't able to tell time, he nevertheless possessed an incredibly precise "inner sense of time." This gift was so reliable that, as an adult, he was able to keep appointments punctually and without needing to be reminded. At the hands of my mother and Rösli, our household help, Peter quickly learned how to make himself useful in domestic matters. He showed himself to be adept at drying the pots and cleaning vegetables. One could also leave him to set the table. Later he discovered what was to become his favorite activity—the laundry. In those days, clothes were washed in a washtub, and he still dedicates himself to the job of hanging and taking in the laundry, as well as to ironing.

Peter and the Parrot

THERE is an episode in Peter's life that I'll never forget. For many weeks a birdcage stood on a low table at home and housed a green parrot. This splendid example of his kind was all too ready to scratch all and sundry. In short, he was particularly aggressive, and for this reason, no one dared place a hand on the bars of his cage. A trespass of this kind resulted in an immediate angry attack. However, the creature behaved quite differently when it came to Peter. With him, the bird was perfectly friendly and trusting. Indeed, a certain fellow feeling—even a kind of love relationship—appeared to develop between them! Whatever it was, the parrot regarded Peter as the only human being in his environment whom he could really consider a friend. Nevertheless, we were all rather concerned about keeping Peter away from the cage. My father once related that Peter had placed the back of his head directly in front of the cage and that the parrot had tenderly caressed it with his beak, a process that Peter thoroughly enjoyed.

One evening we were witness to a moving scene. Peter had been kneeling in front of the cage for a long time. Then he shoved his hand into the cage, and the bird pinched it gently. The more often the parrot pinched his hand, the farther Peter put his hand into the cage. This interplay showed how much the company of this beloved bird delighted him.

Fish in the water and the birds in the air were a pleasure for Peter, too. He knew, of course, that we fed them in the winter. One summer he discovered a large, black-and-gray moth on the floor. He immediately ran to the kitchen to get a few pieces of bread for it and placed the bread in front of it. It was all quite amusing.

As a conclusion to all of this, there is the story of the "owl clock." The eyes of this wooden timepiece used to move back and forth, from left to right, and this would fascinate Peter. Despite being told not to play with this clock, he would do so. The scolding he received for the infraction once gave him an idea. One evening, shortly before going to bed, Peter appeared in his pajamas and sidled over to the clock with a sly smile on his lips, one hand outstretched as though he wanted to pull the fir cone that served as the pendulum. This was a impertinently calculated gesture because he knew all too well that Mother would jump up from her seat on recognizing his intention. This she did as anticipated and so brought the house down in laughter. Because this prank pleased him, Peter never tired of repeating it. It was a pleasure for us all to see that he had developed into a young man who was not above playing tricks on others.

A Life in Homes

MY BROTHER, Peter, has seen the interiors of several homes since his thirteenth year of life. During that time, his state of health has remained stable even though he has suffered from depression and had to stay in a psychiatric unit for twenty-five years.

At first, Peter was accommodated in a home for those who can hear normally but have an intellectual disability. This institution was not far from our home, and here he was lovingly cared for. He spent the weekends and holidays with us, and thus the pain of being apart was somewhat less upsetting. In that home he was thought of as a resident who was easier to care for than others who needed round-the-clock attention. From time to time, Peter in fact proved to be a strong, reliable help to other residents who couldn't walk properly. He had particular success with a pullover that he knitted after he had learned to spin wool. This pullover was exhibited at the home's open house and earned quite a lot of praise.

At twenty-five, Peter entered a home for those who cannot hear and who also suffer from other restrictions. The scope for various activities was appreciably widened here. Both ironing and weaving were his particular province, and he soon began weaving beautiful carpets and was delighted by the work. One of his creations eventually made its way into a first-class restaurant. Along with this, he dedicated himself to little household jobs. In addition, he made good friends during his many walks and stopovers.

For a long time, Peter enjoyed using his field glasses to observe the natural features of the landscape in detail until, that is, he was subjected to another blow of fate. He slowly began going blind. At first, thinking that the lenses of his field glasses had clouded up for some reason, Peter had them cleaned, but when he realized that it was his vision that was steadily deteriorating, he fell into a deep depression. The infinitely long time he was obliged to spend in the psychiatric clinic must have been extremely distressing for him since there he received virtually no personal, loving care. In this unspeakably difficult time, he was also to learn of the death of our father, an event that he was apparently made aware of in some mysterious way and was unable to cope with, which I have already alluded to.

Exactly how my brother dealt with this unhappy period, when there was no hope of an improvement in his situation, I can only vaguely imagine. All I knew was that he was for the most part apathetic and barely approachable, side effects of the high doses of psychotropic drugs he was given. When these were somewhat reduced later on, his general mood brightened, and he could take part in practical activities once more. However, his depression continued to dog him. It was sad for us all to see how his laughter, his jolly breast beating, his rounded "kissing mouth," all of which were signs of his inner happiness from time to time, now seemed to have disappeared altogether. Instead of these, he descended more frequently into fits of fury against the staff looking after him. These were doubtless expressions of desperation against the hopelessness of a situation that was threatening to stifle him and against which he felt forced to rebel. There were even occasions when my brother bloodied his forehead on the walls and doors of the room in his frustration.

In 1991 he was taken to a new home for blind and deaf people, and it was here that he was evidently much happier than he had been in previous homes. He laughed much more often, for example, and bit by bit even came near to regaining his old cheerfulness. The staff there took great care of him, and it wasn't long before he was making himself useful again in the workshop sawing wood, folding brochures, or weaving. There he earned one Swiss franc per day, and this he carefully put away in his wallet. Although my brother had never learned to count, he had nevertheless known the function of money since childhood. He had learned quite early on at the barber's and in cafés to get out his wallet when it came time to pay the bill.

The Death of Our Mother

IN JUNE 2004, as our ninety-four-year-old mother lay on her deathbed, my friends asked me to allow Peter to visit her. Of course, I was only too willing to respond to their request. For my part, I decided to go home and leave him alone with my mother. I learned later that the parting was a very long but peaceful one.

When Peter arrived back at the home, he was overcome with sadness and anger, but on the following day something rather strange occurred, the details of which I received later. While my friends and I were with my mother when she died at half past one in the afternoon, Peter, who at that moment was more than ninety miles away, suddenly burst out laughing. What had moved him to do so? Could it have been a telepathic impulse that he received from my mother's

My beloved Mother at her ninetieth birthday. She supported
my endeavors all my life but also stood up to me. As a result,
she boosted my evolution, my will, and my creativity.

liberated soul at that very instant, a genuine telepathic message?
Today I am quite convinced of the fact.

The sadness Peter felt at the death of our mother would have
been insuperable had it not been for the wonderful gift of intuition
possessed by the nurse who was caring for him at the home. Peter
had a Wedgewood plate that he had placed at our disposal at home
for many years. This was his "treasure," he told us, and the small
plate occupied a special place next to the ashtray and cigarettes
when he came home to visit us on weekends. When he later moved
into a home for those who are deaf and blind, he took this "treasure"
with him. It then became an important element in communication.
For instance, whenever my mother wanted to visit him, this nurse
would show him the small Wedgewood plate as a way of announcing
the forthcoming visit, and Peter would be overjoyed.

In order to help Peter assimilate the idea that his mother had passed away, this particular nurse made use of this plate in another way. She accompanied him to his room, gave him the plate, and demanded that he break it. With a heavy heart, he did so. Then the two of them gently laid the broken pieces in a box. Every day for several weeks they participated in an hour-long ceremony of lighting candles and looking at the broken parts of the plate and various other items he associated with our mother. At these times Peter would cry, I was told, and so it was clear that he realized that his beloved mother would never come to visit him again.

A year later my brother visited our mother's grave at the cemetery in Basel. I was there, too, with a woman friend. The kind nurse at the home was also present and placed the box with the broken pieces and other articles once belonging to Mother on the grave. Peter stroked the gravestone and understood that she had gone. On the journey back to the home, I was told later, Peter was silent—and deeply affected.

Peter and me in a home for Deafblind people in Zürich. Peter has lived there since 1991 and is very well looked after.

TODAY my brother lives a life full of contentment despite the fact that he has to contend with various ailments associated with getting older. He laughs and smiles again, and his good humor is infectious. The broken pieces of the Wedgewood plate are kept safe in a beautiful box. The role once reserved for the announcement of his mother's impending visit is now taken over by a wooden kangaroo, which announces his sister's visit, and whenever the nurse shows him this, he bursts into laughter.

These days, Peter does not regard me so much as a sister but more as a substitute mother, and this not only because I bring him a lot of homemade cakes. When I'm with him, his warm, trembling hand often seeks mine, and it is then that I sense a deep attachment to him—he and I, the last of a family.

20

Aboriginals

WAS it really only the kangaroos that constantly drew me like a magnet to Australia? Were there not people who had been living there for a long time on this huge island at the other end of the world?

These questions, which I had asked myself for some time, were rather unpleasant, if not a trifle embarrassing. I have to admit that I regarded the Aboriginals, the true natives of the continent, with a mixture of shyness and apprehension and never dared to approach them. Secretly, I was always ashamed of myself on this point.

When I was about eleven years old, I gradually became aware of what kind of place my beloved animals came from. It was hot as the tropics of Africa, which I had also learned about at that time. That there were light-skinned people living in Australia was something I also knew. On the other hand, I knew nothing of the language spoken there. In my childlike tendency to simplify everything, I imagined that the people living so far away would speak an appropriately outlandish language. One day I asked my father about this, and he told me that English was spoken there. I was a little taken aback since I had always regarded English as a European language. I declared myself there and then as willing to learn this language one day. So far, so good. At some time or other, I began to consider the question as to whether there were black people in Australia as there were in Africa. The answers I received from my family members on these issues were either evasive or superficial.

One afternoon I recall visiting the Ethnology Museum in Basel, and once there, I pushed my way into the section devoted to Australia. Even the steps to this department were flanked by rows of impressive spears, and I asked my mother whether Australians hunted kangaroos with them. She said yes, although at that time it was not clear to me that she knew extremely little about these matters. She surprised me with a counterquestion: whether I would paint my face and body like the indigenous people. At first I didn't know what she meant until she pointed to the black-and-white photographs on the wall, which depicted these indigenous people. Now it was clear at last that there were dark-skinned people living in Australia. What I also saw did not please me at all. On the contrary. The many, brilliant white lines and points adorning these black bodies, for example, filled me with aversion. A little put off by it all, I said "no" to my mother's inquiry, adding that, as a light-skinned person, bodily adornment of this kind would never please me. But, after all, what did a child of my age know about the cultures and traditions of Australia?

DURING adolescence, I slowly broadened my knowledge about Aboriginal tradition, and every piece of new information was accompanied by a host of daydreams. There was then a period in which I sated my thirst for knowledge by consulting dictionaries about matters Australian whenever I had a chance. In so doing, I discovered pictures and read the histories of a number of different tribes of Aboriginals. The sight of their broad nostrils and prominent, ridged bones over their eyes left a rather shocked impression. What also astonished me was to encounter the occasional blonde or even redhead among them. While looking at these pictures, I was overcome by the conviction that here we had to do with unapproachable, primordial beings that I would never meet. For a long time after this particular visit to the museum, I was dogged by the question of whether these people really belonged to the human species. I began from then on to strictly discriminate between "Aboriginals"[37] and the indigenous peoples of Africa.

A Secret Message from Uluru

WHEN I was about fourteen, I often used to read fairy tales or reports of experiences with animals that contained episodes from Australia. One evening I came across an old book that contained an illustration that, as I looked at it more closely, made my hands shake. The lithograph showed two white hunters in an Australian landscape carrying a pole on their shoulders upon which a kangaroo had been tied by the back legs and forepaws. Its tail dragged along the ground. Although I knew that kangaroos were hunted, this particular picture made me furious. The reason for my wrath was not only that it represented an offense against nature but also that it deeply offended my compassion for an animal I regarded as sacred.[38]

The consequence of this impression was more than one sleepless night. Nevertheless, even when asked why I was apparently in such a bad mood, I said nothing. For a long time after this, I was tortured by the thought that not even in the vastnesses of Australia could kangaroos find refuge. This state of mind peaked in a sad episode that occurred later in a dream:

It is dawn in a desertlike landscape. A gigantic monolith towers skyward from the uniformity of the surroundings. The stone column has the form of a lightly bent kangaroo's back when the animal stoops to place its forepaws on the ground. In the center of the lower half of this monumental pillar is an Eve-like hollow that is strongly reminiscent of an open kangaroo pouch.

37. I was never an advocate of the word "Negro" for the Aboriginal, which was current when I was young. Instead, I tended to use the word "Australian" to indicate the country's dark-skinned inhabitants since my vocabulary was limited at the time.

38. Although, as a teenager, I would never have used a term such as "sacred", I employ it here and associate it with the idea of wholeness or wellness. The word especially encompasses the association of the effects kangaroos have had on me; they have more than once been the means of healing or making me whole.

This picture in my dream had a profound impression on me, and I was from then on firmly convinced that this stone structure was to be found in the very middle of the Australian continent. Imagine my surprise—nay amazement—when, two decades later, I recognized my "dream mountain" in full color in a travel magazine! It turned out to be an illustration of Ayers Rock, the holy mountain of the Aboriginals, which they refer to as Uluru.

A long time after that—in the meantime I had visited Australia six times—I found myself in a dream walking in the countryside:

I walk and walk until there is no more ground under my feet. Then I proceed weightlessly in the air. All around me there is nothing but a bright, turquoise-blue, sprinkled here and there with soft, white clouds of eucalyptus blossoms, whose trees have their roots in nothing. Their stems have the figures of faceless women, though each has a recognizable bosom, waist, and navel! Their outstretched arms are the branches of each tree.

Ayers Rock, called Uluru by the Aborigines. It is a holy mountain located in the center of Australia. I saw it quite clearly and distinctly in a childhood dream.

When I next visited Australia with a small group of tourists, I walked a short way along the foot of Uluru and felt myself transported back to that dream. All around me was a bright turquoise that evoked this effect. But where was I in reality?

I was standing in front of a huge pond. The source of my optical illusion was the reflected light playing on the surface of the water. Then we moved on and to my astonishment discovered the steep, pink-colored rock face of the Uluru mountain outcrop and in it small holes or openings that corresponded exactly to the pouch openings in my dream about the monolith. Was this revelation some kind of extrasensory perception? Had I been subjected to what is called "precognition" or even to the recollection of a reincarnation experience? However, on looking up, I was overwhelmed by a gruesome inkling as to what might be hidden in these cavities. I immediately thought of white stones or what are sometimes called "kangaroo eggs."[39]

BACK home in Switzerland and still under the influence of this experience, I wove two pouches from thick, pink jute yarn, into which I wove irregular black and white stripes. Into each I placed objects made of bright jute thread and wooden balls and then electric light. In this way, I wanted to endow the work with a "sanctified symbol" that was to embody the idea of the coming into being of the kangaroo as a species.

But let us return for a moment to my childhood. Had my soul already been there?

As my desire to read grew, my vocabulary increased, and, to my huge delight, I finally came across illustrations and descriptions of the boomerang even though, at the time, I understood little of the technique of its use. Many years later, a distant relative of mine, who was then living in Sydney, sent a genuine example, and to this day it adorns my doorway. When I look up at it, a creepy feeling comes over me as I ponder the secret forces that invest this hard, old wood.

---

39. I don't know how many people have looked into these crevasses.

I was already quite familiar with the word "Aboriginal."[40] Other, no less mysterious things come to mind such as the magic rituals of the Australian indigenous population, which sent a shudder down my spine. Was it possible that there was some unknown cause for my strong receptiveness to these spiritual Australian "vibrations"?

I was in the plane in 1969 when my mother suddenly announced with a smile that we were now over Australian territory. The information hit me like a stab in the heart, and in the first few seconds after this news, I felt as though I were being "called from below."[41] The feeling was indescribable since, spiritually, it bound me to "those below." At the same time there was a fear accompanying it that perhaps somewhere there was an element of "guilt" about which I knew nothing whatsoever. It seemed to have to do with my devotion to kangaroos, which, as I already knew, were related to Aboriginal totem ceremonies. It seems an odd thing to say, but I was troubled by the question of perhaps having "taken something away" from the Aboriginal people that concerned kangaroos.

Without doubt, something of this reaction can be ascribed to my exaggerated imagination with respect to my wholly new situation. Having said this, it remains a fact that I experienced something odd in these moments. That intrinsic experience, which one could

40. Properly speaking, the term "Aboriginal" is merely an adjective employed as a noun, which, however, because of its negative associations with the word "Aborigine" was used during the course of the brutal and fateful colonization of Australia's indigenous people and was eventually replaced by it. (Female individuals are still referred to as "Aborigines".) At the same time, the term is not without its problems and has been replaced by the correct designation today, which is "Indigenous Australians." I have declined to use this so as not to complicate matters.

41. I first began speaking about the magic, death-inducing practices of Australian shamans relatively recently. The reason for this is that I don't want to spread anxiety, nor do I want to give a negative impression of the Aboriginals.

If, for example, a man disobeys the basic laws of his tribe, the shamans will condemn him to death in some magical way. For this purpose, a bone is "pointed" at him in his absence. At the same time, a chanting takes place, a condemnation that is no way limited by distance, and ultimately brings about the physical death of the transgressor. Just how far this is applicable to whites or those who are not tribal members is a matter of debate. Regardless, I have been told that, in the year 2004, three British tourists were "chanted" in this manner. I was unable to find out what their "crime" in this connection was, but the three people did not meet their death immediately. Only three months after this pronouncement did their boat overturn, and they were devoured by crocodiles.

call a kind of communion or a spiritual affinity, held me in its spell as we began to make preparations to land. Then, despite this, all the pent-up yearnings gained the upper hand and displaced these strange feelings. What a relief it was to go down the gangway and then to tread Australian soil at last and breathe the air of my beloved country!

A few days later, my mother and I went shopping in a suburb of Perth. In one store, my mother pulled at my arm to draw my attention to a couple of Aboriginals. I looked around in order not to stare, but I noticed a shabbily dressed woman with a child. On her broad, strangely furrowed face was an expression of deep dejection. As is the case with many of these uprooted people, it was evident that here, too, alcohol and poverty were her constant companions. This depressing picture remained indelibly engraved on my mind for a long while.

THEREAFTER, during my stay, I occasionally encountered these dark-skinned, despondent beings. My feelings on first seeing them ebbed somewhat, but my inhibitions about seeking contact with Aboriginals were in the main eclipsed by my principal interest in kangaroos. These inhibitions were also an expression of the barrier existing between the "civilized" Western world and an extraordinarily reserved natural people. This reserved attitude is the result of their painful treatment by white people, who robbed them of practically everything they once had. It is a bitter, yet entirely understandable, reaction to British colonialization, under which they suffered constant humiliation and which their descendents were obliged to bear in a state of appalling misery. Although, on the one hand, the fate of the indigenous population deeply disturbed me, on the other I still harbored a certain fear regarding my earlier experience of perhaps being "chanted."

ALTHOUGH I had kept the matter to myself for a long time, it was nevertheless still my wish to come into closer contact with an Aboriginal. There was a possibility perhaps of extending this acquaintance into a normal friendly relationship. Of course, there were also Aboriginals who were oriented to Western ways but nevertheless did not deny their cultural background and who confidently took their place in society, a bearing that was in stark contrast to the general run of widespread depression among them.

Many years after my visit to Uluru, I went to see a well-known Swiss healer in the hope that she could do something to halt my rapidly deteriorating eyesight, but unhappily, she found no remedy. On the other hand, after she had treated my head and body to light hand movements for a couple of hours, she believed that she had found "evidence" that I had once been an Aboriginal chief that had lived in harmony with the people until, for some reason, a rebellion led to the loss of my honorable position.

Since that time I had been banned, she went on. However, before I took leave of my tribe and its village, one of the elders prophesied that I would die at a ripe old age and would, after reincarnation, dedicate my life to the animals that hopped around the countryside, whether this served the interests of research or was for my own personal welfare or pleasure. She had no prior knowledge of my interest in and work with kangaroos. To be honest, these accounts left me a little confused.

At this point, I would like to mention, too, that I was in fact several times taken for an Aboriginal, an error that could no doubt be traced to my untamable curly hair and my brownish complexion.

First Handshakes

ONLY after I had visited Australia ten times did I first come into direct contact with Aboriginals. It took place in an excellent "bush shop" that had an abundance of indigenous products to be admired. Because the interior of the shop was in shadow, I didn't immediately notice that the two obscure figures that offered their hands in greeting behind the counter were Aboriginals. I decided there and then to visit this shop again and that I would view the men in the sunlight, but when I visited the shop a second time they had vanished.

In the meantime, I learned, they had been hired by a tourist organization that offered bush walks.

Then my eleventh Australian trip drew nearer. Again I was accompanied by Ursi. This time it was my firm intention to make contact with Australia's indigenous people. As good luck would have it, I undertook a four-day train trip from Perth to Sydney, and on this journey, my companion got to know an Aboriginal woman, Wolla, and her seven-year-old foster child, John, who were also traveling. In the dining car, we asked politely whether we might sit with them, and they permitted us to do so.

Talk between Ursi and Wolla was quite natural and uncomplicated. Once in Sydney, we arranged to meet each other the next day at the airport since Wolla had planned to fly elsewhere from here. We met each other on time in a room not far from the airport departure gates. Wolla was about fifty years of age, intelligent, open minded, and physically fit. She told us about her trips to Canada, Africa, and other parts of the world she had visited on lecture tours, in which she had talked about the lives of Aboriginals. She took my disability in stride after she had registered the fact that I could communicate with Ursi in a way unknown to her. Shortly after that, I showed her my Lorm glove,[42] which so delighted John that he wanted then and there to tap something onto my hand. He was a good-looking youngster with short, curly hair and dark-brown skin. I learned later that he stemmed from a family of alcoholics. I was pleased to notice that he touched me spontaneously on several occasions.

I can still recall the pleasant, relaxed atmosphere accompanying the conversation between Ursi and Wolla. During their chat I realized that the Aboriginals were in no way different from me. This made it easy for me to overcome my shyness. Ursi communicated Wolla's admiration for me that, in spite of my difficulties, I was able to master all my personal activities with confidence, resolution, and good cheer. This endeared her to me.

---

42. This is a glove that facilitates tactile communication for beginners. The Lorm alphabet, with its corresponding touch points, appears on the inner side. See note 31.

I noticed in passing that Wolla's hair was very similar to mine. Not only was it a mottled gray like my own, but it also had a large spot that was quite white in almost the same place.

A Good Throw

ONE beautiful day we visited an Aboriginal center where there was a lot to see and admire. In addition to dancing, the very old technique of making fire by rotating a piece of wood and the playing of the didgeridoo were demonstrated. For the latter, I was allowed to use my hands to feel the deep, resonant tones these thick wooden pipes produced, an experience that especially pleased me. Later I was informed that one could also use the instrument to imitate the noises made by kangaroos. After that, everyone was invited to throw a boomerang. I knew that to throw this weapon well demanded a certain skill, and, not surprisingly, only a few visitors managed to get the missile to return. Even those were not perfect throws, of course. After lots of waiting my turn came, and I was given the boomerang by a very brown-skinned young man who was heavily painted in colors of red, white, and yellow. He showed me how to stand and how to use my arm to launch it into the air.

Would I be successful? Shouldn't my throw even be perfect so as to be proof of my "tribal identity"? No, that was just silliness. For all that, I wanted my throw to be a more or less correct one, so I concentrated hard on the movement of my arm, then made a wide sweep, and the thing was away in the air. After making a sharp curve, it started on its way back! Now, if that wasn't a sign . . .

Anyway, as acknowledgment of my remarkable performance, I received a fine-looking boomerang as a present. I happily surveyed the young warrior and very gently touched his painted body with my fingertips. He was highly amused at this and laughed, showing his splendid white teeth. His dark eyes lighted up. At that moment, I felt immensely relieved and had now quite forgotten the frightening countenances of those Aboriginals I had seen in old photographs in my childhood.

One could refer to this as my second key insight. From that moment on, it was perfectly clear to me that these natural people were really very peaceful. Every time one of them touched me or took me by the hand, I sensed a feeling of happiness and felt very close to them. In addition, the spiritual, physical, and material misery in which the majority of these people lived had blurred my view of those who resisted this fate.

This second boomerang, which hangs on the wall of my bedroom, is a kind of symbolic handshake that reaffirms my close association with all Aboriginals, with the dark-skinned, the painted, and the poor among them forever.

Toward the end of my visit on this occasion, I went once more to Uluru. After we had recovered from the stress of the long flight, Ursi and I walked to one of the small lookout points, where we had a grand view of the surrounding land. It was a bright, Australian winter evening. Despite my restricted eyesight, I clearly discerned the outlines of the monolith in the distance. One can imagine how surprised I was to discover the similarity between this holy mountain and that in my childhood dream. In fact, it was almost beyond belief.

The bluish anthracite of the colossal rock rose up on the horizon out of the faded gray-green bush, where it blended with the gray-blue of the heavens above. It was a dream picture of quite a different kind, one that only reality was capable of delivering.

21

Eukala

WHEN, in 2006, I set off for Australia, I had an important matter in mind. This time I had firmly decided to get in touch with an Aboriginal. Why? I was determined to learn what my intense concern with kangaroos was all about. I wanted to know definitively why I had felt so drawn to these animals since childhood. Almost as important for me was to understand why I felt so much more at home under the open sky of Australia's countryside than I did in my native Switzerland. Above all, it had been my artistic associations with Australia's earlier inhabitants that had persuaded me to make this decision.

In passing, I had sometimes wondered what would have happened if kangaroos were native, say, to Alaska or the hellish green jungles of the Amazon! Could I, for example, have made up my mind to live for months in an igloo and, stoically ignoring the cold, gone on daylong trips on skis and in snow boots over icy terrain to accompany these creatures on their migrations? Or would I have had the pluck to risk the inferno of South America's tropical rain forests with all their dangers, visible and invisible, in pursuit of my favorite animal? These are questions for which I have no honest answer. Really, they are absurd questions since how is it possible to separate Australia from the kangaroo? Kangaroos are an inseparable part of Australia's natural history. One thing is certain, however: It was kangaroos that drew me again and again to this continent, and it is because of them that this country became the most attractive part of the world for me.

Thanks to the kind mediation of a German friend of mine, Margit, who has lived in Australia for thirty years, I was able to finally have an opportunity to make the acquaintance of an Aboriginal. Margit, who lives in northern Australia, is a trained animal keeper. There

Passion to study tree kangaroos

By Naomi Cescotto

THE Tablelands has played host this past month to an extraordinary self taught expert on the Lumholz tree kangaroo.

Doris Herrmann was born deaf and she is now blind too, but she has never let her personal challenges get in the way of her quest.

Doris saw her first kangaroo as a five-year-old in a zoo in her home country, Switzerland.

She said she had always felt sorry for animals who had to get around on four legs, and she was fascinated to meet a creature who stood proudly on two.

By the time Doris was 11, she knew kangaroos would be a life-long passion.

She kicked off her research with studies in zoology and biology.

Doris has been to Australia a dozen times over the past 40 years to do field observations.

Along the way she has had her research published in university and professional journals and had three books about her experiences with kangaroos published in German.

She has also written and illustrated a children's story *The Laughing Water*, based on an Aboriginal legend.

Doris is now 75, and losing her eyesight 20

years ago put an end to her field studies.

But she still comes back to Australia regularly because she feels at home here, with her beloved kangaroos and the Aboriginal culture.

She said one of her most wonderful experiences had been meeting a local Aboriginal elder through her friend Margit Cianelli, a former zoo keeper from Germany, who now runs Lumholz Lodge outside Atherton.

Margit's B & B is named after the area's Lumholz tree kangaroo.

Dorothy the tree kangaroo charms Atherton's Margit Cianelli and visiting kangaroo expert Doris Herrmann from Switzerland.

Communication experts

BEING both blind and deaf, Doris Herrmann communicates through a professional assistant-translator who travels with her.

They are both experts in a tactile communications technique for deaf-blind people known as "lorming".

While Doris can sign and speak in German, she cannot hear or see to receive information, so her professional lorming assistant uses a manual alphabet spelt out on Doris's hand to let her know what's going on.

It's fast to watch and Doris doesn't miss a beat in her answers.

Her only sadness is that this may be her last trip to a country where she has felt so much joy.

"I feel I have the soul of a kangaroo," Doris said through her translator.

Article about me with my friend Margit Cianelli in the Australian newspaper *Tablelander*, which was published in 2008. Margit keeps a breeding station for tree kangaroos as well as various other kangaroo species.

she lives in a beautiful house in the tropical forest fifteen minutes by car from the nearest township.

Quite a number of animals romp about on her land, all of them brought up by her own hand. Most of them are so-called tree kangaroos and young giant kangaroos. The place is well known in the region and enjoys a good reputation as an animal care station. Because of this, Margit is frequently called upon to take in young animals that have been orphaned when the mother is hit by a car, for example. Her advice on other veterinary questions is also very much valued.

Margit and the Aboriginal woman with whom I was to become acquainted had gotten to know each other years before when they were both involved in saving a seriously injured flying fox that had become entangled in barbed wire. Eukala,[43] the Aboriginal, had contacted Margit, who suggested covering the animal with a blanket and waiting for her to arrive. However, by the time she got there, the animal had died.

For Eukala, this accident was a shocking experience since the flying fox was her totem and for that reason sacrosanct. She felt responsible for the creature's death. In tears, she told her friends about the tragedy and asked for comfort. From this moment on, the two women often met and later became friends.

My meeting with Eukala had been arranged months before my arrival. In addition, I had talked with friends at length about what kind of questions I should ask her. A few of these are listed here:

— Is there an explanation for my great affection for kangaroos?
— What significance does the kangaroo have for the Aboriginals?
— Are there people among the Aboriginals with a penchant similar to mine?
— What differentiates a kangaroo from other animals?
— What role does this animal play in the myths of the original inhabitants?

---

43. "Eukala" is a pseudonym. The real name is known only to me and has been changed at the express wish of the person concerned.

— Is it possible for the human soul to transmigrate into that of an animal and vice versa?

— For an Aboriginal, what does it mean when a human being constantly dreams of kangaroos?

— What would an Aboriginal say to my wish to die in Australia and be buried there?

— Last but not least, could it be that I was once one of them?

This was not to be a matter of simple question and answer. Not at all. Furthermore, I didn't ask all of the questions, nor did I receive an answer to every single question. However, what did happen was deeply impressive—not only for me.

The Great Day

AS THE day of our meeting drew nearer, my excitement grew. What kind of a person would I encounter? Would the answers to my pressing questions bring clarity at last?

I was told that Eukala would come in her own car, and while I waited, Margit put me through a crash course on how to behave correctly in the presence of Aboriginals. The most important rule, I was informed, was to regard the other as a guest and to accord the person the appropriate respect. In addition, it was necessary to wait patiently for an answer and under no circumstances show impatience. Nor should I take it personally if Eukala felt a need to move around during our conversation since this served to make telepathic contact with her people. In this way, I was told, Eukala could ask for assistance from other Aboriginals living in the remotest parts of the country. She needed no technical apparatus for this kind of communication. This telepathic contact was usually facilitated in the sitting position, but if problems arose in communication, walking about made reception easier. Margit's explanation didn't come as a great surprise as I had read similar accounts elsewhere.

These were unusual days. The nearer our meeting came, the more my feelings vibrated on unfamiliar wavelengths. It was as though I was being—how shall I put it?—"chanted." Perhaps these strange vibrations issued from Uluru? That's not to say, however, that I would be condemned to death but rather that this was a beautiful way of opening up the means of bringing about inner healing. These feelings of mine were tuned to the practical issue of my reduced ability to see clearly. I secretly hoped that this anticipated meeting would somehow be an opportunity to normalize my sight, which had much deteriorated recently. However, I can say now that this hope was in vain. My impaired vision remained.

At the same time that my feelings became more intense in this way, my imagination began playing tricks on me. I began to imagine that Eukala lived in the outback where no white person had ever trespassed in circumstances that prevailed at the time of Captain Cook. Later, on a tour by car through the countryside, Margit had put me right on this point by showing me the flat-roofed house in which Eukala and her family lived. "She possesses not only a car but also certainly has a telephone and a computer," I said to myself. So much for my last ideas of Eukala's personality, an odd portrait concocted from a mixture of Western civilization and spirituality born of shamanic lore.

Then, at last, the day of our meeting arrived! It was to be at 11 o'clock. Although the sun shone, the day was not yet hot. I was given a signal that the car was approaching. I waited on the terrace of Margit's house, my heart thumping with anticipation. Margit then appeared with Eukala. She proved to be a chubby woman of about fifty years of age. She was a little smaller than me and was of darkish complexion and wore a pink dress. She came toward me with outstretched arms. It was an unforgettable moment; this woman greeted me with such motherly affection as though I were a long-lost child just returned home! We embraced each other affectionately and stroked each other's shoulders. At this moment, a feeling of deliverance overwhelmed me as though I had labored under an indefinable pressure for decades. I believe that this was certainly the result of Eukala's heartfelt warmth. It was wonderful to touch this woman. Added to this, within the first few seconds we already seemed to be familiars.

Leisurely, we made our way through the yard to seats at a table under the trees of the rain forest. The sky was a little cloudy, and a wind had stirred. A few songbirds and parrots had joined us as though to give us company. All three of us were in the best of moods. Margit, her household help, Sandra, and Ursi, my companion, sat down with us. Eukala had quickly realized my disabilities and made no attempt at superficial sympathy. This, too, did me good. Soon I would be able to ask my questions, and in a way I felt a little as though I were at the doctor's. What "diagnosis" would Eukala make? What would she say about my relationship with kangaroos? However, a second or two later I realized that this was not a fitting comparison and immediately dismissed it.

How surprised and touched I was to learn from Ursi that Eukala was crying. I hadn't been aware of this on account of my bad eyesight. What emotions had overcome Eukala? Apparently, there was a mutual feeling of deep understanding between us; Eukala wept on several occasions during our conversation.

Apropos of this, I quote from a record of what was said on this occasion and later written down by Ursi and Margit: "Eukala several times confirmed that she felt that there was a very strong link between her and Doris. It was for this reason that she often had to cry, so strong were the emotions aroused by this relationship."

Despite our deep feelings, Eukala and I slowly found it possible to carry on a natural conversation. During it, I realized that, from the very beginning, Eukala regarded me as one of her people. Did this conviction have anything to do with my looks? Eukala sought confirmation from those present as to who my parents were. Were they not white Europeans?

Ursi's and Margit's notes have this to say:

Eukala: "Is Doris sure that her parents are in fact her real parents?" Eukala seems to think that Doris's forebears must have been Aboriginals. From the text and when Eukala looks at Doris, she is convinced that, from her feelings, her thoughts, and her outward appearance, she cannot possibly originate from Germany or Switzerland.

Eukala: "I know it; I can feel it. Of course, I believe her when she
maintains that, way back, she stems from Germany, but I have an inexplicable feeling that she is from here. I feel quite certain about this
from the way she describes things and by the questions she asks. . . .
Her books, too, speak quite clearly—the footprints on the dust jacket
of the third book. . . . If, in fact, Doris's ancestors were Aboriginals,
then they must have lived within the last two hundred years—that is
since Captain Cook.

While the others engaged in further conversation, I detached my
thoughts from their concerns and inwardly reflected on the thoughts
and feelings that Eukala had so unexpectedly planted in my heart:
Could it really be true that I was once a member of Australia's
ancient people? I felt all stirred up inside. Where was the basis for
my self-conception, the real basis of my feelings on which I could
build? It wasn't easy in this confusing situation to think clearly. Not
that I had a great desire to assess Eukala's opinion as either right or
wrong. The overpowering emotions accompanying our meeting were
just too unambiguous to doubt. There was a spiritual link between
us that was both strange and inexplicable. Eukala seemed neither
to see the kangaroo researcher nor the artist in me but evidently the
human being in which both were equally at home.

As I could not come to any conclusions in these moments, I
turned to the conversation again and learned from a perfectly relaxed
Eukala that I was once an elder, that is, a wise old woman among the
Aboriginals. This she maintained with great conviction.

Eukala said, "Doris has come home. I feel that she's my elder.
Because she's older, because she has gray hair and has a long journey
behind her, she's an elder, and elders are called 'Auntie' or 'Uncle'
here. I find it difficult just to call her 'Doris'; she's now too near. It
is our 'Auntie Doris' and has nothing to do with blood relationship.
I'll call her Auntie from now on."

But didn't an elder possess knowledge of nature and spiritual
matters allied to great responsibility for the good of the people? And
was this not the reason for an elder's high standing? What did I,
Doris Herrmann, have of all these attributes that might recommend

me for such a position? How could I assert that I had looked after the interests of the Aboriginals in any way? Rather, I had not been greatly persuaded to seek their company and up to now had behaved somewhat circumspectly. Without wanting to be awarded the personal honor of becoming an elder, there was something in this that I found alienating. Yet there was something in it, too, that was worth pondering. But I will not yet say what it was.

I told Eukala about my childhood and recounted how I found two colors especially attractive, colors that created almost a new world for me: salmon pink and ivory. I added that I was more than astonished later to discover that these colors were those of the bark paintings of the Aboriginals. Eukala was not at all surprised at this.

I talked about my relationship to the kangaroo, starting at three and becoming intense at the age of eleven. At five, I made a drawing that included colors that I later found in a rock cave—the exact same colors.

Eukala said, "I'm not surprised about this. These particular colors are important to us. Our artists express themselves through these colors. Doris is one of us. She knows the colors; she has the colors in her. Doris, you didn't choose the colors. The colors chose you. They came to you." There was a pause. In the yard under the tropical trees, the atmosphere at that moment was gentle yet moving. A light wind stirred the trees. One or two large, dry eucalyptus seed capsules fell onto the table. High above us sat Geoffrey, the tame tree kangaroo, looking down at us curiously.

Then came the important question as to my love and passion for kangaroos, and imagine how surprised I was to learn from Eukala's simple response that it was the kangaroos that had chosen me, not the other way around! For Eukala it was a matter to be taken for granted that the kangaroos had chosen me and not the reverse. And in my case it's the gray kangaroo.

It quite naturally occurred to me then that, on my early visits to the Basel Zoo and later at Pebbly Beach, I had experienced how Dora, Jacqueline, and other kangaroos were more than eager to play with me. But Eukala's remarks were not meant in this way. Her

A lucky moment with my beloved kangaroos
during my third trip to Australia in 1978.

perspective was much larger and more all inclusive. She meant that my whole life was oriented to a specific direction by this calling.

I reeled back my memory, arrived at my early childhood, and recalled detesting four-legged animals like dogs, cats, and bears while feeling more drawn to mysterious "two-legged" phantoms. These had a greater influence on me long before I was to see a kangaroo standing upright at the zoo. Could I be fooling myself?

Then I turned my attention again to what was being said and explained to Eukala how acutely I sensed the human element in the kangaroo and how, on the other hand, I often felt myself to be a kangaroo. I went on to say that I often dreamed of talking to them in my own way and that I could read their lips and that they then would transform themselves into friendly fellow human beings.

Eukala said, "Human beings have animal souls, and animals have human souls—there's no difference. All is one." Eukala's reply, here recorded in an abbreviated form, was simple and yet over-whelming in its simplicity. It suggested that all of us, human beings, kangaroos, and all other animals right down to the gnat form one all-inclusive society, a definition that also includes rainbows, plants, and stones.

Eukala's belief is that Mother Earth encompasses everything. There are no exceptions; everything belongs to everything else, and nothing can be separated or excluded. Every thing fits in with every other thing. In this way, Eukala closed this "first chapter," as it were. At first I had difficulty with the conception that the gnat had its rightful place in this commonwealth. I recalled how some of their order had greatly annoyed and even stung me painfully, but joking aside, these, too, were a part of nature's creation of flesh and blood—even when some of the blood belonged to me!

It was an all-embracing concept and, although, at first, perhaps difficult to digest, was nevertheless plausible. After all, I had learned from early childhood to respect and appreciate nature as a whole. The fact that Eukala had gone further and included everything—even stones and rainbows—was unfamiliar but not an obstacle. I had often sensed the mysterious power emanating from stones and the elation that rainbows are capable of producing in us. After all, these are aspects of a force that permeates the universe.

Then the conversation turned to kangaroos as totem and gen-erally to the theme of totem animals. Eukala said, "Clearly, the kangaroo has huge significance in Doris's life. The kangaroos, though, don't stand higher than other animals, trees, leaves, or anything else. The significance here is that the kangaroo is Doris's totem. The spiritual relationship to our own totem can't be sev-ered. [In the past, quite a lot of people wanted to put a stop to Doris's interest in kangaroos. Personal remark made by those tak-ing notes.] To do this would be to cut her vital nerve, so people have to accept this." Eukala added that the Aboriginals establish a child's "nature name" as soon as it is born. (The baby's name will then be accorded a corresponding totem.) Margit and Ursi then noted the following:

— Language name: Among the Aboriginals, a child is immediately given an appropriate nature name at birth, and this
will be its totem (e.g., kookaburra, waterfall, rainbow, frog,
pademelon[44]).
— The totem (e.g., the kangaroo, in Doris's case) is the brother
or sister of this person and must be protected and respected.
A totem is something individual to each person; everyone has a
totem.

I was both glad and relieved to hear Eukala's explanation since
there was something familiar about it. Perhaps this was why I had
failed to relate more about my own totem or my experiences with
it. That was a pity because I would have liked to know what she
thought about it. As for my feelings on this matter, these were not
different from Eukala's. For me, too, kangaroos were brothers and
sisters. Moreover, like Eukala, it was an honor for me to regard
these animals as my brothers and sisters, and the idea filled me
with pride. So it was that Eukala had given precise expression to
my feelings when she said that a totem was to be respected and
protected.

Those who injure their totem—even by accident—or kill it
or even eat it will have to take the spiritual consequences of such
actions. These could result in severe depression. The very idea
that I myself could cause harm to a kangaroo soul had always been
my concern and persuaded me to take precautionary measures. An
example of this is that whenever I go into an Australian restaurant
or, for that matter, a Swiss restaurant or indeed any restaurant in
Europe, I always content myself with a salad or a fish dish. I do this
in order to prevent myself from being sick since kangaroo meat is
frequently on the menu. Those people who are with me know of my
objections in this respect and are nice enough to refrain from eating
kangaroo meat themselves.

In order to add weight to her words, Eukala repeated something
that we might call her creed. For the Aboriginal, she said, the earth

44. Pademelons are a type of wallaby (dwarf kangaroos).

is like a mother who embraces all things. All is one, and each thing belongs to the others. Nothing can separate this affinity without causing harm. Nothing must be excluded; everything complements everything else in the world and fits together as in an orchestra. She also said, "Relationships to our ancestors are not simply to be understood with the mind or intellect but also with the heart and soul. Doris has this relationship and realizes it through her association with kangaroos." I told Eukala that in fact I have a special relationship with kangaroos, and I elaborated by recounting my experiences with Dora, Jacqueline, and other animals.

It seemed as though our conversation had now passed its high point, and again there was silence for a while. The three books I had written lay open on the table. Margit pushed them over to Eukala, who, on looking at the third one showed much enthusiasm. On the dust jacket of this one she recognized the footprints she was familiar with (what was meant was the jacket design, which had employed many colorful spots in the manner of Aboriginal artistic portrayal).

Eukala said the following:

It's easy to see that she's a senior. Her first book describes her longing to know where she came from, and I can see that well. She isn't someone hailing from Switzerland. It makes me sad. She had spent so many years trying to discover her identity. No one showed the way. She spent so many decades finding her place, and she belongs to her home, and that home is here. This is not to speak of reincarnation. Such an idea has no place in our culture. Our forefathers live through us, and we are a part of our forefathers. That's how it's always been. It will never stop.

There is no rebirth in the culture of the Aboriginals; there's only original existence from the very beginning through our forebears in dreams and because they are true to their geographical location and follow in the footsteps of their ancestors and thus acquire their forebears' energy and wisdom.

Each night that passes, our ancestors appear to us in dreams and give us strength, power, spirit, and wisdom on our way.

SUDDENLY Eukala looked at my hair and asked whether she might touch it. I was glad to consent. She pulled at it lightly and remarked that it was as soft as her own . . .

My irritation of a few minutes earlier had not gone unnoticed, and she therefore sought to comfort me. It must have been clear to her that some of her answers to my questions had deeply affected me but had also made me feel insecure. She tried to cheer me up a little. I should not be so concerned about my origins, she said. The most important thing was my relationship with her and her people, with kangaroos and Australia's vast countryside as a whole. Above all, she added with a gentle, happy smile, I shouldn't lose my merry laugh!

Eukala said the following:

Doris has to know that I want to tell her that everything is all right; she needn't worry. There are no more unsolved problems because she has come home. I feel this very strongly. Everything is all right. And everything that you feel now is normal. That's as it should be. That's how we feel things. All of us feel the same way. Aboriginals feel that way, and that's who we are, and that's who she is. Doris is an auntie for me.

We all breathe the same air; we drink the same water. We all do the same things. Human beings are not superior beings; everything is equal to everything else, and everything is part of the whole—one unit, the parts of which belong together. Nothing is better or worse; let there be no discrimination.

I felt that she understood me.

After about two hours, words ebbed. We stood up from our seats, and I stood opposite Eukala for a few moments without a word. We smiled at each other while my glance remained for eternal seconds on her face. I thanked her for this confidential encounter, and we embraced each other most affectionately, stroking each other's backs and shoulders.

Eukala urged me to regard what had been said as her personal viewpoint. Basically, she had followed her grandmother's teaching in her thoughts and in her understanding. "All will be well! Welcome home!" she said.

A few days later Eukala telephoned, asked how I was feeling, and left the following message: "I don't want Doris to worry about her ancestors. I mentioned ancestors because this is the connection to the real issue. Please tell Doris: Live in the now! Now is important, not the past. Doris has a very special gift. She has been given a talent that enables her to communicate with kangaroos and to feel at one with them. It's a gift of the spirit, and not many people have it. A big hug's coming through the phone to you all!"

The days that followed our meeting were full and allowed me little time to mull over the things Eukala had said to me. Yet in a way her statements were still clear in my mind. The fact that she had regarded me as an elder was at first strange, but, bit by bit and with the encouragement of my friends and acquaintances, I slowly got used to the idea.

Of course, I could not be regarded as one responsible for the traditional affairs of the Aboriginals or as someone versed in the solutions to their spiritual questions. Not at all. On the other hand, if one considers the idea of responsibility from the point of view of someone taking an active interest in Australia's crucial affairs from childhood on (if at first passively) and also someone who was enthusiastically committed to them, then the word "responsible" is an apt one. Perhaps one could say that, in my own special way, I *was* an elder.

For example, as a foreigner from faraway Switzerland, I had committed myself to matters such as the protection of Australia's natural environment and its species, with special emphasis on kangaroos, of course, all of which could be regarded as elderlike engagement. Above all, the energy with which I applied myself to these projects and that released in me by these very activities was something I often marveled at.

Where did this energy come from? Was it a sign that I was being "led" and "sheltered" in some remarkable way? Possibly it came from far away, perhaps even the other side of the earth. Was a sincere commitment such as mine at all conceivable without a corresponding sense of vocation? What's more, if I felt very insecure in the presence of Australia's original inhabitants, a feeling of insecurity that even bordered on shame, was this not perhaps the expression of an unacknowledged human kinship? Did not the overpowering childlike impressions I sensed in Australia from time to time when encountering not only eucalyptus woods, kangaroos, possums, and all marsupials but also emus, parrots and other birds, the rocks, and the entire vegetation of the country, which I felt belonged all and only to me, all prove that this place was indeed my home and that secretly I actually knew about the unity of everything?

Dream

MONTHS afterward, when I had long since returned to Switzerland, I had an extraordinary dream:

I live alone in my parent's house in Riehen. My parents are dead. To my surprise and delight, Eukala appears one day in the company of three elderly, gray-haired women. They are light skinned and have wrinkled faces. They have come to visit me and want to spend the night at my house. There is no means of communicating between the elderly women and me, either by word or gesture. Even communication with Eukala is impossible, either by speech or by using the touch alphabet. No, our communication is much more a "speaking sense of feeling." As an unpleasant sensation overcomes me, Eukala notices at once and returns my feelings to a condition of pleasant relaxation by lovingly holding my hands in hers and by massaging them. As soon as I feel the warmth of her hands in mine, I am happy.

Then the parting. My visitors will return to Australia, but I have to leave first, as I have an urgent appointment in the city. It proves to be a silent farewell. Eukala and the women show their understanding of the fact that I have to be off first. I take my white stick—and hop down the garden steps with alacrity. The four women accompany me to the garden gate. A great sense of mutual agreement hangs in the air; it is only the last few moments that are full of sadness and pain.

22

The All-
Embracing Unity

THERE was a phase in my life in which a number of everyday influences did not leave me in peace, let alone allow me to reflect deeply on anything. Above all, this was the kind of time pressure to which I was subjected in my professional life. I found it insufferable. In addition, political events were always clamoring for my personal views on matters. Naturally, family matters also affected me, yet despite all these upsets of one kind or another, the kangaroo never left my heart; its image never faded, not for a moment!

I remember once on the Day of Atonement (Yom Kippur) reading something in the prayer book at the synagogue. A long list of sins was registered there, and yet the meaning of one sin was lost on me. This was the so-called sinning of the heart.[45] I asked my mother for an explanation. With a wink she replied, "That's when you give too much of your attention to kangaroos!" At that moment I felt truly embarrassed and ashamed of myself, but my dear mother had not meant her remark to go home so deeply.

Nevertheless, I took her comment to heart, and every year I felt a certain discomfort on that particular day and would feel disquieted when we came to this point in the prayer book and its "sinning in

45. The actual text reads as follows: "The sin that we have committed through sinning of the heart."

one's heart." The covert accusation in my mother's remark about "idolizing" kangaroos stuck in my mind, although even at that time I sensed that it wasn't justified.

To be sure, some of my friends and acquaintances regard my affection for kangaroos as a bit exaggerated, perhaps even a little odd. My attitude toward kangaroos has indeed always been emotionally colored and has at times certainly assumed the characteristics of a blissful adoration. However, this is not so very different from the admiration of outstanding personalities, works of art, or other things that people greatly appreciate. And, apart from that, I was ever aware of my affection for both animals and people. The most important thing in all this is that my special empathy has never impaired my attitude toward the Creator.

My "Natural Religion"

ONCE, as a child, I was walking in the woods near Riehen with my mother and my brother. In a clearing, my mother showed me two hanging branches next to each other, where something rather odd was happening: They were swinging to and fro, that is, to each other and away from each other as if in conversation, nodding in agreement at this and that, almost as if in a quaint dance, a "leaf minuet," one might say, and all of this when there was apparently no wind blowing! Exactly why they were "dancing" in this manner was not clear. I don't know why, but the sight of this sent shivers down my spine.

The movement of the branches may have made me a little uneasy. That a part of nature that I had always regarded up to that point as "alive" only to a degree had now suddenly taken on life of its own accord. It was not until years later that it became clear to me to what extent life pulses mysteriously through plant life. Realizing this, I could no longer think of plants as "dead" material. I have come to learn in the meantime what many-sided, finely adjusted, varied forces are at work in plant organisms in keeping them alive and healthy. A whole library of books has been written about the mysterious inner life of plants, and some of them even talk of a "plant soul," a term I find rather revealing.

As plants demonstrate, the secret processes that go on in organic material suggest the presence of a Creator, and it's for this reason that I don't just leave my observations at a superficial level but press to know more about that which is hidden. Especially in the smallest particles—for us generally of the least interest—do we find the greatest power. This has been proven in the splitting of the atom and in the atrocious results of dropping a nuclear bomb on Japan.

What's more, even the stones at our feet are not "just dead matter." The fact that ores "grow" was known even to our ancestors. Today we know that crystals "grow" as well, and we use them as synthetically cultivated objects for integrated components in electronic memories. In the Middle Ages people knew very well that precious and semiprecious stones possessed healing attributes that one could make use of, and when I think of Japanese culture and the almost sacred role that stones play in it, one can almost speak of a "stone consciousness." Unfortunately, I know much too little about this Far Eastern culture.

My ideas of religion have changed greatly during the course of my life. I have realized that they are much more in line with nature than the Jewish religion acknowledges—at least as far as I can determine. My many and varied experiences in nature have taught me to realize and accept that the forces at work there are those of a universal Creator, or at least they are a reflection of this. During these experiences I have also come to see how idiotic and illusory it was (and is) to represent Western civilization as superior in many ways to that of natural peoples. It doesn't take much thought to realize how removed Western people are from their roots and so much more in need both of a home for the mind and of spiritual stability and identity than are so-called primitive peoples. This lack of a spiritual bond in Western societies is plain to see for anyone who has watched the systematic destruction of nature that has taken place in the last century.

It is just as reprehensible and inappropriate to unthinkingly assume that the generations of people who have preceded us were per se less informed than those in our present one. Unfortunately, this assumption is still very much in vogue. The pride inherent in this disdain for everything in the past and for things that stem from different cultures is both stupid and revolting. Our current "civilization" has perpetrated not only the most stupendous wars but also the uniquely arrogant view that we are cleverer than the whole of humankind at any prior point in history.

THANKS to traditions handed down from generation to generation and to their intimate closeness to nature, indigenous peoples have very often been able to sense the imminence of a catastrophe and seek refuge before it struck. This is all the more so with animals. Their instincts tell them often days before that something is in the air and that they must flee.

I myself have had an opportunity to witness such a thing, although the cause was not dramatic. It concerned an almost mature, male tree kangaroo that had been brought up by my friend Margit and that actually shared her bedroom. It slept there on a high, broad windowsill. One night the animal became very restless. Noticing this, Margit sent it outside. A few hours later, the house was hit by a violent tornado!

My thoughts and experiences have taught me that God is to be found in nature—in trees, clouds, stones, rivers, mountains, plants, and in all living creatures. For me, God lives in them all. Nature as a whole is a reflection of God's activity. It is the immediate presence of another, higher being that fills me with awe and makes my heart beat faster. I refer to my belief as a "natural religion" without the need to regiment my feelings into some system or press them into some kind of religious armor. And why shouldn't I acknowledge this when it is true? A good part of my spiritual being is filled by kangaroos since I have them to thank for giving my soul so much. When I was troubled or sad, they often healed me, and in this sense I see them as "holy." When I see them and stroke them, it is like a refreshing bath for me, something that relaxes me and gives me new strength. These animals delight me, and, as with every delight, one feels quickened and invigorated.

The Cosmic Essence

MY SPIRITUALITY has been constantly deepened as the result of cultural contact with people of the most varied religions, as well as with atheists. I can still remember well how I held impassioned talks on philosophy with Julia, an atheist kangaroo researcher, on Rotamah Island. For the most part we carried on passionate philosophical conversations in English[46] for hours at a time, so that they simply flew by, even making us forget our kangaroo studies for a while. Julia told me that she was disappointed in her church and felt that she had been left in the lurch by her own confession; as a result, she had turned to other forms of faith. She had carried on searching until she finally found what she called her "nature religion." Openly and symbolically, she demonstrated her allegiance to this belief by not marrying in a church but in the middle of the bush, surrounded by friends and relatives. The fact that the bride and groom did not decline to wear a wedding dress and formal jacket, respectively, and that an uncle of Julia's officiated at the ceremony (incongruously standing in for a priest on this occasion) gave the whole affair a rather bizarre touch.

The subject of spirituality was deepened as we walked the miles of Rotamah Island's wooded shoreline. On one occasion, Julia asked how it was possible to pass on one's spirit to another human being. This is a question of education, she said, answering her own query. She wanted, she said, to bestow her spirit on the child she one day intended to have. She told me that in the mind itself lay the real link with nature and in my case above all was represented by kangaroos. What she said to me was, I must admit, here and there a little strange, but we shared many other conclusions, concepts, and wishes. One of these was that, in the long run, humankind must one day make peace with nature.

As I grew older, my spiritual concepts took a direction in which heavenly beings and the distinction between heaven and hell after

---

46. At that time I could still see well enough to lipread. It was only now and again that I needed Julia to write out an unfamiliar English expression for me.

life have no validity. My interest was centered on finding my real self. What were the basic principles, and where was this "I" before it appeared in the world? Was there any trace of my "I," some kind of evidence of my soul before the first living things began to populate the earth? Was my "I" there at that time as a single-celled creature and later as a small worm and so on? Could it move, consciously or unconsciously, eat and void and eat again over an infinite length of time? Was there such a thing as "nothing," and if so, would my soul return to it after death?

Anyone who has pondered such fundamental questions knows that the answers are rare—if, indeed, there are any answers at all. At the same time, it is important for me to contemplate them because in this way I remain alert to everything that happens in daily life, boring though it unfortunately sometimes is. The most delightful thing would be to have absolute assurance on these matters one day! But it is not in our power to gain certainty by ourselves. Sometimes, when I ask myself where there is a beginning and an end to everything, I'm afflicted by the thought that we cannot do anything else than think in terms of beginnings and ends. Perhaps we are forced to think this way because our lives are bounded by birth and death. Even if the soul is immortal, our lives are limited. A life that would go on boundlessly without a beginning or an end would in all likelihood be too much for our imagination.

Once I had a strange, yet wonderful, dream. I was a light-filled gene, something akin to a "light seed," drifting about in a myriad of other illuminated particles somewhere in space. Were these the souls or "soul nuclei" from which countless millions of human beings and animals would one day develop?[47]

47. One can perhaps imagine how astonished I was when I learned recently that this dream has a remarkable resemblance to the concept entertained by the Greek philosopher Heraclides Ponticus, one of Plato's disciples. I quote what was said to me: "He [the philosopher] maintains that souls populate the Milky Way before they 'sexually' enter human existence. He describes them as illuminated, fine ethereal essences." Evidently I touched upon an area of preknowledge in my dream.

A Siesta for My Soul

ONE afternoon at Pebbly Beach, I look all around me, and everywhere are beautiful green meadows in which kangaroos are standing, resting, or grazing. At one or two places, small, pink-flowered plants are growing, but the kangaroos avoid these as inedible. Clumps of eucalyptus trees, acacias, and banksias appear all over the place. At the upper edge of the sloping meadow is a row of trees with slender trunks with branches that stretch upward, and in one of these a pair of magpies has made a nest. A kangaroo with a starling on its back, perching there like a small monarch, hops leisurely by. A second starling flies overhead, and a quarrel about place breaks out. They argue on the back of the kangaroo, who, quite unperturbed, takes not the slightest notice. The air is filled with bewitching, refreshing odors issuing from the trees, the bushes, and, above all, the bark, the leaves, and the yellow and white blossoms of the eucalyptus trees. They are enhanced by the wonderful, natural, delicate scent of the kangaroos. I am perfectly happy and fulfilled. I feel a smile creeping over my face.

Time passes without my noticing. It is already late afternoon. One after another, the kangaroos get up slowly and move down toward the beach meadow. I carry on with my observations in great spirits, and soon the sun begins to sink behind the bush hills. I stand at the seashore and look out thoughtfully at the surging sea. The sky is a pale, azure blue, punctuated here and there with a few strands of cloud. A strong wind whips up foamy waves. The crashing of the breakers remains silent for me, and yet I can feel the never-ending coming and going, while the charging water circulates deep in my soul. A tingling sensation runs over my body, and my heart beats wildly. Somehow I have the feeling that my soul is leaving me for a short while and lingering above in the air, where, for a moment, it joins the souls of the kangaroos, which are also hovering over the restless sea.

Acknowledgments

MANY good friends and acquaintances have accompanied me on my literary path, helping me in the most varied ways by encouraging, inspiring, and correcting me or directing my thoughts in this or that direction with curiosity, interest, and affection, standing, so to speak, around the "cradle" of my latest creation as it greets the world in hopeful anticipation.

The first attempts at this creation were accompanied by the loving perseverance of Bettina's aunt, Dagmar Wüst, who brought the very first manuscript into an acceptable form, but, unfortunately, our "baby" was not accepted by the publishing world. However, Dagmar's efforts were not in vain. She was able to lay down the necessary foundations for Volker Jäger. It was with him that I once again prepared my autobiographical elements against the background of my experiences with kangaroos. Apart from this, he, like a therapist, helped me come to grips with my experiences so as to become more conscious of them and thus to be able to lend them more emphasis, thereby giving them a new focus.

I wish to acknowledge the help of Maya Bräm, with whom I consolidated my field studies of wild kangaroos into one book.

With Michael Gaida I was able to process my twenty-three-year correspondence with Christel Jacobi, my friend in the former GDR. That became my third book. In his capacity as coauthor of this, my fourth book, and with his innumerable questions, he managed to virtually squeeze me like a lemon for information!

Jeannine Lehmann, who has been my loving, caring guide in all my book projects and for whom I'm sure I was not always the easiest partner, somehow managed to magically transform a "headstrong swain" into a gentle, fine-feeling "kangaroo lover."

My career as a kangaroo researcher has been kindly and sympathetically furthered by a number of people, some of who are now deceased. In this, my first guide and mentor was Dr. Robert F. Schloeth, zoologist and one-time director of the Swiss National Park in Graubünden. During my short stay at an animal reserve in the Camargue (south of France), where I was privileged to observe the bulls there on horseback, a horsefly stung my leg. Afraid of falling from my great height, I did not bend down to brush away the insect; I was later to learn to deal with all sorts of pitfalls that Robert warned me were awaiting me in Australia.

Professor Heini Hediger assessed my first scientific work on pouch cleaning. It was he that made me into a kangaroo researcher overnight, so to speak. The fact that he once offered me salt for my fruit muesli at breakfast time I took as the gesture of a friendly colleague.

Something similar is true of the occasion of enjoying vegetable soup together with the director of the Zoological Garden in Basel, Professor Ernst Lang, with whom I also enjoyed many an intellectual exchange on topics of mutual interest.

I wish to acknowledge Professor Geoffrey Sharman, a well-known researcher who works at his kangaroo center in Canberra. He once reported that, on a trip to Europe, one of his friends lit a eucalyptus leaf and inadvertently singed Sharman's beard. On that occasion, the friend spoke of "the wonderful Australian air in Europe." It was as if I smelled it, too.

In addition, I would like to thank Professor Adolf Portmann of the Zoological Institute, Basel, who introduced me to Dr. Vreni Germann-Meyer, who was at the time a student zoologist. I studied with Vreni at the Basel Zoo, and she became my "kangaroo friend." I am grateful as well to Dr. Hans Wackernagel, zoologist and curator of the mammal department at the Basel Zoo, who helped me with his encouraging words before TV appearances and also by promoting my work at book displays by announcing that "Doris Herrmann and her kangaroos are a shining example to us all."

I am also indebted to Pebbly Beach and in particular to Uschka Schwallbach, whose image as an old woman from tsarist Russia I retain and who was the "good spirit" of that settlement and indeed brought it to life. Her activities run through many unforgettable moments in my dreams.

Dr. Roman Mykytowycz, former director of the Institute for Animal Wildlife Research at Canberra, and his son, Marc, must not be forgotten. The two of them often caught wonderful fish for breakfast and even tried to teach me how to fish, a kind but futile endeavor because of my lack of talent. I will always remember them.

I remember, too, the many happy hours spent with Margit Cianelli from Atherton/Tableland, in Queensland, and the tree kangaroos she brought up herself. It was a pleasure to watch these climb the curtains or devour spaghetti in the kitchen!

Last but not least, I would like to thank those kind people who accompanied me on my trips to Australia:

— Dr. Bettina Becker, veterinary surgeon, who took me on like an old friend, encouraged me and helped me overcome my fears and insecurities. Her spontaneity was a continuous source of refreshment and inspiration.

— Her husband, Professor Max Becker, who shares the same profession, photographed the interior of a pouch of a sick kangaroo for me in Pebbly Beach, which gave me much pleasure.

— I would also like to acknowledge the kindness of Christel Jacobi from Dresden, Germany, with whom I spent time in "paradise" on Rotamah Island and whose equableness and easygoing attitude toward life, even in ticklish or uncomfortable situations, served as a balm to my soul. What I failed to see or instantly note down she had already photographed or placed on video!

— My thanks are also extended to Ursula Weiss, with whom I visited Australia three times and whose lightning swiftness at tactile communication fascinated all who were witnesses to it. I am grateful as well to Kathrin Zimmermann, with whom I spent a wonderful six months in Australia.

In addition, I would like to acknowledge the late Dr. Heinz Schmid, the disabled husband of my best friend, Lilly, who at one time directed the residence and office center for people with disabilities in Reinach and who did so much to facilitate my professional emancipation in the areas of art and graphic design. His powerful, sunny personality and engaging smile I'll never forget.

Finally, I would like to thank all of those who are not mentioned here but who should know that their advice, assistance, criticism, inspiration, tolerance, and recognition have helped me along the way. Through them I have taken in love, trust, respect, and modesty, and I hope that my efforts have been worthy of their support.